Paradigm Lost

Paradigm Lost

From Two-State Solution to One-State Reality

Ian S. Lustick

PENN

UNIVERSITY OF PENNSYLVANIA PRESS

PHILADELPHIA

Published by
University of Pennsylvania Press
Philadelphia, Pennsylvania 19104-4112
www.upenn.edu/pennpress

Printed in the United States of America on acid-free paper
10 9 8 7 6 5 4 3 2 1

Library of Congress Cataloging-in-Publication Data
ISBN 978-0-8122-5195-1

For Terri, the love of my life,
and to the memory of my brother David

Sounded like the truth
Seemed the better way
Sounded like the truth
But it's not the truth today
—Leonard Cohen

Man plans and God laughs.
—Yiddish proverb

Contents

Flaw in the Iron Wall

Introduction

Zionists saw more clearly than anyone else the catastrophe facing the Jews of Europe and the need for a refuge. Their campaign to transform all or most of Palestine into a Jewish state succeeded in 1948. The Israeli-Palestinian conflict arose from that success and from two refusals. The first, when Israel refused to allow three-quarters of a million Palestinian Arabs to return to their homes, created the Palestinian refugee problem and ensured deep and continued challenges to its peace and security. A second and far more protracted refusal stretched over decades following the Six-Day War of 1967. In this period, Israel prevented a Palestinian state or entity of any kind from being established in the West Bank and the Gaza Strip. Israel thereby destroyed the one option available for a negotiated compromise capable of ending not only the Palestinian-Israeli dispute but also the larger Arab-Israeli conflict. This second decades-long refusal and its consequences are the focus of this book.

The odds of a two-state solution (TSS) were never favorable, but opportunities to negotiate were present from soon after the 1967 war to the collapse of the Oslo peace process in 2000. By the early twenty-first century, however, it became impossible to explain how a TSS could materialize and deeply implausible to expect one. TSS diehards still say that splitting the country into two states can be done and that the establishment of a single state is impossible. In principle, two states might someday emerge in Palestine. But the hard truth is that such an arrangement will not and can no longer come about from negotiations. Partly by design and partly by accident, Israeli policies have established another hard truth. There is today one and only one state ruling the territory between the Mediterranean Sea and the Jordan River, and its name is Israel. To be sure, the government of Israel rules different territories and groups of people "between the sea and the river" according to different laws and norms and with different degrees of authority and regularity. But if a state is defined to mean an entity with ultimate control over the security of life and property, then no inhabitant of this area, whether in Tel Aviv, Nablus, Haifa, or Gaza, lives in any state other than Israel. So, not only is one state that rules large Jewish and Arab populations in Palestine/the Land of Israel not impossible, it is also reality. It already exists.

No blueprint for the resolution of the Zionist-Palestinian Arab or Israeli-Palestinian conflict has had better prospects for success than the creation of "two-states for two peoples in one land." Such an arrangement would have protected the most cherished objective of the Zionist movement—a viable, recognized state in the Land of Israel inhabited by a large majority of Jews—while providing Palestinians with the protection and satisfaction of a viable state. The failure to achieve some version of that scheme before it became impossible to achieve through negotiations is a great historical and political tragedy that requires much deeper examination and an explanation compelling enough, perhaps, to push Israeli-Palestinian politics in a new direction.

Although the TSS is dead, its ghost remains, not as an inspiring blueprint for action but as distracting dogma. The ghost of the TSS haunts the conflict and obscures the reality that all of Palestine is controlled by one state, and the name of that state is Israel. With the false but seductive promise of its own resurrection, the TSS diverts attention from key questions about the nature of the Israeli state today and about whether or how the nature of its rule over the different territories included within it could change. The mirage of the TSS justifies the treatment of an increasingly oppressive status quo as a necessary but temporary evil. It prevents those who favor a democratic future from working effectively to bring that about while abetting those who favor nondemocratic outcomes.

The false belief in a negotiated TSS survives because advocates and opponents both cherish it as a useful fiction, the former as a yearned-for fantasy and the latter as a usefully conjured nightmare. The baleful legacy of the TSS—which blocks useful thinking about the future and abets the unannounced consolidation of a regime based on discrimination and coercion—can only be counteracted by an equally strong understanding of the structural barriers in Israel—cultural, psychological, and political—that crippled its chances for success. These obstacles are much more fundamental than the widely appreciated difficulties posed by more than 620,000 Israeli settlers in the West Bank (including expanded East Jerusalem) and other well-documented processes of "de facto annexation." They include the historical consequences of Zionism's initial failure to address Arab requirements, the way that the Holocaust and its "lessons" were eventually construed and enshrined in Israeli political culture, and the drastic distortion of Israeli politics resulting from an American foreign policy implemented mainly in conformity with the demands of the Israel lobby in the United States. This book examines the contribution of each of these obstacles to the failure of the TSS, leading up to an exploration of how that analysis can guide new thinking about the future of all the people living between the river and the sea, no matter what their ethnicity, religion, or citizenship status.

From the late 1960s to the end of the first decade of the twenty-first century, I was an active participant in the TSS project and considered it a worthy struggle. Certainly, the TSS would have brought its own problems, but these would have been more manageable than those in its absence. A Palestinian state could have been established and could have coexisted peacefully alongside Israel, but the opportunity to establish it was historically perishable and is no longer available.

Neither Zionists nor Arabs were ever uniformly and sincerely committed to a TSS. Certainly, Israeli leaders are not the only ones who contributed to failure of the TSS project. Nevertheless, given Israel's overwhelming political and military power vis-à-vis the Palestinians, and its virtually complete control of developments on the ground in the West Bank and Gaza, the TSS's failure to launch was primarily a function of Israel's behavior.

This disproportionate responsibility is obvious not just in hindsight. It was obvious a hundred years ago that getting Palestine's Arabs to reconcile with a Jewish state in their country would be difficult if not impossible. Most Zionists early in the twentieth century knew it was completely unrealistic to imagine that the indigenous population of Palestine would welcome the colonization of their country and its deliverance into the hands of another people. "I don't know of a single example in history," said Vladimir Jabotinsky, leader of the right wing of the Zionist movement, "where a country was colonized with the courteous consent of the native population."[1] Jabotinsky's political foe on the Zionist Left, David Ben-Gurion, agreed. "There is no solution to the question of relations between Arabs and Jews. . . . And we must recognize this situation. . . . We as a nation want this country to be ours; the Arabs, as a nation, want this country to be theirs."[2] At the inception of the movement, Zionists well knew that if the Arabs of Palestine were ever to accept Zionism, it would be the result of bitter resignation after decades of fierce resistance.

That prescience—and scenario—comports with the dismal fate of other states founded by Europeans in heavily populated non-European countries (Rhodesia, South Africa, French Algeria, etc.). So, the real question is not why Palestinian Arabs have not been more accommodating to a TSS but rather why Israel did not exploit any possibility to bring it about. Why did Israeli governments repeatedly reject opportunities to move decisively in that direction when a stable partitionist outcome was most available or least improbable, which is to say between 1967 and 2000? Why instead did Israeli governments systematically implement policies designed to prevent a viable Palestinian state from ever being realized?

Israeli Decisions and the Decision Not to Decide

Even a partial list of missed or torpedoed opportunities for movement toward a solution based on trading land for peace illustrates the unrelenting pattern.³ In 1967 in the first weeks after the Six-Day War, Palestinian no-tables from the West Bank wanted to negotiate the establishment of a Pal-estinian entity that would coexist peacefully with Israel. Israeli military, intelligence, and policy officials drafted half a dozen proposals to the gov-ernment that responded positively to the Palestinians by permitting public meetings to discuss and promote the idea. Every one of these proposals was ignored or rejected by Defense Minister Moshe Dayan, who was sup-ported by Prime Minister Levi Eshkol. Instead, the military government was instructed to ban Palestinians from engaging in any public political ac-tivity. Despite inclinations on the part of a number of senior ministers, the Labor-led coalition governments of Eshkol, Golda Meir, and Yitzhak Rabin, from 1967 to 1977, steadfastly abided by a "decision not to decide"—the phrase used standardly to describe policies by each of these prime ministers to avoid having to determine the final disposition of the territories occu-pied by Israel in 1967. As a result, during the first decade of the occupa-tion, the political status of the West Bank and Gaza drifted toward de facto annexation.

In 1968, King Hussein of Jordan told Israeli leaders that he would ne-gotiate a bilateral peace treaty if Israel withdrew from the West Bank. Israel responded with an informal offer to withdraw from two-thirds of the terri-tory but keep the rest—including a greatly expanded Jerusalem—as part of Israel. That ended negotiations.⁴

In 1969, U.S. secretary of state William Rogers announced a plan spon-sored by the Four Powers (the United States, the Soviet Union, Great Brit-ain, and France) to achieve a comprehensive peace between Israel and its neighbors that would include return of the West Bank to Jordan, with mi-nor territorial adjustments, and transformation of Jerusalem into a united city with shared municipal government. Israel "flatly rejected" the plan as "an attempt on the very existence of Israel."⁵

In 1971, Israeli diplomats prepared a response to peace offers made by Egyptian president Anwar Sadat in the context of an initiative launched by UN secretary-general Gunnar Jarring. The plan they submitted to Prime Minister Meir was a unanimous recommendation for Israel to achieve a comprehensive peace by returning the Golan Heights to Syria and the Sinai

Peninsula to Egypt and by withdrawing from the Gaza Strip, most of the West Bank, and East Jerusalem. Known as the Yakinton Plan, it was summarily rejected by the prime minister.[6]

In 1972, the Jordanian king offered Israel a peace agreement that would have included the West Bank and the Gaza Strip in a federated "Hashemite Kingdom of Jordan." Despite disagreement from some ministers, Meir's government rejected the plan and shortly thereafter endorsed the Galili Plan, which called for extensive infrastructural investment, increased land acquisition including private purchases, and expanded settlement of the West Bank and in the southern approaches to the Gaza Strip.[7]

In 1973 in the American-sponsored negotiations following the Ramadan/Yom Kippur War, Israel returned portions of the Golan Heights and Sinai to Syria and Egypt, respectively, as interim steps toward comprehensive peace agreements. However, despite personal appeals by President Richard Nixon in July 1974, the new Israeli government of Yitzhak Rabin refused any withdrawals from parts of the West Bank that would have set in motion a similar process with Jordan and the Palestinians.

No one can guarantee that any of these opportunities, no matter how enthusiastically pursued by Israel, would have produced the kind of stable, if imperfect, peace between Palestinians and Israelis that partitionists imagine. But it is obvious that the option of peace based on a two-state framework never got a decent chance, first and foremost, because of Israel's decisions and policies. Especially in the first decade of the occupation, Israeli governments had considerable latitude to pursue territorial compromise. Arab demands that Israel cede areas it had conquered in 1948 had effectively ended. Polls regularly showed that wide sectors of Israeli society opposed the absorption of large Arab populations from the West Bank and the Gaza Strip and were therefore willing to entertain territorial compromise. From the mid-1970s on, Israel had unquestioned military superiority over all its potential enemies, including a regional monopoly on nuclear weapons, that allowed Israeli governments to operate from a position of confidence in the country's security. It was also always clear that any Israeli government committed to territorial compromise would have enjoyed the generous and enthusiastic support of the international community.

Meanwhile, the Arab world's readiness for a peace based on territorial compromise and a political solution to the Palestinian problem was registered by the emergence of the "acceptance front," including Jordan, Syria, Saudi Arabia, Lebanon, Tunisia, and Morocco. These countries, supported by Palestinians in the occupied territories and a growing number of Palestine Liberation Organization (PLO) leaders, accepted Security Council Resolution 242, which recognized the right to peace and security by all states in the region and was based on the principle of trading lands occupied by Israel in 1967 for peace. As all scholars of the conflict agree, even the Egyptian and Syrian attacks in 1973 on Israeli forces in the Golan Heights and the Sinai were designed to convince Israel of the importance of negotiating withdrawals from these territories while encouraging the United States to take a more active role as a peacemaker.

In 1974, the PLO made its first official statement in favor of an "independent fighting national authority" on any part of Palestine relinquished by Israel, quickly moderating its tone by removing the word "fighting" and agreeing that the Palestinian entity could be achieved by political as well as military means.[8]

In 1977 the PLO's legislative body, the Palestinian National Congress, described its goal as an "independent Palestinian state" without characterizing that objective as a transitional stage toward a "secular democratic state in the whole of Palestine."[9]

In August 1981, Saudi crown prince Fahd (soon to become king) proposed a comprehensive peace agreement with Israel based on establishing a Palestinian state in the territories occupied in 1967. Over the next decade the PLO, strongly influenced by West Bank and Gaza sentiment in favor of an independent Palestinian state alongside Israel, moved with increasing clarity toward acceptance of the TSS. In 1988 that acceptance was made official.

In 2002 Saudi Arabia revived the Fahd proposal by launching its own initiative, a plan endorsed by the Arab League for ending the Arab-Israeli conflict based on establishment of a Palestinian state in the West Bank and Gaza. Though by this time it hardly mattered, Arab League summits held in 2007 and 2017 reaffirmed support for the proposal.

In other words, from the late 1960s on, Israel had significant opportunities to negotiate with both Palestinian and Arab world representatives who had made clear their readiness to sign and implement a comprehensive peace based on trading occupied territories for a TSS.

Of course, the same power position that gave Israel the discretion to compromise also gave it the option of pursuing instead larger territorial and ideological ambitions. By stonewalling responses to negotiating opportunities while facilitating settlement expansion in the West Bank and the Gaza Strip, Prime Ministers Eshkol, Meir, and Rabin had for a decade protected the Labor Party from grappling with internal disputes between hawks and doves. These prime ministers also forestalled threats by coalition partners (in particular the National Religious Party) to bring down the government should it seriously pursue options for peace with the Palestinians. But the drift toward de facto annexation and suppression of Palestinian political mobilization also encouraged Israelis to believe that their country could keep most or even all of the lands captured in 1967. Ten years of the "decision not to decide" thereby preserved opportunities for governments desirous of permanently incorporating the West Bank and the Gaza Strip to act decisively toward that end. In 1977, opportunities to do so were fully exploited by the openly antipartitionist governments of Likud prime ministers Menachem Begin (1977–1983) and Yitzhak Shamir (1983–1984, 1986–1992). Proudly committed to extending "Jewish sovereignty" over the "whole Land of Israel," these governments implemented massive programs of settlement and infrastructural development to bind the territories to Israel while preventing emergence of any Palestinian state west of the Jordan River. While often seeking to camouflage their objectives with ambiguous formulas and complex negotiations over procedures or terms of reference, these governments as well as the those led by Benjamin Netanyahu (1996–1999, 2009) never seriously entertained any future for the country that would or could feature a viable Palestinian state.[10]

The Labor Party next led an Israeli government in 1992, by which time it had become vastly more difficult to negotiate a TSS. Instead of "simply" having to overcome risks to the ruling coalition and the risk of losing an election—obstacles that had pushed Labor Party governments in the 1960s and 1970s to the "decision not to decide"—the Rabin government of 1992 also faced daunting risks of violent challenges to the regime by settlers and their supporters, outbreaks of intra-Jewish political conflict if not civil war, and threats to the legitimacy of state authority. From a purely political point of view, a TSS had become an order of magnitude more difficult to pursue than it would have been in the first decade of Israel's rule of the West Bank and Gaza.[11]

It is certainly true that Arab and Palestinian elites were at times inept, ambiguous, or insincere in their proposals for peace with Israel.[12] They were certainly never united. However, from the beginning of the occupation of the West Bank and the Gaza Strip, Israel made it difficult, if not impossible, for the moderate Arabs whom Jabotinsky had predicted would emerge to organize or persuade wider segments of their own community, or of the Arab and Muslim worlds, that pursuing compromise with Israel was a realistic option. Banning all political activity by Palestinians in the West Bank and Gaza was part of Israel's determined policy to exclude Palestinians under its control from any role in the determination of their political future. Although at one point the military government tried to set up a "Village Leagues" organization of puppet Palestinian strongmen willing to work for the Israeli government rather than against the occupation, the scheme lasted less than a year, at which point Israel reverted back to its traditional policy of discrediting as a terrorist any Palestinian leader with a mass political following.

Until January 1993, Israel treated the PLO as a terrorist organization. Until that date, it was illegal for Israelis even to meet with PLO members. In the West Bank (including East Jerusalem), Arab newspapers were heavily censored. Any sites of organized activity with the potential to become political, such as local governments, professional associations, student groups, unions, and religious institutions, were subject to intensive surveillance and strict regulation. The incarceration rate in the occupied territories became the highest in the world, with more than 800,000 Palestinians imprisoned in the fifty years between June 1967 and May 2017.[13] Combined with deportations and killings, Israeli control policies neutralized thousands of Palestinian leaders and prevented tens of thousands more with the necessary talents and ambition from becoming leaders.

To be sure, under Israel's interpretation of the 1978 Camp David Accords, signed by Israel, Egypt, and the United States, Likud governments were willing to discuss "administrative autonomy" arrangements for "Arabs of the Land of Israel living in Judea, Samaria, and the Gaza District." But these ideas were of little interest either to Palestinians or to Jordan. Jordan boycotted the prolonged negotiations over the "powers and responsibilities" to be included within Menachem Begin's "full autonomy" scheme, negotiations which involved only Israel, the United States, and Egypt. The PLO was excluded. The "autonomy negotiations" collapsed after years of fruitless encounters.[14]

For two decades after the Six-Day War, many Palestinians, including most of those inside the occupied territories, were anxious to negotiate interim or permanent arrangements based on the vision of a Palestinian state alongside Israel. Yet it was not until the aftermath of the First Intifada—a mass Palestinian uprising in the West Bank and the Gaza Strip—and the election of a Labor Party government in 1992 that some Israeli leaders were willing to engage in political negotiations with Palestinians in general and the PLO in particular. From 1993 to 1995, negotiations between Israel and the PLO did produce arrangements that might have led to a TSS. But the terms of what became known as the Oslo peace process included no guarantees for Palestinian statehood, no agreement on boundaries within which Palestinians might exercise political authority, no limits on Israeli settlement activity in the West Bank and the Gaza Strip, no imagined solution to the Palestinian refugee problem, and no enforceable timetable for the implementation or conclusion of the agreement. That the PLO would accept such a framework for negotiations suggests how ready, if not desperate, Palestinians were for compromise. This also highlights the extent to which the fate of the peace process depended on Israel's curtailment of its own ambitions to dominate the entire area between the Jordan River and the sea.

In the end, these ambitious were not curtailed. A settler massacre of Palestinians in the Ibrahimi Mosque in Hebron in 1994 and Prime Minister Yitzhak Rabin's assassination in 1995 by a Jewish fundamentalist began a spiral of escalating violence. Burdened by unprecedentedly rapid expansion of Israeli settlements in the West Bank and systematic efforts by the governments of both Benjamin Netanyahu and Ehud Barak to discredit the Oslo Accords and avoid scheduled withdrawals, the Oslo process collapsed. This led to the bloody Second Intifada (2000-2005).

From 1967 on, Palestinians ready for territorial compromise had few cards to play other than making themselves available for whatever kind of negotiated solution Israel was willing to contemplate. However, Israel's policy—with the partial exception of the first few years of Oslo process—was systematically to belittle, discredit, or ignore Arab peace initiatives. Israel blocked nearly all efforts to move toward a future of Israeli-Palestinian relations that would have entailed the establishment of a politically viable Palestinian state. Yet it would be a serious mistake to attribute the failure of a TSS to specific discrete decisions, particular events, or the timidity, short-sightedness, or designs of individual leaders or to flaws in this or that diplomatic process. Blaming particular leaders or their policies does not answer the crucial questions: Why did Israel never produce a government capable of implementing a TSS, and why have those leaders who favored the idea been unable to achieve it? Nor can these questions be answered by treating Zionist and Palestinian objectives as intractably and entirely contradictory, since each side has shown flexibility in the definition of its objectives and dynamism in their pursuit.

Instead, the record of TSS failure owes much to the mechanism of unintended consequences. Zionism's strategic logic unintentionally institutionalized a political incapacity to discern or exploit Arab willingness to compromise.

The Iron Wall and Its Partial Success

As is true of any organized movement, Zionism was both a tool for affecting the world and an arena within which members struggled and cooperated with one another. As an ideology, Zionism offered members a guide for analyzing the world, a blueprint for changing it, and a culture for living in it. Zionist culture included archetypes, vocabulary, myths, heroes, villains, and styles. Within Israel, Zionism has been so successful that even today no ambitious Israeli leader can justify important national policies except in a Zionist vocabulary and unless they can be described as deriving from Zionism's founding principles. Thus, in 2014 when the Labor Party sought desperately to find a way back to power, it joined with breakaway elements from Likud to form the Zionist Camp (HaMachane HaTzioni), popularly but less accurately translated as the "Zionist Union." But more than a century after the movement began, the thoroughness of Zionism's victory within Israel has had the profound and unintended consequence of forcing the country to act as if the outside world still presents Jews with the same circumstances and challenges they faced in the late nineteenth century and the first half of the twentieth century. This disconnect between nineteenth-century Zionist ideology and the vastly new challenges and opportunities of the twenty-first century is enormously important for understanding the failure of the TSS and Israel's growing isolation in the world.

The Zionist movement arose in Europe in the late nineteenth century with a controversial but brilliant solution to what it called the international "Jewish problem," by which it meant the problem of Jews and Judaism in Europe from Britain to the Urals. Zionism, like all ideologies, advanced a definition of the problem that it had been organized to solve.[15] But ideologues often forget or pretend they do not know what political scientists know well. Because the world constantly changes, ideologies can offer only partial analyses and ultimately incorrect or at least only temporary solutions.

Virtually all classical Zionists identified the existential condition of Jews, as a minority everywhere and a majority nowhere, as abnormal and even pathological for Jews. It was the taproot of anti-Semitism and the cause of what Zionists considered the ugly distortions of Jewish culture and Jewish life. Zionists proposed to solve this problem through the normalization of Jewish life by concentrating Jews in a country where they would be the majority. Because of traditional Jewish attachments to the Land of Israel and imperial control of the territory (first Ottoman, then British), Palestine was the place on Earth where that solution was most feasible.

The centerpiece of the Zionist plan for ensuring Jewish survival was a country with a Jewish majority that would implicitly or explicitly be governed by a Jewish state. But Zionism had no solution to an obvious problem.

What was to be done with the Arabs living in Palestine whom even in Zionist eyes were firmly attached to the country as their native land and political patrimony? Deep-seated Arab opposition to Zionism was unmistakable. Arab demonstrations and riots were commonplace by the 1920s. In addition to Muslim-Christian associations, a number of clan-based nationalist organizations and parties emerged, all opposed to the growth of the Jewish national home. Palestinians unanimously rejected the idea of a Jewish national home in Palestine, as set forth in the Balfour Declaration in 1917, and therefore also opposed the British mandate over Palestine that began in 1920. Instead, they demanded a plebiscite to implement Wilsonian principles of national self-determination for the country's inhabitants. Multiple British investigating commissions identified Zionism itself—and the Jewish immigration and land transfers associated with it—as the root of chronic and often violent Arab discontent.

Zionism's refusal to deal directly and honestly with the Arab problem should not be surprising. Given the desperate circumstances that surrounded Jewish life in the first half of the twentieth century, it was natural as well as typical of national movements for Zionism to launch its national independence and state-building project before solving all outstanding issues. But the question of what to do with the indigenous population of the territory was uniquely difficult to avoid. Among other things, the Arab problem was closely related to the deepest division within the Zionist movement—the struggle over whether to accept some rather than all of Palestine as space for the Jewish state. Everyone understood that the more territory Zionism aimed to rule, the more Arabs it would have to displace or incorporate.

Even if Zionists disagreed on the territory issue, all knew that what they wanted and believed was right clashed fundamentally and unavoidably with what Arabs wanted and believed was right. Though its official leadership tried hard not to say so publicly or officially, the Zionist movement fervently wished that Palestine had been or could become free of Arabs. Most Zionists, however, believed that to be an unattainable fantasy.[16] They could not imagine an acceptable role for a large, free, and growing Arab population within the future Jewish state, but they also believed that peace with the Arabs, including those of Palestine, would be necessary to permanently enshrine Jewish sovereignty in the Middle East. Zionists also realized the importance of fostering the belief within the international community that their success would not mean permanent war. They made this case before every investigating commission that ever looked into the Arab-Jewish conflict in Palestine.[17] David Ben-Gurion's testimony before the Anglo-American Committee of Inquiry in 1946 illustrates the sometimes desperate form of this argument. Ben-Gurion conjured a bright future for Arab-Jewish relations, assuring the committee that the Arab problem would vanish in the wake of the decisive establishment of Jewish statehood:

> We are not afraid of the present tragic conflict between us and the Arabs. It is a passing thing. . . . I know that the Arabs, at least some of them, don't want us to return and I understand it. I merely am convinced that their opposition is futile, but it is natural. We will return, and there will be understanding between us and the Arabs.[18]

> There is now tension, perhaps a little more, between us and the Arabs. It is very unfortunate, but it is a passing thing. It is not a danger.[19]

> I want to say a few words to the Arabs. . . . The conflict between us today is the most tragic, for it is in a way a family conflict. But it will not last long.[20]

Ben-Gurion's attempt at nonchalance was as ineffective as it was disingenuous. Conflict between Arabs and Jews, violent or otherwise, had for a quarter of a century dominated international consideration of the Palestine problem. His testimony also belied the Zionists' own maddening (if publicly suppressed) inability to find a formula for reconciling inevitable Arab demands with Zionism requirements. Contrary to legend, Zionists had never seen Palestine as "a land without a people." The Arab problem was apparent from the very beginning of Zionist settlement in the 1880s.[21] By the 1920s, its daunting significance was obvious. Lengthy debates of various Zionist Congresses reveal scarce discussion of the Arab problem, as Israeli historian Benny Morris has shown, only because the minutes were systematically censored to hide the fact that the movement knew it had nothing acceptable to offer the Arabs as a basis for peace.[22]

Yet Zionism did come up with its own theory of how peace could be achieved. It set aside wishful thinking that Arab political aspirations would wither away or that an effendi class of backward elites was only temporarily misleading the Arab masses of Palestine into believing that Zionism was a threat to their way of life. Instead, Zionist leaders from across the political spectrum agreed on a theory and a strategy for action that would prove central and momentous: the strategy of the Iron Wall.

The theory was formulated in its earliest and most influential form in an article published in Russian by the Revisionist (maximalist) Zionist leader Vladimir (Ze'ev) Jabotinsky. "On the Iron Wall" ("O Zheleznoi Stene") appeared in the journal *Razviet* in Berlin on November 4, 1923. Jabotinsky made an honest and forceful argument. Given Zionism's ambitions to transform Palestine, he recognized that Arab opposition was inevitable and natural. He condemned Zionist "vegetarians" anxious to negotiate with Arabs and ridiculed their dreams of satisfying Arab ambitions with promises of a better standard of living.[23] The Arabs of Palestine would feel and act precisely as would any other "indigenous people." They would "regard their country as their national homeland where they want to live and constantly remain its sole owners. And such a people will not voluntarily submit to new owners or even to a partnership." Given that Zionism would always insist on unlimited Jewish immigration, he declared that down deep all Zionists knew that "there is not even the slightest hope of ever obtaining [Arab] agreement to transform Palestine from an Arab country to a country with a Jewish majority." He insisted that this simple truth be made an "essential part of our basic thinking on the Arab problem. . . . Colonization is self-explanatory and what it implies is fully understood by every sensible Jew and Arab. There can only be one purpose in colonization. For the country's Arabs that purpose is essentially unacceptable. This is a natural reaction and nothing will change it."

Under the circumstances, although peace was necessary, it would have to wait. The only way for Zionism to "achieve an agreement with [the Arabs] in the future," wrote Jabotinsky, "is by absolutely avoiding any attempts at agreement with them at present." The crucial instrument for transforming the Arab question would be systematic, coercive pedagogy—erecting an "Iron Wall" against which Arab opposition would be so crushingly and so regularly defeated that eventually the "gleam of hope that they will succeed in getting rid of us" will be driven from their eyes. Jabotinsky summarized:

> Only when they [the Arabs] have given up all hope of getting rid of the alien settlers and can make no breach in the iron wall . . . will extremist groups with their slogan "no, never" lose their influence and only then will the moderates offer suggestions for compromise. Then only will they begin bargaining with us on practical matters, such as guarantees against pushing them out, and equality of civil and national rights.[24]

The Iron Wall strategy can be divided into five stages, each stage a requirement for advancement to the next:

Stage 1: Construction of the Iron Wall.
Stage 2: Crushingly successful defenses of the Iron Wall against attempts to breach it.
Stage 3: Power shifts within the adversary's camp from intransigent extremists toward moderates willing to compromise.
Stage 4: Defenders of the Iron Wall perceive the shift toward moderation within the adversary camp and shift their own policy toward negotiation and compromise.
Stage 5: Negotiations lead to a settlement of the conflict based on equality of collective rights.

Together, the five stages are a plan for moving from categorical Arab rejection of Zionism to a negotiated compromise based on satisfaction of Zionism's minimum requirements. Much of the story of the Arab-Israeli conflict can be told as the successful Zionist/Israeli implementation of the first three stages, followed by failure to advance in a timely manner to Stage 4 and a consequent disappearance of a key formula (the TSS) as a framework for consummating Stage 5.

By the 1930s Jabotinsky's Iron Wall strategy toward the Arab question was embraced by Ben-Gurion and the Labor Zionists who controlled the central institutions of the movement and of what it termed the "state on the way."[25] The policy of the Iron Wall consisted of treating the Arabs (of Palestine and of the surrounding Arab world) as an enemy with whom compromise might ultimately be possible, but only after their will had been broken by successive and painful defeats. Constructing an Iron Wall against Arab opposition was the first task. Jabotinsky preferred the British army to serve as the Iron Wall, and indeed the overwhelming use of British military force in the late 1930s to crush the Arab Revolt was a blow from which the Arabs of Palestine never recovered. Ultimately, however, it was the military arm of the Zionist movement and especially the Labor Zionist movement's armed formations, the Haganah and the Palmach, that formed the Iron Wall. Under the auspices of the Histadrut labor federation, the main Labor Zionist parties, together with their settlement movements, smuggled and manufactured weapons, trained thousands of part-time soldiers, developed an elaborate command and control structure, and erected watchtower and stockade outposts in strategic outlying areas. This was the military and infrastructural basis for the emergence of the Israel Defense Forces in 1948.

Zionism's preeminent leader, David Ben-Gurion, served as both prime minister and defense minister for most of the first fifteen years of Israeli statehood. He channeled enormous resources to the military and related security services. Emphasis was placed on aggressiveness, qualitative superiority, universal service, and offense rather than defense. By the late 1960s, top-level decisions made a decade earlier to develop an Israeli nuclear weapons capacity added a new dimension to the Iron Wall.

The second stage of the Iron Wall strategy called for Israeli military power to inflict repeated and grievous defeats on Arab attackers. As anticipated, the Arabs of Palestine (with help from Egypt, Iraq, Syria, Transjordan, and elsewhere) repeatedly attacked the Yishuv, the prestate Jewish community in Palestine. Major disturbances occurred in 1921, 1929, and 1936–1937, although low-intensity scattered attacks began before World War I and continued through the entire period of the British mandate. Following the UN's approval of the partition of Palestine in November 1947, full-scale civil war erupted. Irregular Palestinian Arab groups waged a fierce struggle to conquer isolated Jewish settlements, take control of key roads, force the capitulation of Jewish Jerusalem, and make the UN plan unenforceable.

Exploiting its advantages in organization, military training, and national unity, the Yishuv held its ground. By April 1948, the Jews of Palestine went beyond defense toward punishment of the Arabs and expansion of the territory allotted to the Jews by the UN. Fighting intensified again in May 1948 when Egyptian, Syrian, Iraqi, and Transjordanian troops invaded Palestine. But with arms from Czechoslovakia and with Jewish ranks refreshed by thousands of new immigrants, the Iron Wall began producing the devastating blows that Jabotinsky had prescribed. Apart from the Arab Legion of Transjordan, which abided by strict limits in its engagement with Israeli military units, each Arab army suffered embarrassing defeats. Israeli forces prevented the loss of any Jewish settlements from within the territory allotted to the Jewish state; added substantial territories in the Galilee, the northern Negev, and the "Little Triangle" (along the new country's narrow waist); secured Jewish Jerusalem; uprooted hundreds of thousands of Palestinian Arabs and seized the villages and lands of three-quarters of a million refugees. The attempt to breach the Iron Wall had not only failed but also resulted in precisely the kind of disproportionate losses to both Palestinian Arabs and the Arab states that, it was thought, would encourage Arabs to accommodate themselves to Jewish sovereignty in the Land of Israel.

The use of war to teach the enemy that the Jewish state should be and could be accommodated continued after 1948. Refusing to negotiate with Palestinian representatives, Israel (with Jordan's cooperation) blocked emergence of the Arab state that the UN had envisioned in parts of Palestine. Once armistice agreements were signed with the Arab states in 1949, Israel did all it could to bar the return of refugees. Thousands of those seeking to return to their homes or harvest their crops were deported or shot.[26] Unsatisfied with the aggressiveness of some units assigned reprisal and retaliation missions, Ben-Gurion commissioned Moshe Dayan and Ariel Sharon to form a special detachment for this purpose: Unit 101. The policy of brutal reprisal and collective punishment implemented by Unit 101 was part of a general effort to infuse the army and the populace with a siege mentality and norms of ruthlessness in the defense of Israel's borders. The intent was not only to demonstrate the futility of attempts to breach the Iron Wall but also to encourage Arabs in general and Palestinians in particular to abandon hopes of ever benefiting from violence against Israel.

In this context, Israel's attack on Egypt in October 1956 and its capture of the Gaza Strip and the Sinai Peninsula was a reprisal raid on a massive scale. It was also an effort to unseat Gamal Abdel Nasser and discredit the militant brand of Pan-Arab nationalism he represented. Thus did Ben-Gurion seek to strike at what Jabotinsky had referred to as "extremist groups with their slogan 'no, never'" and hasten their replacement, at least in principle, by more moderate elements ready for peace negotiations.

Although the war did reassure Israelis of the effectiveness of their military and the integrity of the Iron Wall, it was a political failure. American and Soviet pressure forced the British and French troops reoccupying the Suez Canal into a humiliating evacuation. Within five months the Dwight D. Eisenhower administration forced Israel to withdraw from both Sinai and the Gaza Strip. Although ships were again free to sail through the Tiran Straits to Eilat and although Sinai became a demilitarized buffer zone, the war raised Nasser's prestige in the Arab world to astronomical heights. Nor had Israel destroyed the idea among both Palestinians and Arabs that in a genuine second round of real warfare, without Israel benefiting from great power assistance, they might still destroy Israel by Arab arms.

With this idea in mind, Syria, Jordan, and Egypt joined forces in May 1967 to threaten Israel with a war of destruction. Whatever the actual intent of Nasser and other Arab leaders in early 1967, the definite impression created for Arab publics was that the hour of decision was approaching and that this time Israel would not catch the Arabs off guard or be saved by imperialist intervention. Israel smashed these hopes and expectations in the war it launched on June 5, 1967. Within hours the Egyptian Air Force was almost entirely destroyed, ensuring Israel's victory. Egypt again lost Gaza and Sinai. Israeli forces took the West Bank, including Arab Jerusalem, from Jordan and the Golan Heights from Syria, generating another wave of more than 250,000 refugees on these two fronts.

The Arab world was in shock. Nasser's closest friend, the chief of staff of the Egyptian Army, committed suicide. Nasser himself resigned (though after mass demonstrations, he returned to office). Almost 20,000 Arab soldiers died in the fighting, more than twenty times the number suffered by Israel. Despite hard fighting by some Arab units, Israel's military superiority was painfully obvious. The territorial losses were incontrovertible evidence of Israel's military dominance in the region, even bracketing its nuclear weapons. The Six-Day War, as it was known in Israel, dramatically illustrated the premise of the Iron Wall strategy: Israel could not be destroyed by Arab military force, and every attempt to do so would result in greater and more costly defeats.

Thus, in 1967 the second stage of the Iron Wall strategy was complete. In its third stage, the theory held, moderate political forces within the Arab world would react to this reality by gaining ground against and then displacing die-hard extremists. Indeed, whatever trends in this direction had been present after 1948, the impact of the 1967 war was unmistakable. Following the war, Israeli defense minister Dayan described his government as "waiting for a telephone call from the Arabs."[27]

Although not immediately apparent, the Six-Day War sounded the death knell for ambitious Pan-Arab unity schemes advanced by Nasserists, Baathists, and Arab socialists. Egypt and Jordan accepted UN Security Council Resolution 242, which required recognition of the "sovereignty, territorial integrity and political independence of every State in the area and their right to live in peace within secure and recognized boundaries." This was the first clear diplomatic signal that the confrontation states were ready to accept Israel's presence in the Middle East within the 1949 armistice lines. Syria did the same once the radical Baathist regime of Salah Jedid in Syria was replaced by the pragmatic authoritarian, Syria-oriented rule of Hafez el-Assad in 1970. In that same year Nasser died but not before beginning a retreat from his grand ambitions. His successor, Anwar Sadat, changed the country's name on its postage stamps from the "United Arab

Republic" to the "Arab Republic of Egypt" and eventually to "Egypt." Soon after taking power he launched successive initiatives to gain a nonbelligerency or interim peace agreement with Israel. These movements toward recognition of Israel's indestructibility, though not its legitimacy, included the nascent Palestinian campaign in the West Bank and Gaza to reach a political accommodation with the Jewish state, even if the PLO itself did not officially endorse a political solution to the conflict until 1977.

The fighting did not end, of course. In 1969 and 1970, the bloody War of Attrition erupted in the Jordan Valley between Jordanian artillery and Israeli artillery and aircraft and along the Suez Canal, where Israeli planes responded to Egyptian raids into Sinai by attacking Egyptian forces and by destroying military and economic targets deep within Egypt. Rapid escalation led the Soviet Union to send tens of thousands of "advisers" and pilots into Egypt. The antiaircraft system they constructed inflicted heavy damage on the Israeli Air Force. The fighting ended in the summer of 1970 when Israel and Egypt agreed to a cease-fire, and under American and Soviet pressure Israel accepted Security Council Resolution 242. An uneasy peace prevailed until late 1973. In these three years Egyptian, Jordanian, American, UN, and Four Power peace initiatives were rejected by an Israeli government unwilling to risk internal fissures by beginning talks about trading territory for peace. In October 1973 Syria and Egypt, with support from Saudi Arabia and other Arab countries, launched successful surprise attacks on Israeli positions along the Suez Canal and in the Golan Heights.

Ironically, the Arab attack on Israeli forces in 1973 was a vivid and ironic affirmation of Arab perceptions that Israel was for all intents and purposes a permanent feature of the Middle East. Indeed, both the War of Attrition and the Ramadan/Yom Kippur War of 1973 were vastly different from previous conflicts. Neither was fought by the Arabs to destroy Israel, and neither was fought by Israel to establish its indestructibility. The Arabs' objectives in these wars was to spur Israel to negotiate, to puncture what Israelis later came to call their *conceptsia*—a complacent belief that Israel enjoyed such overwhelming military superiority that it could safely ignore Arab opposition, stay on the 1967 cease-fire lines indefinitely, and gradually absorb the occupied territories. Simultaneously, the Arabs wished to draw the great powers, particularly the United States, into a more energetic role in the mediation of a peace agreement. Financed by Saudi Arabia and with the postattack participation of Iraq, Jordan, and Morocco, the Ramadan/ Yom Kippur War showed that the Arab world as a whole had learned the lesson that the Iron Wall had intended to teach: the Zionist project would not succumb to Arab violence.[28]

It is here that a crucial flaw was revealed in the Iron Wall strategy, which assumed that the Arabs would respond rationally to defeats but did not consider how Jews would respond to victories. To review, Zionism had concluded that it could offer the Arabs of Palestine or even the Arabs of the Middle East nothing that would satisfy them or justify peace with the Jewish state-on-the-way. It was therefore necessary to defeat Arabs so decisively and so often that Arab opinion would moderate, and Arab leaders would then come forward to negotiate based on mutual compromise and settle for much less than what they believed they deserved.

That is what the Iron Wall strategy explicitly expected of the Arabs. But it also *implicitly* required something of the Jews, something aside from building and mobilizing a victorious military machine. It was assumed that Zionism's political descendants would regularly assess and update their beliefs about Arab readiness for peace. For the strategy to work, Zionist (i.e. Israeli) leaders would have to promptly discern signals of Arab readiness to compromise. They would have to respond to such inevitably ambiguous opportunities for negotiations by strengthening Arab moderates and isolating the "no, never" extremists. Victorious and secure, Israelis would have to recognize that moderates did exist on the Arab side who were prepared to make peace based on equality of national rights and compromises that would satisfy the minimum requirements of each side. Political echelons behind the Iron Wall would also have to publicly treat Arab moderates as sincere and not dismiss them as wolves in sheep's clothing out to destroy Israel by other means or under other slogans.

But as realistic about the eventual responses of Arabs to successive defeats as Jabotinsky was, he was just as *unrealistic* about the eventual responses of Jews to successive victories. If a "normal" people (as he described both Arabs and Jews) would respond to repeated defeats by a grudging and painful moderation in its minimum demands, Jabotinsky should have understood that a normal victorious people would come to despise enemies responsible for decades of suffering and death and would follow up repeated victories over them by enthusiastic and easily justified escalation in the victors' demands. Those who adopted Jabotinsky's analysis correctly believed that successive and devastating defeats inflicted on Arabs would eventually produce psychological and political change toward moderation of Arab demands. But neither Jabotinsky nor adherents to his strategy realized that fighting Arabs so often and defeating them so decisively would push Jewish psychology and politics toward more extreme demands for the satisfaction of Zionist objectives. This would reduce the desire for peace agreements and encourage psychological disregard of both the rights and abilities of the Arabs. In short, failure to anticipate the unintended consequences of successful implementation of the Iron Wall strategy's first three stages prevented Israel from swift and effective movement to the fourth and fifth stages.

This was a development never anticipated or intended by the Iron Wall strategists, though it can be understood by applying psychological and political assumptions about how normal peoples react to chronic failure or exaggerated success. In this sense, the strategy called upon Jews to act abnormally. They did not. Instead of responding to signs of Arab moderation by moving from the third to the fourth and fifth stages of the Iron Wall strategy, Israeli governments escalated their demands for territory, security guarantees, and eventually recognition for the legitimacy of Zionism—a demand never before advanced as a condition for a peace agreement.

Zionism realized at its inception that it had no solution to the Arab problem. It coped by devising a strategy that made it both unusually important and unusually difficult for Israelis to separate emotion from politics, exercise restraint and generosity toward their enemies, and learn to see opportunities for peace amid ambiguous threats to their security and existence.

In this context it is certainly impressive that Israelis, including some Israeli governments, made significant efforts toward negotiating a compromise peace with Palestinians. Their efforts proved to be too little too late, but given the odds against their success, the fact that they were made at all is a credit to the critical intelligence of many Israeli Jews, their genuine yearning for peace, and their ability to change. However, even this (inadequate) readiness to acknowledge and respond to Arab moderation was only possible as a result of the losses and pain inflicted by what can appropriately be understood as the Arab Iron Wall.

In 1971 I was in my senior year at Brandeis University. Yitzhak Rabin was Israel's ambassador to the United States and came to speak on campus. In the crowded auditorium, I asked him a question: "Why shouldn't Israel negotiate with the PLO, since the whole idea of peace negotiations is to settle problems with enemies, not with friends?" Rabin's response was characteristically blunt. "We will not negotiate with the PLO because doing so would mean accepting the idea of a Palestinian state, and Israel should not and will not do that." In his capacity as defense minister in the 1980s, Rabin became known for his "iron fist" policy toward West Bank and Gaza Arabs and for his advice to soldiers during the intifada as to how to treat Palestinian soldiers: "Give it to them! [*tachnees bahem*]" and "Break their arms and legs." By 1993, however, his outlook changed. Israelis had been tragically slow to learn the need for compromise or to appreciate the role of the Arab Iron Wall in making this learning possible.

Rabin was elected to the premiership in June 1992. After secret negotiations in Oslo, Israel and the PLO exchanged letters of official recognition, setting the stage for Rabin and Yasser Arafat to shake hands on the White House lawn. In October 1994 Rabin spoke before the Israeli parliament, defending the peace process with both Jordan and the Palestinians and explaining why it had taken so long for Israel to respond seriously to offers of territorial compromise. He reminded his audience of Moshe Dayan's dismissive comments in response to post-1967 Arab peace proposals that "We are waiting for a telephone call from the Arabs" and that "I prefer Sharm al-Shaykh without peace to peace without Sharm al-Shaykh." Referring to Israel's rejection of Sadat's peace offers before the 1973 war, Rabin reminded Israelis that

we responded to the Egyptian President's remarks with ridi-
cule and arrogance. A bloody war with Egypt and Syria and
thousands of fatalities among IDF [Israel Defense Forces]
soldiers dear to us and among soldiers in the Egyptian and
Syrian Armies were needed for Cairo to reach the correct
conclusion that peace is preferable to war and for Jerusalem
to reach the correct conclusion that peace is preferable to
Sharm al-Shaykh.[29]

By most accounts, Rabin was initially unenthusiastic about using Oslo to
lay the groundwork for a viable TSS, although there is evidence that by the
fall of 1995 he looked more favorably on striking a TSS deal. But the odds
against Oslo's success were enormous. In 1992, more Jews had voted for
parties opposing negotiations with the Palestinians than had voted for parties open to the idea. Rabin's coalition held a minority of seats in the Knesset and depended, controversially and unprecedentedly, on the support of
Arab parliamentarians. Settlements were rapidly expanding, while cycles of
massacres and bombings by both Jews and Arabs polarized public opinion.
In mass demonstrations Likud and other right-wing, religious, and ultranationalist parties vilified Rabin as a traitor and even a Nazi. On November 5,
1995, after speaking to a pro-peace rally in Tel Aviv, Rabin was assassinated
by a religious Jew with close ties to the settlement movement who was con-
vinced of Rabin's treason against the Jewish people.

In 1996, cycles of targeted killings of Palestinian leaders and bloody
acts of terrorism brought the Likud Party to power. Its leader, Benjamin
Netanyahu, was a fervent opponent of a TSS. He expanded settlements,
used elaborate stonewalling tactics to halt progress toward the implementation of the Oslo Accords, and worked intensively to undermine Israeli
faith in the peace process. By the time Ehud Barak replaced Netanyahu as
prime minister in 1999, the Oslo process was already widely discredited. It
collapsed entirely with the failure at Camp David and the outbreak of the
Second Intifada at the end of 2000.

Barak has been roundly criticized for the tactical errors that led to
this outcome. He intensified settlement and bypass road building in the

West Bank, abandoned a schedule of partial withdrawals for an "all or nothing" summit with President Bill Clinton and Yasser Arafat, and escalated Israeli demands far beyond those informally agreed to by Israeli and Palestinian leaders.

However, the political basis for a successful outcome to the Oslo process had already all but disappeared. Zionism's desperate embrace of the Iron Wall strategy to finesse an otherwise unsolvable Arab problem and its partially successful implementation had drastic if unintended consequences. Victories produced expansionism, not the generosity based on strength that Jabotinsky had imagined. That unseen flaw in the Iron Wall strategy sabotaged peacemaking such that after the 1967 war when the opportunity for a two-state compromise arose, it was missed.

Chapter 2

The Cost of Holocaustia

In early March 2014 General Benny Gantz, then chief of staff of the Israel Defense Forces, responded to a mass protest by ultraorthodox Jews against conscription of their young men. In a widely publicized meeting, Gantz told dozens of ultraorthodox soldiers that "in Auschwitz they did not differentiate between us; we all went to the crematoria regardless of who wore a kippah and who did not wear a kippah, and they did not distinguish between those with beards and those without beards."[1] Gantz's point was that the essence of Jewish life in the contemporary world is that all Jews are threatened equally by Nazi-style genocide. Two years later the same idea was presented by the president of Israel, Reuven Rivlin. Speaking on behalf of the Jews of Israel, he addressed the 6 million Jewish dead. "Today, seventy years after the liberation of the death camps, we stand before you and we swear an oath, and promise: All of us, each and every one of us, has a number tattooed on his arm."[2] In November 2006, Likud leader Benjamin Netanyahu told the United Jewish Communities General Assembly in Los Angeles that "it's 1938 and Iran is Germany."[3] In February 2013 Prime Minister Netanyahu repeated his warning, describing Iran's nuclear program as a Holocaust threat growing out of

> the millennial desire of the enemies of the Jews, fired by Jew
> hatred in antiquity and medieval times and in modern times
> to eradicate the Jewish people. That has not changed. It may

have taken a back seat for a few decades after the Holocaust,
it was politically improper, but it has come back with full
force, in the renascent Islamist anti-Semitism, the anarchist
left and that strange bond between them.[4]

These three—an Israeli president, prime minister, and chief of staff—offer
Holocaust-like threats of annihilation as the essence of what it means to be
a Jew in a gentile world. Such depictions are dramatic and extreme, but they
also represent how the Holocaust is understood and imagined by the vast
majority of Israeli Jews. They present the Holocaust as a template for Jewish
life—the Nazi destruction of European Jewry tells Jews most of what they
need to know about being a Jew—that governs how Israelis think about
themselves and their country. This widespread and naturalized conception
of the Holocaust has helped paralyze Israeli responses to the Palestinian
problem and is crucial to understanding Israel's failure to embrace negotiated routes to resolve the Israel-Palestine conflict.

Given the sensitivity of this topic and the danger of misinterpretation,
I want to stress that analysis of how the Holocaust is understood and interpreted is not in any way a form of the despicable practice of Holocaust
denial—the rejection of the historical fact of the mass murder of 6 million
Jews by the Nazis during the Third Reich. However, analyzing alternative
conceptions of the Holocaust as they have emerged in Israeli political culture and shaped collective memory does depart from a dominant approach
that imagines the Holocaust's influence on subsequent generations of Jews
as being akin to the direct effects of trauma. For example, in his widely read
1971 book *Israelis: Founders and Sons*, Amos Elon described the Holocaust
as "a basic trauma of Israeli society." Its effects were "impossible to exagger-
ate," accounting for

> the prevailing sense of loneliness . . . the obsessive suspicions,
> the towering urge for self-reliance . . . the fears and preju-
> dices, passions, pains, and prides, that spin the plot of pub-
> lic life. The lingering memory of the holocaust makes Arab
> threats of annihilation sound plausible. . . . The trauma of the

holocaust leaves an indelible mark on national psychology, the tenor and content of public life, the conduct of foreign affairs, on politics, education, literature, and the arts.[5]

The prominence that Elon attributed to the Holocaust in the life and culture of Israeli Jews was and is correct. The term "holocaust" (*shoah* in Hebrew) was not yet commonly capitalized when his book appeared. From that fact alone we can glean that it later grew to occupy an even more powerful place in the culture and political imagination of the country. However, Elon wrongly suggests that the impact of this "basic trauma" was expressed within Israel immediately, profoundly, and uninterruptedly and that its meaning has remained constant. It is not the event itself but rather the collective memory of it, indeed the *changing* collective memory of it, that has so powerfully shaped Israeli politics and policy and limited its diplomacy. Thus, understanding the Holocaust, what happened to Jews in Europe between 1933 and 1945, means understanding Holocaustia—how the events of those awful years have been culturally and psychologically absorbed to distort what Jews, especially Israeli Jews, believe about themselves and the world.

"The Holocaust Is Not What It Used to Be"

In Israel's early years, the Holocaust was not prominent in public life.[6] Until the 1960s, textbooks contained virtually no information on the topic.[7] Although the Knesset did pass the Holocaust and Ghetto Revolt Day Law in 1951, legislation to require and regularize its observance—the Memorial Day for Holocaust and Heroism Law—did not appear until 1959. Not until the late 1990s did leaders of the state use this occasion for public appearances and major speeches on the topic. The museum of the Holocaust, Yad Vashem, was not commissioned until 1953, in part prompted by news of a plan to establish such a center in Paris. Before its construction, the only Holocaust memorial site was a tiny chamber on Mount Zion near the (highly disputed) Tomb of King David, where Ministry of Religion officials had established a small religiously themed collection of relics.[8]

These absences do not mean that the Holocaust's effect on the new state and its population was minimal. In the early 1950s approximately 350,000 survivors comprised fully one-third of the Jewish population of the country. But what Israelis in recent decades have experienced as "the Holocaust" has dramatically changed. Its prominence in public life has vastly increased. Its uses for guidance, inspiration, and disquisition are the product of particular processes, policies, and choices. Most Jews in Israel and in the diaspora may now experience the Holocaust as the single most important focus for thinking about their place in the world and their responsibilities as Jews. But this was not always so. I contend that the ascendance of a very particular, intense, and pervasive collective memory of the Holocaust has severely limited the political imagination of Israelis and made negotiating a compromise with Palestinian Arabs even more difficult and unlikely than it would have been otherwise.

The Holocaust as an unquestioned template for Jewish life has come to dominate Israeli political culture, but Israeli thinking about the Holocaust in the aftermath of World War II was also shaped by three other representations: as proof that the Zionist analysis of the Jewish condition was correct, as an asset to gain support from the non-Jewish world, and as an object lesson in universal human values. Although primarily influential before the 1980s, their presence lingers, and as Chapter 5 will discuss, at least one of these may yet play a crucial role in opening paths from the present to a very different kind of future.

The Holocaust as Proof That Zionism Was Right

Because of the genocidal scale and industrial form of the Nazi crimes committed against Jews, it was exceedingly difficult for anyone to believe news reports as they trickled out of German-occupied areas in the early 1940s. For Zionist leaders, the challenge was especially complex. On the one hand, the Ben-Gurionist and Revisionist streams that had dominated the movement since the 1930s emphasized that to survive, the Jewish people needed a state. It was a cruel and fundamental truth that the Nazi destruction of so much of European Jewry required first stripping victims of their citizenship or otherwise rendering them stateless.[9] No feat of verbal or intellectual agility was required to connect the absence of a state controlled by Jews with their awful fate or to convince Jews the world over, including most of those who had staunchly opposed Jewish statehood, that the disappearance of 6 million Jews made it more difficult to establish a strong Jewish state but also made it more necessary. In this sense, the Holocaust was seen as powerful validation of Zionism and, in particular, of statist Zionism. On the other hand, Zionism had always counted on millions of European Jews in desperate need of refuge as the demographic foundation of the society it imagined building and the state, economy, and army it would require to survive against large and hostile Arab populations. After the Holocaust, those Jews were no more. The reservoir of what Zionists traditionally called *homer anoshi tov* (good human material) had practically vanished. In this respect, news of the scale of the tragedy hit the Yishuv like a sledgehammer, plunging many into deep depression. With the wholesale destruction of millions of European Jews, even Chaim Weizmann and David Ben-Gurion began to wonder if perhaps Zionism had come too late.[10]

In testimony more to their iron will than their realism, Zionist leaders did not abandon their project. Despite the nightmarish reports they received and moments of despair about the future, they continued disciplined work toward the objectives they had long pursued. Saving Jews from the Nazi onslaught was important but not decisive. The failure of Zionism would be the one and only completely devastating loss.

Basic Zionist principles were readily available and offered useful categories for making sense of the awful present while holding out some hope for the future. After all, at the very core of Zionist thinking had been analysis of the fundamentally pathological nature of diaspora Jewish life and the imperative for Jews to respond to this danger by leaving as quickly as possible to build a state of their own. Men and women raised on ferocious denunciations of diaspora Jewish culture dominated Jewish life in Palestine, now the center of and dominating force in the Zionist movement. Indeed, radically anti-Jewish diatribes are to be found throughout the work of leading Zionist writers and poets, such as Chaim Nachman Bialik (the movement's poet laureate), Yosef Chaim Brenner, Micha Berdichevsky, and Shaul Tschernicovsky. For many Zionists, it was psychologically compelling and politically convenient to treat Holocaust victims—those who died "over there"—as having perished because they failed to embrace the truths of Zionism. By this logic, those killed in the camps and even those who survived could be referred to derisively in Hebrew slang as *sabon* (soap), typical diaspora Jews whose inbred cravenness led them to submit without resistance to their oppressors, marching to their deaths "like sheep to the slaughter."[11]

The Holocaust as Zionist prooftext (i.e., direct evidence of the validity of Zionism) had three key elements: rejection of the Jewish life in the diaspora as a viable form of existence, diagnosis of Jewish ills as stemming from a cowardly and embarrassing unwillingness to fight, and the inevitability of persecution against Jews in any country other than their own. As Zionist ideology had long affirmed, life in the diaspora was too dangerous for Jews; Jewish statelessness was a recipe for disaster; no amount of prayer, acquiescence, flight, or diffidence could protect Jews as individuals; and only a Jewish state, wielding its own military and political power and acting as a vehicle for the psychological and physical rehabilitation of the Jewish people, could offer a future to the Jewish people. Against this overall conception of the Holocaust, its "lessons" were distilled by Ben-Gurion and his avatar for this purpose, Ben-Zion Dinur, appointed as minister of education and culture and the first president of Yad Vashem. In their formulations, the behavior of non-Zionist Jews during the Holocaust became an example for citizens of the new state of how *not* to behave, even as rare but important acts of violent Jewish resistance to the Nazis were honored and credited to the fighters' Zionist commitments.[12]

Thus, the Ben-Gurion/Dinur construction of the Holocaust worked as prooftext in two ways. First, the annihilation of Jewish life in Europe served to validate the fundamental Zionist analysis that the very structure of Jewish life had to be transformed and based on independent statehood if the Jewish people were to survive. Second, Zionist postures of bold action, defiance, and physical heroism, in contrast to the docility of the masses of Jewish victims, could be valorized by evoking and giving special honor to armed Jewish resistance to the Nazis, especially resistance offered by Zionist movements. Textbooks concluded their narratives of the ghetto revolts by describing Zionism as a "call for rebellion" and "the heroic position of the ghetto Jews . . . as compensation for the shameful surrender of the Jews who were transported to the death camps."[13]

The unintended result of this framing of the Holocaust was to encourage among young Israelis a deep revulsion toward the behavior of Jewish victims and even toward the victims themselves, a revulsion that came to extend to all Jews living in the diaspora and even toward Jewishness itself. An official committee on Israeli Jewish consciousness was established in 1956 to reconsider curricular treatment of the Holocaust. The impetus for the committee's work was noted in a protocol acknowledging that "anyone involved in children's education will admit that when we talk to our youngsters about exilic Jewry, we find their hearts shut."[14]

In this context the government's steps to gain reparation payments from Germany were important: they not only helped secure desperately needed resources for the fledgling state, but the effort also required Israel and Jewish Israelis to identify at least indirectly with all the victims of the Holocaust, not just with armed resistors. This stance implied a distinctive second conception of the Holocaust, suitable to a campaign for reparations and for political and diplomatic support for Israel based on Jewish suffering and gentile guilt, that treated the Holocaust as a wasting asset, a political resource whose effectiveness would decay with the passage of time.

The Holocaust as Wasting Asset

Post-Holocaust sympathy for Jews was vital to the postwar Zionist campaign for independent statehood. Historically, this was a rare and temporary circumstance—an opportunity that no politician as shrewd as Ben-Gurion could ignore. One standard tactic used by Ben-Gurion throughout his career was to search in the face of every reversal or setback for a silver lining—a way that the goals of Zionism and his personal goals could be advanced precisely as a result of the problem itself. He fashioned himself as the indomitable Leninist, ready to subordinate all other considerations to what was necessary and expedient for the achievement of Jewish statehood in Palestine under his leadership. His biographer explains that Ben-Gurion sought to treat the mass murder of millions of European Jews the same as other setbacks. He would find ways to treat it as a "beneficial disaster."[15] In January 1944, Ben-Gurion advised the Mapai central committee that after the war "the world's conscience will awaken" and that "gentile guilt" at not "lifting a finger" to stop the "incessant flow of our blood" would be an important Zionist resource.[16] The Holocaust was a *wasting* asset, however, since the "guilt" and horror of European and American gentiles would decline rapidly over time and needed to be exploited while it was available.

Leaders used gentile guilt and horror at Jewish suffering to boost Zionist prospects and later Israel's economy and its position among gentiles. For the masses, however, the wasting asset view meant a psychological and emotional shift from shame and anger at Jewish weakness to compassion for Jewish victims. Indeed, identification with Holocaust victims was necessary for Israeli Jews—and for Israel as a state—to become beneficiaries of their suffering. This was a major perceptual shift from seeing the Holocaust as a prooftext of Zionist theory to seeing it as a theater of Jewish suffering.

Construing the Holocaust as a wasting asset was important in two spectacularly successful campaigns. The first was conducted by the Zionist movement against the British blockade of Palestine to support immigration into the country of 100,000 Holocaust survivors from displaced persons camps in Europe. The Haganah ship *Exodus* was a freighter carrying more than 4,500 Jewish refugees. The ship was forcibly boarded by British Royal Navy troops, and its wretched cargo was returned to Germany. This cruel story triggered worldwide sympathy for the refugees and for Zionist demands for a state in Palestine. The incident led rather quickly to British abandonment of the mandate and to the United Nations (UN) Partition Plan that followed it, which created the legal basis for a Jewish state.[17]

The second campaign was to establish the State of Israel as the appropriate recipient of massive German reparations for Nazi atrocities. Ben-Gurion and his foreign minister, Moshe Sharett, again drew heavily on the wasting asset interpretation of the Holocaust. In 1951 they began secret negotiations with the Federal Republic of Germany that ultimately yielded nearly $89 billion in compensation paid to Jews between 1952 and 2012, most of it directed to the State of Israel or Jewish citizens of Israel.[18] The negotiations and the reparations agreement itself were extremely controversial in Israel. Both Sharett and Ben-Gurion responded that the Germans should not be able "to both murder and inherit," a slogan that epitomized the emotional shift from treating victims of the Holocaust as grist for the Zionist ideological mill to empathizing with their fate. Both the wasting asset conception and the psychological changes associated with it were necessary to justify demands that reparations for Jewish suffering in Europe be paid to Israel and to Israeli Jews.

The Holocaust as Human Rights Object Lesson

After the war, the Nuremberg Court did not convict or punish Nazi leaders for killing Jews, Roma, Slavs, homosexuals, or the disabled but did convict them for committing "crimes against humanity." For people around the world, the Holocaust is most prominently understood as a gigantic criminal act, an insult and a challenge to civilization itself. Survivor testimonies and advocacy groups most frequently identified the imperative to teach the world what happened to the Jews at the hands of evildoers so that evil would never again be visited on any other people.[19] This is not the most prominent or influential way that Israeli Jews have thought about the Holocaust, but the Holocaust as an object lesson in universalist values is a third distinctive and important conception of it in Israeli political culture.

Undoubtedly, the most spectacular dramatization of the Holocaust as object lesson was Israel's trial of Adolf Eichmann, the Nazi official responsible for ensuring a constant supply of Jewish victims for the extermination camps. For survivor organizations, the 1961 trial was an invaluable education in man's potential inhumanity, the fundamental importance of civilizational commitments to individual human dignity and the rule of law, the protection from genocidal attacks that every people deserved, and the immorality of the bystander role in the face of monumental evil.

For Ben-Gurion, the Eichmann trial also served other purposes. It burnished his anti-Nazi and anti-German credentials and those of the ruling Labor Party in the aftermath of allegations that Labor Zionist leaders had in some ways collaborated with the Nazis.[20] Ordering Eichmann's apprehension and trial also served Ben-Gurion's urgent efforts to deepen Israel's military relations with Germany (by distinguishing between "Nazi" Germany and the "new" Germany). Meanwhile, he and other Israeli leaders hoped that the sympathy aroused during the trial would overcome some of the alienation from diaspora Jews and Judaism occasioned by earlier unsympathetic portrayals of diaspora Jews and Holocaust victims. In other words, the trial as staged reminded the world of the scale of Jewish suffering and the inadequacy of international responses so as to extend the period of usable gentile sympathy and guilt.[21]

One of the many consequences of Eichmann's trial in Jerusalem was the prominence it gave to universalist principles that encouraged Israelis to interpret and understand the Holocaust as an object lesson for all who valued civilized life and respected human dignity. Hannah Arendt's firsthand account of the trial, *Eichmann in Jerusalem*, received enormous attention. It became and still is the best-known and most influential argument in favor of treating the Holocaust as a human rights object lesson. This theme, among others, was also emphasized by Gideon Hausner, who served as chief prosecutor. In his opening address to the court, Hausner referred repeatedly to the Nuremberg Tribunal "whose decision is binding upon us according to our Law."[22] Hausner pointed to Adolf Hitler's rejection of

> the existence of a common basis for all humanity. According to his doctrines there is no mutual responsibility between men. In place of the injunction 'And though shalt love thy neighbor as thyself,' we find 'Crush him that is unlike thyself!' Instead of the ideal of human brotherhood, we have the principle of race superiority.[23]

The trial lasted four months. Graphic and emotionally exhausting testimony broadcast live on the radio gripped the entire nation of Israel. Hausner's strategy and prosecutorial style were dramatic and passionate. Ironically, however, the most far-reaching effects of the trial were not to serve the multiple interests that animated Ben-Gurion. Nor did the trial make the Holocaust as a universalist object lesson into the dominant Israeli or Jewish interpretation of the disaster. Instead, the trial's most important effect was unintended. It laid the groundwork for the fourth and most consequential construction of the Holocaust: as a template for Jewish life.

The Holocaust as Template for Jewish Life

Within Israeli collective memory, the Holocaust as a template for Jewish life became dominant in the 1980s and was consolidated in the 1990s. It remains ascendant. I do not refer here to an extreme and specifically religious view prevalent among some ultraorthodox sects that the Holocaust was an unusually horrific but tragically familiar persecution, authorized by God, of his chosen but wayward people.[24]

Instead, "template for Jewish life" refers to a collective memory of the Holocaust as a reliable political and moral guide for all Jews, whether secular or religious, to what it means to be Jewish in an overwhelmingly non-Jewish world. By this logic, the Holocaust revealed the unbridgeable abyss that separates Jews and gentiles and the ferocious anti-Semitism lurking in the hearts and cultures of all non-Jews. These realities make the Holocaust understandable—both the industrialized and genocidal slaughter of millions of Jews by the Germans and their allies in almost every occupied country and the widespread refusal of refuge to Jews seeking to escape.

Jews do not have to be religious to experience the Holocaust as a template for Jewish life. Reduced to a simple slogan, the categorical imperative of this construction for any Jew is "Don't be a "*frier!*" (a sucker) by trusting non-Jews, relying upon their goodwill, or taking risks with Jewish interests or objectives to serve supposedly universalist purposes.[25] It is this Holocaust interpretation that has largely displaced the other three, becoming deeply and pervasively institutionalized in contemporary Israel and among Jewish diaspora communities. Beliefs associated with treating the Holocaust as a template for Jewish life became unevaluated and virtually unevaluable axioms of Israeli political discourse and deeply inform the self-experience of Jewishness for millions of Israeli and non-Israeli Jews.

Four events contributed decisively to the victory of this conception of the Holocaust over the other three: the trial of Adolf Eichmann in 1961, the three-week waiting period before the Six-Day War of June 1967, the Yom Kippur War of 1973, and Menachem Begin's premiership in the late 1970s and early 1980s.[26]

As noted, in the mid-1950s Israeli elites had begun to worry about the intensity of the state's rejection of Jewish life in *galut* (exile) and the near disgust with which the new sabra generation (Jews raised in Palestine or Israel) treated the experience and behavior of Holocaust victims. Leaders of Jewish educational and cultural institutions as well as governing elites thought that the trial of Eichmann, by exposing the Israeli Jewish public via live national radio broadcasts to heart-wrenching survivor and expert accounts, would help replace scorn with empathy for the victims of the final solution.

Indeed, Israeli Jews were emotionally overwhelmed by the ghastly and terrifyingly inescapable conditions imposed on European Jews during the Holocaust. Survivors' dramatic testimony collapsed the psychological separation that had been maintained between "them," the mass of Jews who had allowed themselves to be victimized by the Nazis without resisting, and "us," a healthy courageous nation of Jews who lived in the Land of Israel and founded the Jewish state.[27] Yehiel Dinur, a writer also known as Ka-Tzetnik, was a survivor of Auschwitz. He fainted on the stand during his testimony but not before describing experiences so remote from anything human and familiar that it might as well have occurred on another planet. One scholar describes Dinur's phrase "Planet Auschwitz" as "one of the most thoroughly absorbed of all terms in the Israeli discourse." It enabled individual Israelis to believe that had they been *there* they also would have succumbed, no matter how Zionist or courageous they imagined themselves to be.[28] The Eichmann trial propelled Israeli Jews toward a profound, direct, and personal identification with the mass of Holocaust victims. Survival was the imperative. Heroism encompassed anything done for that purpose, not just armed actions against the oppressor. Hanna Yablonka has written that the Eichmann trial, more than any other event, "turned the story of the Holocaust in Europe into an Israeli story."[29] Thereafter, Israeli Jews, whether of European, Middle Eastern, North African, or sabra extraction, identified personally with the victims of the Holocaust—not just with the partisans and ghetto fighters but also with the slaughtered masses.[30]

Five years after the Eichmann trial, tension between Israel and the Arab states escalated. Arab capitals responded to dogfights in the skies over Syria with threats of annihilation. A new alliance among previously quarreling Arab leaders led to a united Arab military command dedicated to the liberation of Palestine and the destruction of Israel. Following Gamal Abdel Nasser's order to evacuate the Sinai, the UN Emergency Force disappeared as a buffer between the Egyptian and Israeli armies. The Egyptian announcement of closure of the Gulf of Aqaba to Israeli shipping and signs of dithering in Europe and North America made it seem as if Israel would be standing alone against a credible threat of disastrous defeat and even genocidal slaughter.

Israel's prime minister at the time was Levi Eshkol. His popular image was that of a pre-Zionist Jewish politician with expertise in practical matters (as minister of agriculture and finance). Eshkol had none of the brio of Ben-Gurion and his coterie of sabra warriors. Eshkol was widely suspected of being afraid to lead the country to war, and his halting radio address during the crisis reinforced the public's angst and sense of doom. The Eichmann trial had stimulated Israeli Jews to identify themselves with the fate of Jews murdered by the Nazis, but it was only during this anxiety-filled three weeks (the waiting period) that masses of Israeli Jews came to see their collective political predicament as corresponding to the Nazi menace that had overwhelmed European Jews.

As a direct result of moral panic among both the masses and elites, Eshkol was forced to appoint Moshe Dayan as defense minister. Chief of staff during the 1956 Suez War against Egypt and closely allied with Ben-Gurion, Dayan was the iconic image of the new aggressive Israeli Jewish hero. Many historians now believe that Israel was never in the kind of existential danger attributed at the time to the Arab threat, and Eshkol's diffidence is now widely judged to have been wisdom, but Dayan's appointment made war inevitable. With Dayan in command Israel launched a surprise attack, destroying the Egyptian Air Force in a single blow and ensuring a victory that dramatically exposed the Arabs' weakness and disunity. The victory was so quick and seemed so complete that the waiting-period angst in Israel was replaced by euphoria and a triumphalist attitude toward the Jewish state's ability to impose peace on its terms, including Israeli rule of most or all of the territories acquired in battle from Syria, Jordan, and Egypt.

The mood was short-lived. The anxiety of the May 1967 waiting period was rekindled, this time as a fixture of Israeli political culture, by the 1973 Yom Kippur War. The Eichmann trial had shifted the psychological stance of Israeli Jews toward the victims of the Holocaust from alienation, stigmatization, and disgust to empathy and identification. Next, during the waiting period this empathy and identification had encouraged Israelis to draw an equivalence between the Nazi threat during the Holocaust and the Arab threats against Israel while the world stood by and watched. But it was not until the 1973 war that the implications of this change in political psychology became clear. In this war Israeli losses were more than triple those suffered in 1967. Intense fighting lasted for weeks. Hostilities and the mobilization of reservists dragged on for many months. At one point early in the fighting, Defense Minister Dayan panicked and recommended unleashing Israel's nuclear weapons. Combined with the scale of the losses and rumors of even larger defeats and breakdowns in leadership, despair gripped the Israeli public as the outcome of the war seemed in doubt. Regardless of the greater damage inflicted by Israel on the Arab armies, Israelis experienced the outcome of the war, including withdrawals from territory in both the Golan Heights and the Sinai, as an agonizing defeat.

The prolonged sense of weakness and vulnerability that followed the 1973 war, coupled with disillusionment and distrust, solidified the Holocaust as a template for Jewish life. From October 1973 onward, Israeli Jews' affinity with Holocaust victims came to fundamentally inform popular political understandings of the predicament of the State of Israel and its Jewish population as chronic and existential.

It was only a matter of time before politicians positioned to exploit this way of thinking would reap its benefits, and that time was not long in coming. Four years after the military earthquake of the Yom Kippur War, Israel experienced a political earthquake—the replacement of the Labor Party in the elections of 1977 by Menachem Begin's Likud Party. Instead of a single-party dominant system anchored by the Labor Party, a competitive party system emerged that oscillated between center-left and center-right governments. This pattern continued for almost three decades until the reestablishment of a single-party dominant system in 2009, with Likud as the dominant party.

Likud's leader in 1977, Menachem Begin, had been more passionate and consistent than any other major Israeli politician in evoking the Holocaust as emblematic of the permanent condition of the Jew. His Holocaust-dominated gestalt had both personal and political dimensions. Begin's parents and brother were killed by the Nazis. He himself narrowly escaped, spending years in Soviet prisons before arriving in Palestine. Though it was not as central to his political message as it would become later, the Holocaust was always a personally defining event for Begin in a way it never had been for Ben-Gurion and most leading Labor politicians. "The Holocaust," Begin said in a 1977 interview, "lives within me. And I live within it. And I will live with it until the last day of my life." It was "the prime mover," he said, "of all that we have done in our generation."[31]

After the 1948 war Begin transformed his underground Irgun military organization into the Herut (Freedom) political party, basing its appeal on calls for maximalist territorial expansion. Expecting to emerge as leader of the opposition to Ben-Gurion's Mapai Party, Begin was stunned by Herut's poor showing in Israel's 1949 election. After an even worse showing in 1951, Begin resigned as party leader. But he shortly returned, basing his comeback on Holocaust appeals. He denounced the reparations agreement with Germany as a humiliating acceptance of blood money and fully exploited the Kastner trial in 1955, during which Labor Party leaders suffered devastating attacks for their alleged willingness to negotiate with the Gestapo.[32] Begin emerged from the 1955 elections as head of the largest opposition party. He was mindful of how much his success was tied to the Holocaust as a basis for attacking Labor Party rule, constructing Israel's conflict with Arabs as equivalent to its struggle with the Nazis, and portraying relations between Jews and gentiles as intractably hostile.

Thus, the Eichmann trial and the wars of 1967 and 1973 supplied Begin with a spectacular opportunity to anchor appeals to Israeli voters strongly and broadly enough to bring his new Likud Party to power and, except for seven years of Labor and Kadima governments, keep it there. The key was garnering support from the Mizrahim (Easterners), the great mass of Jewish working-class and lower-middle-class voters whose families had immigrated to Israel from the Middle East and North Africa. Mizrahim harbored intense resentment about mistreatment as new immigrants in the 1950s and the discrimination, condescension, and even racism exhibited toward them by many members of the predominantly Ashkenazi (European American) Labor Party and bureaucracy. Few Mizrahim featured prominently in either Herut or the broader Likud, but Begin could mobilize them en masse, in part by drawing directly and dramatically on the common identification of all Israeli Jews, including Mizrahim, with Jewish victims of the Holocaust.[33]

Key to Begin's success was the change in Israeli sentiments toward Holocaust victims and an extension of the category of "we who have survived" to include not only those who had been in the camps or had fled Europe but also to all Jews whom the Nazis had failed to kill, including Mizrahim. Begin exploited Mizrahi desires to avoid identification as or with Arabs (despite their appearance, key aspects of their culture, and the prominence of the Arabic language in their homes and families). To do this, he used the Holocaust to instruct all Jews and warn them of their precarious, frightening position. With powerful melodrama Begin portrayed Jews, including Mizrahim, as forever isolated and exposed to slaughter in an intrinsically anti-Semitic gentile world. Drawing directly on the anxieties, fears, and furies associated with the waiting period and the losses and disillusionments of the 1973 war, he missed no opportunity to identify Arab terror and Arab military or political mobilization of any kind as an ineluctable recapitulation of Nazi genocide. His success with this tactic led one of Israel's shrewdest political observers to remark that it was Menachem Begin "who released the genie of the Holocaust from the bottle."[34]

A sampling of Begin's rhetoric reveals how many of his tropes have become staples of Israeli political discourse. During a September 1969 election rally in Safed, Begin spoke to a mostly Mizrahi audience and devoted nearly his entire speech to a portrayal of Jews as standing alone and isolated in an anti-Semitic world and to an analogy between the threats posed to Jews and Israel by the Arabs and those faced by Jews during the Holocaust.[35] It was a theme he repeated endlessly. Arab threats before the 1967 war "threatened another Holocaust." After the war, trading occupied territories for peace would lead to another slaughter of 1.5 million Jewish children.[36] "The PLO [Palestine Liberation Organization] Covenant was . . . *Mein Kampf* no. 2, and 'the organization of murderers' [the PLO] and its leader were the modern-day equivalent of the SS and Adolf Hitler respectively."[37] The Soviet Union's support for the PLO reprised its alliance with Nazi Germany. UN responsiveness to the Palestinian cause as well as European and American tolerance for PLO offices in their countries proved that the Holocaust's lessons had not been learned. On the eve of Israel's invasion of Lebanon to destroy PLO forces there, Begin told his cabinet, "Believe me, the alternative to this is Treblinka, and we have decided that there will not be another Treblinka."[38] When Israel bombed the Iraqi nuclear reactor in 1981, Begin equated radioactivity with the poison gas used in the extermination camps, declaring that the raid had protected "Israel and her people" from "another Holocaust.[39] While Israeli soldiers were attacking Beirut in 1982 in search of PLO head Yasser Arafat, Begin characterized himself in a letter to President Ronald Reagan as "a Prime Minister empowered to instruct a valiant army facing Berlin where, amongst innocent civilians, Hitler and his henchmen hide in a bunker deep beneath the surface."[40]

In this fashion, Begin led the way for generations of politicians to use "Holocaustia" as vocabulary for political analysis. Advocates of the "Greater Land of Israel" were especially effusive in its use to advance their political program. By their lights, only an expansive and militant State of Israel would be prepared to do battle against inevitable and recurrent Holocaust threats.[41] In this respect, Benjamin Netanyahu has been Menachem Begin's most faithful disciple, treating the destruction of 6 million Jews as a kind of forever Holocaust. Since at least 2006, Netanyahu has railed against Iran's nuclear technology development program as a repeat of Nazi Germany's mobilization. Over a period considerably longer than the twelve years between Hitler's rise to power and the end of World War II, Netanyahu continued to declare, "It's 1938 and Iran is Germany."[42]

To be sure, Israeli intellectuals have roundly accused politicians who use this kind of rhetoric of trivializing the catastrophe with self-serving attempts to instrumentalize its memory.[43] But those who beat the Holocaust drum at every opportunity do so because they appreciate its effectiveness in mobilizing the Israeli Jewish population. Their success shows how saturated the society is by Holocaustia and how hegemonic—which is to say "natural"—it has become for Israeli Jews to understand the Holocaust as a template for all one needs to know about what it is to be Jewish.

At least ten major museums and memorials to the Holocaust are now open in Israel. In 2017 the biggest of these, Yad Vashem, welcomed 925,000 visitors, including de rigueur visits by virtually every foreign leader visiting Jerusalem.[44] According to Yad Vashem's director, in 2011 alone 6,000 books were published in Israel on the Holocaust—more Hebrew books than appeared in any other thematic category.[45] In 2014 this flood of books included a gigantic coffee-table volume containing nothing but 6 million instances of the word "Jew."[46] In June 2014 more than half the books in the Judaica section of the main store of Tel Aviv's largest bookseller were devoted to various dimensions of the destruction of European Jewry and its legacy.

The Israeli educational system paid limited attention to the Holocaust during the 1950s and fluctuated in its approaches during the 1970s and 1980s, but once Holocaustia took hold in the 1980s, public schools became powerful vehicles for its transmission. Visitors to a Holocaust museum in Israel on almost any school day are sure to see classes of youngsters or teenagers being led through the exhibits. In 1988 the Education Ministry began sponsoring carefully scripted, subsidized, weeklong trips to the death camps in Poland for Israeli students in their penultimate year of high school. The initiator of this program chose the following passage to begin the guidebook provided to participants:

As we stand by the crematoria . . . opposite the flag of Israel raised on high and over the death pits and ovens of destruction, we stand erect and our lips whisper—the people of Israel lives! . . . And we swear to the millions of our murdered brethren—if I forget thee, O Jerusalem, let my right hand forget its strength! In the ears of our spirit we hear their souls calling to us—through our death we have commanded you to live! Guard and protect the State of Israel like the apple of your eye! And we answer wholeheartedly—long live the State of Israel forever![47]

The final ceremony of the trip is conducted in Warsaw, where the participants recite a passage from Haim Gouri, one of Israel's most famous patriotic poets. The melding of Jew-Holocaust victim-defender of Israel is succinctly accomplished:

And sometimes it is I that suffocated in the gas chambers;
And a minute later, I am the partisan in the forests . . .
And I am the Mussulman,
And I am the IDF [Israel Defense Forces] paratrooper taking revenge
    against his enemies . . .
And I know that this is my people.[48]

By 2008, 250,000 students had completed their *masa* to the death camps.[49] In 2012 a kilometer-long connecting path was opened between Yad Vashem and Mt. Herzl, where the military cemetery and a shrine to national heroes are located. A sign erected at the beginning of the walkway announces that it was "constructed manually by members of Israel's youth movements." Echoing the theme of student trips to the death camps and back to Israel, visitors are told that "passage along it is a symbolic voyage in time from catastrophe to rebirth. It represents the journey from the Diaspora to the homeland of the Jewish people, from exile and destruction to a life of endeavor and hope in the State of Israel." Ministry of Education events organized for Holocaust Memorial Day include a hike along this path for thousands of students.

There is strong evidence that these programs, along with the dramatic shift in Holocaust memory and discourse in Israel that I have described, have had a major effect on young Israeli Jews. As early as 1993, a survey found that the prominence of the Holocaust in the psychological and cultural consciousness of students in teacher-training colleges had increased markedly since the mid-1980s. Respondents were more likely to see the Holocaust as the source of their personal identity than any other factor, to view it as the most important event in Jewish history, and to identify more strongly with Holocaust victims than with Jews living in the diaspora.[50]

A study of Holocaust imagery used in the Israeli press corroborated the survey's findings. During the 1991 Persian Gulf War, 230 Israelis were injured by Iraqi missile strikes, and 2 others were killed. But fearing poison gas attacks that never came, millions of Israelis took shelter for significant periods in sealed rooms, where they also wore gas masks. In a landmark study of the Hebrew press during this period, Moshe Zuckerman showed the domination of Israel's public consciousness by Holocaust thinking. According to Zuckerman, reporters and commentators deployed Holocaust metaphors and categories during the war so routinely that they threatened to dilute the Hebrew language itself to such an extent that actual catastrophes could no longer be described, gauged, or appreciated.[51]

We might expect that the Persian Gulf War, with its threat of poison gas, would prompt more than its share of Holocaust associations, especially in a rightist-leaning popular press, but a subsequent study of the liberal *Haaretz* newspaper yielded similar results. From October 2007 to September 2008 an average of 132 Holocaust references per month were recorded, compared to 140 monthly uses of all different phrases referring to the "Israeli-Arab conflict."[52] A 2009 survey asked Jewish Israelis about the "guiding principles of their life." The results showed found that almost all respondents—98.1 percent—reported "remembering the Holocaust" as one of those guiding principles. This was the most often cited guiding principle—advanced more frequently than "feeling part of Israeli society," "living in Israel," or "having a family."[53]

One of Menachem Begin's biographers observed that when it came to the Holocaust, Begin "was entirely sincere, entirely impassioned and entirely haunted."[54] The hegemony of the Holocaust as a template for Jewish life means that millions of twenty-first-century Israeli Jews, who did not experience or suffer what Begin did, nevertheless have acquired the same haunted perspective. Visitors to the office of Meir Dagan, head of Mossad—Israel's clandestine intelligence and operations agency—from 2002 to 2011, found a picture on the wall featuring his grandfather kneeling near a trench just seconds before being shot by an SS officer. In 2003, pilots of the Israeli Air Force, each a descendant of a Holocaust survivor, flew Phantom F-15 fighter-bombers in a simulated bombing run over Auschwitz. The air force added text to the official video of the event it posted on the Internet: "We rose from the ashes of millions of victims, carrying their silent cries, saluting their heroism, and promising to be a shield, to the Jewish people and its land, Israel."[55] Young Israelis tattoo numbers on their arms and pose for pictures with their grandparents who received tattoos in the death camps.[56] A schoolgirl of Iranian descent cries to her mother, wondering if she is really Jewish since she does not have an aunt who died in the Holocaust.[57] In 2014 the minister of education announced that Holocaust education would begin in the first grade.[58] Paraphrasing a key portion of the Passover seder, the philosopher Adi Ophir aptly portrayed the centrality of the Holocaust template for translating Jewishness into meaning in contemporary Israel and thereby transforming every Jew into both a Holocaust survivor and a witness. "A familiar commandment appears here: in every generation, each individual is bound to regard himself as if he had personally survived Auschwitz, as if he had witnessed the revelation of Evil."[59]

Although Prime Minister Moshe Sharett spoke briefly to commemorate the Holocaust in 1953, it was not until the mid-1990s that Israeli prime ministers and presidents made official speeches on the subject. Once the template for Jewish life displaced other interpretations of the Holocaust, however, the national calendar was filled with occasions of all but mandatory public memorialization of the catastrophe. Holocaust and Heroism Remembrance Day is observed in the spring near the anniversary of the Warsaw Ghetto Uprising. Israelis stand silent while a siren sounds throughout the country for two minutes. This occasion follows shortly after Israel observes its official memorial day for military casualties and victims of terrorism. International Holocaust Memorial Day is observed on January 27. For many religious Jews, Tisha B'av (the ninth of the Hebrew summer month of Ab) is used as the traditional occasion for mourning great national tragedies, now including the Holocaust. Others commemorate the Holocaust on the tenth of the winter month of Teveth. The key trope of Jewish martyrdom in the early twenty-first century joins victims of the Holocaust and all Israelis—soldiers and civilians—who have died as a result of hostile actions.[60] In recent years large groups of Israeli leaders have gone to Auschwitz to lead an annual March of the Living, featuring a two-mile hike from the Auschwitz concentration camp to the extermination center at Birkenau. In January 2014, fifty-four members of the Israeli parliament—nearly half—flew to Poland for this purpose.[61]

Holocaustia—intense, pervasive, and relentlessly reproduced—is protected from critical scrutiny by an aura of sacredness and a presumption of universal agreement about its claims. This makes it extremely difficult for Israeli Jews to appreciate the narrow confines of their thinking and spot distortions in their view of the world associated with belief in the forever Holocaust. In 2010 a leading Israeli historian of the Holocaust was dismissed from her post as chair of the national committee to advise the government on history textbooks. Hanna Yablonka, a professor at Ben-Gurion University, was fired after she criticized the Education Ministry's established Holocaust curriculum for its "superficiality," "mistaken emphasis," and absence of a "critical approach."[62]

From Nazis to Arabs and Back

To live forever in the expectation that Holocaust-scale threats could be imminent brings continuous traumatization. Constructing the Holocaust as both the greatest crime in human history and the permanent epitome of what it means to be Jewish creates a culture that marinates Israeli Jews in

Holocaustia images, associations, emotions, and "lessons." Intrapsychically, this produces hundreds of Holocaust hyperlinks in the minds of Jews so that ordinary words, objects, and experiences—barking dogs, ovens, gas, barbed wire, smokestacks, railroad cars, trucks, carbon monoxide, showers, soap, lampshades, camps, nakedness, fear, baby shoes, hunger, humiliation, and so on—lead immediately to Holocaust thoughts and Holocaust emotions. This reality of Israeli Jewish consciousness is unignorable for politicians, journalists, writers, artists, and performers who want to communicate with or arouse their audiences.

The Holocaust template also powerfully stamps Israeli foreign policy. When the common sense of the Jewish masses in Israel is that the gentile world is fundamentally out to get Jews and the Jewish state, the fortunes of any foreign policy position publicly advanced by Israeli elites will be heavily determined by whether it echoes the terms of that worldview. Policies based on appreciating risks but seeing them outweighed by the benefits of cooperation and trust in other peoples and countries will be systematically disadvantaged, often devastatingly so, in competition with policies based on extremely pessimistic assessments of the intentions of potential adversaries and the possibilities of productive cooperation.

This reality is well known to politicians who affirm Holocaustia assumptions in their public speeches and in the rationales they offer for policies. This in turn restricts the kinds of analyses and recommendations that experts and elites think useful or wise to advance. Whether the questions relate to Israeli support of white South Africa, Pahlavi Iran, Phalangist Lebanon, implementation of the Oslo process, Iran's nuclear technology program, arguments over disproportionate use of force or collective punishment, votes and initiatives at the UN focused on Israeli settlement policies, discrimination against Arabs, or responses to European and other campaigns of boycotts and sanctions, the result is more or less the same. The lessons and precedents marshaled to justify or reject policies, along with the memes and tropes to embed them, are drawn from the Holocaustia dictionary—1938, Kristalnacht, Auschwitz, Never Again, Judenraat, ghetto, yellow stars, *Judenrein*, and so on. In this context, official Israeli policies are naturally drawn, often irresistibly, toward rejection of initiatives whose attractiveness is based on positive-sum images of Jewish or Israeli relations with the non-Jewish world. When cooperation is pursued or justified in any but short-term or technical arenas or when initiatives are publicly accepted—for example, Prime Minister Netanyahu's Bar-Ilan University speech formally endorsing the two-state solution—a double discourse is usually deployed, which ensures that the Israeli public and its key groups understand that such declarations are mere public relations strategies, easily reinterpreted as ploys to keep Israel from being played for a sucker.

In the public policy domain, the Holocaustia template has had its largest and most destructive effect on the capacity of masses of Israeli Jews to empathize enough with Palestinian Arabs to deal effectively with their demands and discontent. The basic syllogism holds that all enemies are Nazis and that Arabs or Muslims are enemies, so Arabs and Muslims are Nazis, effectively disqualifying them as objects of humane concern.[63] The process of transforming Palestinians, Arabs, and, more recently, all Muslims or even all those who oppose Israeli measures against Arabs or Muslims into Nazis if not logically syllogistic is at least psychologically so. Consider how six inferences flow from the initial premise, resulting ultimately in a principle for guiding foreign policy (meaning, effectively, policies toward non-Jews) that together trump any nontactical or ethical argument for restraint:

> *Premise*: "There can be nothing more evil than what the Nazis did to the Jews; it was absolute and infinite."

> 1. Therefore all measures to weaken or destroy Nazis or potential Nazis are legitimate.
> 2. Those who oppose measures taken against potential Nazis increase the potential for absolute evil.
> 3. Therefore all measures taken against those who oppose measures taken against potential Nazis are legitimate.

4. Since the Nazis attacked Jews, anyone who attacks Jews is a potential Nazi.
5. Arabs and Muslims attack Jews and therefore are potential Nazis.
6. Therefore, all measures taken against Arabs and Muslims and against those who oppose measures taken against Arabs and Muslims are legitimate.

The other three Holocaust constructions described briefly at the beginning of this chapter are still relevant, but the ascendancy of Holocaustia has driven most successful Israeli politicians to speak and act in ways that reinforce Israeli Jewish understandings of their world as intractably and existentially threatening. In this way the Holocaust as a template for Jewish life powerfully contributes to vicious cycles of violence and hatred between Israel and the Palestinians. To the extent that Arabs and Muslims are automatically seen as Nazis or are expected to act as Nazis and to the extent that gentiles are always liable to "revert to type" as anti-Semites, then every problem faced by Israel is most convincingly portrayed as potentially another Holocaust that the state must guard against.

To be sure, the hegemony of Holocaustia does not mean that all ordinary Jewish Israelis, intellectuals, and leaders see their world exclusively or primarily through the lens of the darkest hour in human history. For decades there have been Israeli Jews ready to recognize Palestinian rights and Jewish responsibility for Palestinian suffering and to find compromises that might fulfill the fundamental requirements of both peoples. These positions have emerged not because the Holocaust was forgotten but because it has been differently remembered and interpreted. In Chapter 5 the surprising potential of the consciousness of evil associated with Holocaustia to encourage radically new Israeli Jewish perspectives on the conflict with the Arabs will be discussed. Here it is simply worth considering the acclaimed 2008 Israeli film by Ari Folman, *Waltz with Bashir*. The movie is a mostly animated treatment of the experiences and traumas of Israeli soldiers during the 1982 Lebanon War and their indirect complicity in the massacre of Palestinians by the Phalange militias under the leadership of Israel's ally, Bashir Gemayel. *Valtz eem Bashir*, as the title reads in Hebrew, conjures directly the idea of "doing something German" with Bashir. Indeed, the entire film, from the ravenous dogs in the first scene to the emaciated naked bodies of Israeli soldiers rising from the sea and trucks piled with Palestinian bodies, is constructed on the knowledge that Israeli viewers will automatically make the connections linking Israelis to Germans that cannot be made explicitly.

Ultimately the Holocaust is "unmasterable." Charles S. Maier said this about the perpetrators—the Germans—as they sought to understand their past.[64] But it is true for Jews as well as they confront their present. It is just too immense an event, too protean, too subversive of all purposive narratives, for it to be contained or disciplined by a formula. In the battle over the meaning of the Holocaust in Israeli political culture, Holocaustia has benefited from its affinity with Iron Wall belligerence. As we shall see in the next chapter, it has also thrived in a context of complete American protection from the consequences of the policy excesses it encourages. Yet one of its rivals, the Holocaust as moral object lesson, may be poised for a comeback.

Holocaustia has prompted Jewish fundamentalists to condemn Prime Minister Yitzhak Rabin to death with caricatures of him in a Nazi uniform. It has also led settlers evacuated from Gaza to don yellow stars to accuse the Israeli government of Nazi policies. Defenders of the conception of the Holocaust as a template for Jewish life have condemned such uses of Holocaust imagery to criticize Israeli policies or officials, but what they term "Holocaust inversion" is a natural if unintended consequence of the immersion of Israeli Jews in Holocaust imagery.[65] Triggered to view acts of cruelty and oppression in Holocaust terms, an increasing number of Israeli Jews find themselves drawn to images of the Warsaw Ghetto's liquidation when witnessing Israeli military assaults on Gaza or to images of SS troopers forcing Jews to humiliate themselves when hearing of Israeli soldiers debasing Palestinians at checkpoints or in detention centers. Just as the Zionist prooftext and wasting asset conceptions of the Holocaust were eventually undermined by efforts to promote them, so too Holocaustia's influence may eventually be transformed by its own devices into a basis for appreciating the common humanity of Jews and Palestinian Arabs. Israeli Jews may always need to understand their world in relation to their understanding of the Holocaust, but under conditions that force them to worry seriously about their future and the consequences of their actions, other ways to interpret the Holocaust are available, ways that can open doors to cooperation and peace rather than keep them shut.

Chapter 3

The Lobby and the Cocoon

Nothing that the United States does about Israel is likely to endanger the integrity or future of the United States. By contrast, the implications *for* Israel of U.S. policy *toward* Israel can be and have been immense. Combined with the legacy of the Iron Wall and the impediments to compromise associated with Holocaustia, the Israel lobby's hammerlock on U.S. foreign policy toward the Arab-Israeli conflict doomed prospects for a negotiated two-state solution (TSS).

A Most Special Relationship

The lobby's grossly disproportionate influence over U.S. policy in all matters relating to Israel is the best example in American history of what President George Washington's Farewell Address warned against. Washington was fully cognizant that the constitutional order encouraged ferocious factionalism on domestic issues, thereby checking the voraciousness of any one interest by the countervailing power of others. He also knew that this would not work in foreign affairs, since conflicting international interests were not represented in domestic politics. He therefore advised Americans against politicizing foreign policy, warning them "to steer clear of permanent Alliances, with any portion of the foreign world." Washington condemned

both "inveterate antipathies against particular Nations and passionate attachments for others" and stated that

> a passionate attachment of one Nation for another produces
> a variety of evils. Sympathy for the favourite nation, facilitat-
> ing the illusion of an imaginary common interest, in cases
> where no real common interest exists, and infusing into one
> the enmities of the other, betrays the former into a participa-
> tion in the quarrels and Wars of the latter.[1]

Washington treated the threat of excessive partiality for and special attachment to a foreign country as dangerous because he well understood
how vulnerable the new nation's domestic political structure made it to
the influence of a passionate faction unchecked by similarly animated opponents. The Israel lobby's domination of foreign policy toward Israel and
the Arab-Israeli conflict is definitive proof not of the lobby's malevolence
but instead of the compelling character of Washington's original analysis.
American policy toward Israel violates his advice more dramatically than
any other bilateral relationship in the country's history. According to one
scholar, the "special relationship" maintained by the United States with
Israel is "the *most* atypical bilateral bond in [the history of] inter-state
relations."[2]

The full measure of the extravagant specialness of that relationship
and the "passionate attachment" that Washington forewarned is beyond
the purview of this chapter. So is consideration of the usually partisan,
partially valid but fundamentally weak objections to the directly political
analysis offered here for what has produced and maintained the relationship. But before examining the effects on Israel of the lobby's influence in
Washington, D.C., it is crucial to register just how strong that influence is
and how unusual is the relationship it has produced. From 1948 to 2018
more than $50 billion flowed to Israel as charitable contributions, mostly
from American Jews but increasingly from evangelical Christians, which
the U.S. government has subsidized with tax-exempt status.[3] In that same

period, Israel received $134.7 billion in direct military and economic aid from the U.S. government, with another $38 billion pledged over the decade beginning in 2019.[4] Ever since 1976, Israel has been the single largest recipient of American aid and regularly receives more than half of all U.S. military aid delivered worldwide (leaving aside Iraq and Afghanistan, where U.S. troops have fought for many years). Since 1980 annual U.S. aid to Israel has averaged more than $3 billion, and since 1985 that aid has never dipped below this figure.[5] The amount of U.S. aid to Israel is particularly impressive when considering the small size of Israel's population and the relatively high standard of living it enjoys. For example, U.S. aid to Israel for 2017 was eighteen times the per capita aid from the United States to Haiti, forty-eight times aid to Colombia, and seventy-seven times aid to South Africa. Israel is not just more favored by U.S. aid. It is best thought of as being in a category all its own.

The way Israel receives aid also distinguishes it from all other recipients.[6] Israel receives lump sums rather than installments and also receives U.S. surplus military equipment at heavily discounted rates. For many years Israel was allowed to spend up to 26 percent of the military aid on contracts with its own defense industry, not with U.S. companies, and is exempt from having to draw on loans and grants equally. Israel is still not required to account for how its aid money is spent. This means that the aid is almost entirely fungible and can be used by Israeli governments and planners for budget relief or to pursue the ruling coalition's high-priority policies.[7] Beyond direct military and economic assistance, the United States has also provided loan guarantees to Israel—approximately $10 billion in the early 1990s and $9 billion in 2003. In fact, the vehicles for providing aid to Israel are so complex that the actual amounts of aid substantially exceed publicly available figures.[8]

Another vivid measure of Israel's unique status in American politics and foreign policy is invitations to foreign leaders to address special joint meetings of the U.S. House and Senate. Since Israel's creation in 1948, foreign leaders have been asked to speak to a joint session of the House and Senate seventy-nine times. Eight of those occasions featured Israeli leaders—more than for any other country.[9] When Prime Minister Benjamin Netanyahu addressed the U.S. Congress on March 3, 2015, his speech was interrupted by ovations thirty-nine times. One commentator summarized: "If there is one word to describe Congress's response . . . it would be 'ecstatic.' In the drug-addled sense. A bit too ecstatic—verging on the delirious. Maniacal, almost."[10]

Between 1973 and 2013, U.S. senators and representatives offered 938 nonappropriation congressional bills and resolutions "supportive of Israel, many unanimously."[11] For example, in November 2012, the Senate unanimously approved a resolution with sixty-three cosponsors reaffirming U.S. commitments to Israeli security and Israel's right to defend itself against terrorism emanating from the Gaza Strip.[12] Less than two years later senators again voted unanimously to support a war that Israel launched against Gaza based on what turned out to be false pretenses.[13]

Israel's outlier status among all U.S. bilateral relationships is also apparent in the record of American protection of Israel at the United Nations (UN).[14] In just 2015, for example, the United States opposed eighteen resolutions in the UN General Assembly that it said "were biased against Israel." On five occasions in 2014 the United States cast the only "no" vote against measures taken up by the UN's Human Rights Council that the U.S. government deemed unfair to Israel.[15] Since 1967 the United States has exercised its UN Security Council veto, unaccompanied by the negative vote of any other permanent member of the UN, fifty-three times. Forty-one of those vetoes—77 percent—were against draft resolutions deemed too critical of Israeli policies.[16] The decisiveness of American domestic politics on U.S. behavior at the UN with regard to Israel is equaled only by the exceptional pattern of U.S. voting on the issue of the embargo on Cuba. Substantively, Cuba and Israel have virtually nothing in common. What they do share is that they both have a strategically positioned, extremely influential, single-issue lobby active in Washington. The domestic politics imperative behind U.S. policy in these cases is nicely illustrated by the contrast between militant American opposition to the principle of international boycotts against Israel and Washington's lonely stance in favor of the embargo on Cuba.[17]

The Political Dominance of the Israel Lobby

The Israel lobby's preferences, explicit promises of rewards, and (usually) implicit threats of punishment are overwhelming factors in the daily experience of those engaged in U.S.-Israeli policy. The vast majority of these political leaders, legislators, aides, bureaucrats, and commentators operate within a narrow and closely enforced zone of politically acceptable thinking. The central address for the Israel lobby is the American Israel Public Affairs Committee (AIPAC). AIPAC's most concerted activity is to carefully record the behavior of U.S. senators and members of Congress[18]—who votes which way, who cosponsors bills, who backs AIPAC-sponsored resolutions, and who uses AIPAC talking points when they comment on relevant issues.

AIPAC makes legislators unambiguously aware that if they toe the line they will be rewarded with recognition as part of the "pro-Israel community," and if they do not, their careers will suffer if not end. In a bipartisan 1997 poll by *Fortune* magazine of 2,200 Washington "insiders," AIPAC was ranked number two among influential lobbies out of more than one hundred, surpassed only by the AARP.[19] By 2002 AIPAC had already been "long regarded as the most effective foreign-policy lobby in Washington."[20] This is also AIPAC's standard depiction of itself.[21]

AIPAC mobilizes and directs campaign funding to exert political pressure on individual legislators. It does not directly fund campaigns but provides policy guidance to senators and representatives. AIPAC then uses the funds raised by the scores of public affairs committees it has helped, via networks of bundlers and donors, to arrange financing for those whose loyalty has been proven while encouraging or supporting primary and electoral challenges against those who do not comply.

The crucial role of political funding, rather than votes, was well understood by Tom Dine, who served as AIPAC's executive director from 1980 to 1993.[22] By his own account, in the 1980s and 1990s AIPAC-directed contributions comprised "roughly 10 to 15% of a typical congressional campaign budget."[23] Respondents to the 1997 Fortune 500 survey identified control over contributions to politicians as *the* crucial lever of power used by AIPAC.

It is a misperception that AIPAC's power is concentrated in states or districts with high proportions of Jews, that it seeks to elect Jews to public office, or that it is, for that matter, committed primarily to electing politicians who above all care very deeply and genuinely about Israel. For example, AIPAC has brought down senators in states such as Nevada and Kansas that lack large Jewish populations. AIPAC's response to any sign of defiance is reliable and known to be such by every member of Congress: find and fund challengers to the offending legislator. The more sparsely populated the district, the cheaper it is for AIPAC to mount devastating challenges. In other words, representatives from states or districts with few actual supporters of the Israel lobby and relatively little interest in the Middle East are precisely those where AIPAC's influence is likely to be greater and easier to maintain.[24]

AIPAC has also targeted powerful politicians representing populous states, since the overall purpose of the tactic is to establish clearly in the minds of all legislators—and of those seeking to succeed them—that the lobby is capable of ending political careers of even well-established leaders. The most important example is Charles Percy of Illinois, a two-term Republican senator with presidential ambitions unseated in 1984 by an explicit high-profile AIPAC campaign to punish him for his support of an arms sale to Saudi Arabia in 1981. Percy's fate has weighed heavily on senators and congressmen ever since. The *Washington Post* shorthanded this effect of AIPAC's influence as the "Percy factor."[25]

In 1992 a prospective donor, Haim (Harry) Katz, secretly recorded a telephone conversation with AIPAC president David Steiner. Steiner was recorded bragging about AIPAC's network of operatives embedded within both the George H. W. Bush administration and Bill Clinton campaign, the influence AIPAC would have over appointments in the new administration such as secretary of state and national security adviser, and its ability to dictate the details of Israel-related legislation. Steiner assured Katz that the sole criterion of interest was whether candidates are loyal to AIPAC preferences on Israel, and this was ruthlessly enforced. The impact of donations would be multiplied by AIPAC's strategy of helping friends and punishing enemies in states with small populations and small campaign budgets. Playing the Holocaustia card, Steiner stressed that Katz should support AIPAC because "if we had AIPAC in the '30s and '40s, we would have saved millions of Jews."[26]

AIPAC quickly forced Steiner to apologize and resign for portraying it as an intimidating and self-satisfied political enforcer. But how accurately the recording captured AIPAC practices and its self-image was strongly corroborated by a subsequent episode. In 2005 AIPAC fired Steven Rosen, its top foreign policy official. A Pentagon sting operation had caught Rosen and one of his associates receiving and distributing classified information. AIPAC fired them both for "conduct that was not part of their jobs and because this conduct did not comport with the standards that AIPAC expects of its employees." Under indictment, Rosen sued AIPAC for defamation and $21 million in damages, charging that he had only done what AIPAC had rewarded him for doing for decades. The case dragged on for years, resulting in the publication of voluminous documentation of AIPAC's standard procedures. "I was indicted," said Rosen in 2010, "not because I violated AIPAC policies, but because I followed them.[27]

Both Steiner and Rosen operated fully within the culture and expectations established by AIPAC for its employees. Both the recorded phone call with Katz and the reams of documentation offered by Rosen in court provide unfiltered access to AIPAC's role, its self-perception as a dominant player in Washington on the issue of Israel, and the obeisance it expects to command.

Thanks to AIPAC and other Israel lobby affiliates, "America is," as Benjamin Netanyahu put it, "a thing you can move very easily, move it in the right direction."[28] Legislative aides, foreign policy staffers, journalists, and other insiders know how resentful and even humiliated many American politicians and officials privately feel about having to toe the lobby's line in public. In 2007 Representative Tim Moran, a veteran moderate Democrat from northern Virginia and former mayor of Alexandria, resisted AIPAC's elaborate and detailed manipulation of the terms of a supplementary aid package to Israel. In 2007 Moran explained why four hundred representatives followed AIPAC's instructions, compared to the thirty who resisted them:

> If you cross AIPAC, AIPAC is unforgiving and will destroy you politically. Their means of communications, their ties to certain newspapers and magazines and individuals in the media are substantial and intimidating. Every member knows it's the best-organized national lobbying force. The National Rifle Association comes a close second, but AIPAC can rightfully brag that they're the most powerful lobbying force in the world today. . . . AIPAC considers the voting record only as it applies to Israel.[29]

Even the most candid of politicians often wait until the end of their careers to express their true feelings about the lobby.[30] Senator Ernest (Fritz) Hollings represented South Carolina for thirty-nine years. When he announced his retirement in 2004 he criticized the cruel bind the Israel lobby placed on presidents as well as senators. Known as "the tartest tongue in the Senate," he declared in his last speech to that body that "You can't have an Israel policy other than what AIPAC gives you around here."[31] Capitol Hill insiders report that he had "eloquently stated what many members of Congress believe but are too afraid to say."[32]

Mike Lofgren worked for twenty-eight years as a senior staffer on Capitol Hill. In his study of special interests in Washington he relates a telling episode in 2014 at the height of Congress's inability to act on almost any legislation, no matter how crucial. Despite the gridlock, he notes that following the war in Gaza launched by Israel in 2014 as Operation Protective Edge, Congress moved swiftly on its own initiative and with unanimous consent to add an extra $225 million to Israel's Iron Dome antimissile program.[33] Lofgren attributed this "miraculous" performance to the Israel lobby and, quoted *Slate* journalist Jim Newell as being guilty of only "minimal exaggeration" when he commented that when it came to Israel,

> If there was another Civil War and a batch of states seceded from the union but Israel still needed its war money, the two sides would call a cease-fire, the seceding states would

temporarily rejoin the union, go to Congress to pass the funding, and then re-secede and continue fighting.[34]

Beyond Policy: Socialization, Agenda Control, Censorship

According to a 1994 book on the Israel lobby by two Israeli investigative journalists, by the mid-1980s the Israel lobby had become "a muscular behemoth with roots planted in all corners and all levels of U.S. society."[35] Now the lobby is even stronger. In 1992 there were 3,000 attendees at AIPAC's annual policy conference in Washington, and in 2011 there were 10,000, including well over half of both houses of Congress. In 2018, the number of participants hit 18,000. Indeed, the influence of the Israel lobby now extends well beyond the Beltway and well beyond the institutions of government. The single most prominent American source for talking-head comment on Israel and Arab-Israeli affairs is the Washington Institute for Near East Policy (WINEP). According to an AIPAC staffer who was present at the meeting where the decision was made to do so, WINEP was created in 1985 precisely in order to "disseminate the AIPAC line in a way that would disguise its connections."[36] Its founding director was Martin Indyk, who served as a high-ranking foreign policy official in the Clinton and Barack Obama administrations, including two stints as ambassador to Israel.

The scale of the lobby's success is reflected in the expansion of its mission. Beyond ensuring policies that accord with its view of Israel's interests, which except in rare cases is a given, AIPAC seeks to control agendas, exclude potential question raisers from rising to political prominence, and patrol the boundaries of discourse against categories, questions, and comparisons regarding Israel or the Palestinians the lobby deems inappropriate. This means monitoring and placing limits on opinions voiced by not only politicians but also journalists, academicians, media celebrities, and even students. Accordingly, AIPAC's field of activity has expanded well beyond the executive and legislative branches of the federal government to state legislatures, municipal government, and key elements of civil society, namely colleges and universities.

To support this general effort, Israel lobby organizations need activists on campuses. This requirement is met by a vast propaganda, recruitment, and socialization effort featuring, as a core element, a multitude of programs sponsoring heavily subsidized tours of Israel. Space allows only a brief survey of this truly immense effort. Between 1999 and 2017 more than 500,000 young Jews (between the ages of eighteen and twenty-six) were awarded ten-day all-expense-paid visits to Israel in a program known as Birthright (Taglit, meaning "discovery). Similarly purposed junkets include the Onward Israel program,[37] Masa Journeys,[38] Hasbara Fellowships, and many separate programs offered by Aish HaTorah (which aims at returning nonobservant Jews to the fold).[39] Alumni from these programs are channeled through funding and coordinating groups such as the Israel on Campus Coalition and Students Supporting Israel to Israel advocacy groups on campus named, for example, Huskies for Israel at Northeastern University, Buckeyes for Israel at Ohio State University, and so on. Israel and Co., which is closely related to the U.S.-Israel Business Initiative, sponsors conferences in Israel and three different kinds of heavily subsidized "I-Trek" seven- to ten-day tours for students in high-prestige graduate and professional schools.[40] AIPAC itself sponsors three all-expenses paid missions per year to Israel.[41] Israel advocacy junkets with economic networking opportunities or military or political tourism dimensions also abound.[42]

The lobby also invests heavily in bringing government officials, politicians, and candidates to Israel for luxurious, exciting, and carefully scripted visits. As early as the 1980s, according to a former AIPAC executive director, ninety-nine of the one hundred sitting U.S. senators had visited Israel.[43] In 2012 the *New York Times* identified the American Israel Education Foundation, "a non-profit offshoot of the American Israel Public Affairs Committee," as being the leading organizer of what one "pro-Israel advocate in Washington" described as "the Jewish Disneyland trip." In 2015 lobby affiliates arranged for all but three incoming congressmen to take a tour of Israel.[44] Two-week tours for academics in prestige institutions specializing in topics other than the Middle East include five-star accommodations and meetings with top Israeli officials.[45] Similar *hasbara* junkets are provided for state and local government officials. For example, in December 2016

the governor of Massachusetts and a dozen members of the state legisla-
ture were treated to six ten-day all-expense-paid tours of Israel paid for by
the Combined Jewish Philanthropies of Boston and the Jewish Community
Relations Council.[46] In 2016 every top-category Oscar nominee received a
swag bag with vouchers for a $55,000 ten-day deluxe trip to Israel.[47]

As noted, the dramatic growth in the Israel-junket enterprise was
linked to the expansion of the lobby's mission, the lobby having come to enjoy virtually complete domination of U.S. foreign policy on matters related
to Israel. But the lobby's emphasis on patrolling the boundaries of debate
and socializing new generations of American influentials was also spurred
by the transformation in Israel's international image from David to Goli-
ath.[48] In 2012 a BBC poll including more than 24,000 respondents ranked
Israel as being tied with North Korea in regard to its negative influence in
the world. Only Iran and Pakistan were judged more unfavorably.[49] Five
years later, the same poll reported Israel as the fourth most disliked country
after Iran, North Korea, and Pakistan.[50] Israeli policies of settlement expansion and stonewalling against progress toward a negotiated peace have
resulted in a flood of unfavorable press and a drumbeat of criticism by the
UN and human rights groups. In this climate the visibility of Palestinian-
led mobilization has risen, especially in the form of the boycott, divestment,
and sanctions (BDS) movement. Although BDS has gained more traction
in Europe, Asia, and Africa than in the United States, the attention it has
achieved in America has helped the lobby amplify its mission by pressing
federal agencies, state legislatures, municipalities, and universities to sup-
press, delegitimize, or even outlaw support of boycotts targeting Israel or
Israeli policies.

As the Palestinians have switched from armed struggle to negotiations
and nonviolent economic and legal campaigns, the lobby has changed the
label it mainly uses to stigmatize Palestinians and discredit critiques of Israel. Instead of blanket accusations of terrorism, the lobby's most prominent tactic recently has been to condemn virtually all but the most anodyne
criticism of Israel as anti-Semitic.

For example, Stephen Walt of Harvard University and John Mearsheimer of the University of Chicago, two renowned scholars with expertise

in national security and foreign policy, were vilified and publicly and repeatedly accused of anti-Semitism following publication of their article and then a book on the influence of the Israel lobby on U.S. foreign policy. Their prestige made them a particularly spectacular object lesson for the lobby's intended audience—younger and less well-established scholars, commentators, and journalists. Having witnessed the punishment and ostracism of Mearsheimer and Walt, they would doubtless hesitate before they applied their critical faculties to policies regarding Israel.[51] A long list of scholars have experienced fundamentally similar treatment, including Joseph Massad, Rashid Khalidi, Edward Said, Norman Finkelstein, Nadia Abu-Haj, Juan Cole, Tony Judt, David Palumbo-Liu, Stephen Salaita, Lila Abu Lughod, and Judith Butler.[52]

This strategy for patrolling and limiting debate was designed by Natan Sharansky, a famous Soviet refusenik who became a prominent right-wing politician in Israel and eventually head of the World Zionist Organization. Sharansky advocated treating as anti-Semitic and therefore as beyond the pale for public debate any speech or writing liable to "delegitimize" or "demonize" Israel or that treated Israel according to a "double standard."[53] However, both the Three D's (delegitimize, demonize, double-standard) slogan and the concomitant charge that "anti-Zionism is the new anti-Semitism" are disingenuous. Their main purpose is not to combat anti-Semitism but instead to weaponize the anti-Semitic label to deter, outlaw, or punish any strong criticism of Israeli policies.[54]

The Three D's device for excluding criticism of Israel from public debate had its origins in concerns that American college campuses were becoming the crucial battleground for defending Israel and its future.[55] A primary organizational framework for waging this war against criticism of Israel is the Israel Campus Coalition (ICC). Founded by the Schusterman Foundation in 2002, it provides resources and coordination to more than thirty different organizations to monitor and counter Israel-related activities on American campuses. The ICC prides itself on a network of four hundred faculty members supporting its activities on 175 different U.S. campuses and a program offering fifty $1,000 stipends to undergraduate activists. In its report for 2016–2017 the ICC stated that despite a 40 percent decline in the number of "anti-Israel lectures and speakers" and an increase in the number of "pro-Israel" events, the anti-Israel movement had strengthened in sophistication and intensity."[56]

Of course, every point of view has a right to organize support on American college campuses, and groups critical of Israel also receive significant assistance from outside academia. But the vigilantism of the Israel lobby effort, associated with its effort to limit the bounds of acceptable discourse, is distinctive. Various lobby-affiliated organizations have made it increasingly difficult to criticize Israel without fear of lawsuits, accusations of anti-Semitism, demands for political balance in the staging of events, blacklisting of participants, or other forms of personal or institutional harassment. Across the country, groups such as Students for Justice in Palestine, Jewish Voice for Peace, and activists affiliated with the BDS movement have borne the brunt of these attacks.

One specific tactic is to treat criticism of Israel as hate speech liable to cause discomfort to Jewish students. In 2011 more than 150 American colleges received warnings that Title VI complaints were being considered as a result of what multiple Israel advocacy patrol organizations alleged were hostile environments for Jews on their campuses—complaints to the federal government that could leave them liable for "massive damages."[57] In 2015 Robert Satloff, executive director of WINEP, posted a twelve-minute video on YouTube advising parents of Jewish college students about how to help their children shield themselves from disturbing ideas about Israel and how to help the lobby by taking blacklists of pro-BDS professors into account when choosing courses and reporting to Israel advocacy organizations when they think they may be negatively impacted because they are Jewish or Israel supporters.[58]

In June 2015, three wealthy lobby donors—Sheldon Adelson, Haim Saban, and Adam Milstein—headlined a Las Vegas summit that raised $50 million to fund an anti-BDS campaign on U.S. college campuses "to demonize the demonizers."[59] The strategy has been to avoid substantive debate on Israeli policies in favor of preventing events with critical potential from occurring and, failing that, to deploy sophisticated propaganda techniques to shift the focus of public discussion to nonsubstantive issues.[60] Canary

Mission, whose self-described purpose is to disseminate pejorative information about individuals (mainly academics) so as to punish them by damaging their career prospects, has sought to conceal its source of funding, but in 2018 that source was identified as the Israeli-American billionaire Adam Milstein.[61]

Other arms of the lobby have carried the fight to both state and national legislatures. They have tried to enact laws and prompt administrative measures to deprive institutions of funding if their campuses are used for activities characterized as anti-Semitic. By the end of November 2018, twenty-six states had taken official action to discourage, punish, or prevent participation in boycotts targeting Israel.[62] Typically, executive orders and legislation bar state agencies, including pension funds, from participating in any boycott or divestment targeting Israel and/or preventing state agencies from signing contracts with organizations or companies that boycott Israel or support the BDS movement.[63] The overwhelming if not unanimous margins by which anti-BDS resolutions and legislation have been passed in state legislatures are not based on free trade principles per se, which have been compromised for other boycotts such as those protesting anti-Catholic discrimination in Northern Ireland in the 1990s, but instead result from effective mobilization by the Israel lobby.[64]

The lobby has also strongly promoted discourse patrol and anti-BDS policies and legislation in Congress by making it a federal crime to support a boycott of Israel and by applying sweeping definitions of anti-Semitism to limit activities of Middle East study centers that receive federal funding. In 2017, 2018, and 2019, Congress debated bills outlawing support of a boycott against Israel or Israeli settlements.[65] As assistant secretary of civil rights at the Department of Education, Kenneth Marcus, founding president of a Washington-based center dedicated to patrolling the boundaries of discourse on Israel, showed his intention to make the lobby's mission to limit American discourse on Israeli and Palestinian official government policy. In September 2018 he reopened a seven-year-old case against Rutgers University, accusing it of sponsoring an anti-Semitic event. The case had been dismissed for lack of evidence by the Obama administration.[66]

I am not making an argument here that the Israel lobby never fails or that it is the only factor shaping U.S. foreign policy toward Israel. Amy Kaplan has demonstrated the important political implications of how myths and sentiments favorable to Israel have been absorbed by American popular culture.[67] The United States has also enjoyed strategic benefits from its relationship with Israel even while regularly suffering from association with Israeli policies that American presidents have almost all opposed. Nor am I painting a sinister image of a Jewish lobby. Evangelical Christian influence is powerful within lobby circles, and in any case American Jews are far more diverse in their opinions about Israel than the positions advanced by the lobby. Nor do I contend that single-issue lobbying is un-American or a betrayal of U.S. national interests. The argument and evidence I have presented are not an indictment of the Israel lobby or of those American citizens whose passionate efforts and dedication to their beliefs stand behind its success.

What I do assert is that successive American administrations have given vast support to Israel because, due to the lobby's sophistication, clout, and single-mindedness, it is in their political interests to do so. If blame is to be assigned for the resulting distortions in U.S. policy, it must be directed at the founding fathers. The citizens who built and are active in the Israel lobby have behaved exactly as James Madison and his colleagues in Philadelphia expected them to behave—selfishly, strategically, and with a narrow vision of the problems confronted by the overall community. While the proliferation of factions with opposing views would ordinarily prevent any one faction's domination of policy, George Washington's warning against excessive partiality toward a foreign country was based on his insight that in foreign policy this mechanism of countervailing power would not work. The Israel lobby's domination of foreign policy toward Israel and the Arab-Israeli conflict is definitive proof of Washington's prescience.

I now move from demonstrating the lobby's power over U.S. foreign policy toward Israel to an almost entirely overlooked corollary of that power—the drastic and fateful deflection of Israeli democracy from compromise and peace toward maximalism and belligerence.

The Dutch Disease, Israeli Style

It is not always the case that the more resources a country has, the better for that country. As with children, too many gifts or too few limits spell trouble.[68] And trouble is what fifty years of virtually unlimited American economic, diplomatic, and military aid has meant for Israel. Instead of encouraging Israelis to make tough decisions toward peace, American policies of fulsome and unconditional support drove Israeli democracy— and the governments it produced—in the opposite direction. It did this by shaping the incentives operating on Israeli politicians and parties and making it easier for both elites and the public to believe that Israel would always be able to have its cake and eat it too.

Political economists have long observed that when a country is the beneficiary of gigantic rents arising from its command of a commodity with extremely strong global demand—cotton for Egypt in the 1860s and oil for OPEC countries in the late 1900s and early 2000s—it experiences short-term benefits and long-term disasters. The syndrome of economic distortions and failures that results from such bonanzas is known as the Dutch Disease. The term was coined by Terry Karl in her analysis of the effects of a natural gas boom in the Netherlands. In 1959 a field containing 100 trillion cubic feet of natural gas was discovered in the northeast region of Netherlands. The field was intensively exploited in the 1960s and 1970s, during which time the Dutch economy suffered from declining manufacturing, severe pressure on wages, enormous waste, and long-term decline in productivity.[69]

For my purposes, Karl's economic analysis has an analogy in the political realm of Israel and the United States. Essentially, the United States has given Israel a political version of the Dutch Disease. The constant availability of American political, diplomatic, military, and economic protection shaped the incentives operating on Israeli politicians and parties, thereby systematically affecting the political perspectives that became dominant. Those Israeli politicians who favored policies of settlement and territorial expansion were freed from restraints and hesitations that otherwise would have been associated with the cost and international obloquy those policies entailed. These parties and groups competed by outbidding one another on platforms of being tough with the Palestinians, settling in the West Bank, and opposing initiatives with potential for a viable TSS. Doves lost, moderates became hawkish, and hawks became more hawkish. The right-wing Likud Party, purged of its liberal wing and increasingly aligned with its ultranationalist and religious allies on the Far Right, became the dominant force in Israeli politics.

Tragically, both the legacy of the Holocaust and the poisonous generosity of the United States encouraged—or if not did not virtually impose—a trained incapacity to learn from outsiders. Yet Israel needed this capacity to read external signals and adapt in order to escape from its long-term predicament and fulfill the last stages of the Iron Wall strategy in the years and decades after 1967. Given the legacy of Zionism's initial failure to find a solution to the Arab problem other than the Iron Wall, the weight of Holocaustia, and other factors arising from developments in the Arab world, the prospects for attaining a comprehensive peace agreement in the decades after 1967 were probably remote to begin with. But the smothering cocoon of unconditional American support, implemented mostly as a function of the Israel lobby's influence, undermined and eventually destroyed what modest chances for that outcome did exist.

The Defeat of Israeli Moderates

A key argument on the Israeli liberal dovish Left has always been that territorial expansion and refusal to take Arab requirements seriously would lead to a confrontation between Israel and the international community. In particular, the Left warned repeatedly of a fateful clash with the United States, committed as Washington was to the principle of trading Israeli-occupied land for Arab-Israeli peace. On occasion in public but mostly in private, doves pleaded with leaders in Washington to exert the pressure on Israel necessary to convince the Israeli public and in turn politicians of the need for concessions. In public, both Israeli and diaspora Jewish doves used forecasts of U.S. pressure to spur Israeli concessions.[70] In the aftermath of the 1973 war Nahum Goldmann, one of the foremost leaders of the Zionist movement prior to the establishment of the state, was told that Israelis had been tragically misled to believe that "whatever we may do, we will have the full support of the United States of America." He blamed the failure of American diplomats to push Israel toward negotiations during that period for "freezing the status quo"—a policy of doing nothing that was "largely responsible for the Yom Kippur War."[71] Writing for the left-wing newspaper *Al-Hamishmar*, Naftali Ben-Moshe told his readers in November 1973 that doves had always known that one day the United States would act toward Israel as the superpower it was. Now they were about to be proven right. The hawks had "erred." Israeli doves, on the other hand,

> had no illusions that the United States of America would be prepared to abandon its global policy of détente and cooperation with the SU [Soviet Union] for the sake of Israel's territorial demands. . . . [I]t is today clear to all that Kissinger's statement that the USA is prepared to defend Israel but not her military conquests, is now his country's policy. We are now almost totally dependent on the USA; it may be expected that this policy will be forced on us whether we like it or not.[72]

In some cases, doves offered explicit analyses of the relationship between Israel lobby power in America and political paralysis in Israel. Before becoming president, Jimmy Carter had referred to the right of Palestinians to a homeland. After his election in 1976, one editorial writer hoped that perhaps the U.S. government could sustain a rational policy toward Israel long enough to prevent the war that would otherwise certainly occur:

> There is a way out—peace through withdrawal, Palestinian self-determination and mutual recognition . . . . [T]hough Israel's leaders seem unwilling to take the necessary initiative themselves, there is some hope that despite the apparent requirements of the campaign, President Carter will not delay too long in defusing a new round of hot war.[73]

After Israel invaded Lebanon in 1982, occupying most of the country south of Beirut and destroying much of the capital itself, the United States became deeply involved in diplomatic efforts to end the fighting and extricate the leadership of the Palestine Liberation Organization (PLO) from Beirut. When that was accomplished President Ronald Reagan, whose foreign policy team had until then studiously avoided public criticism of Israel on the Palestinian issue, gave a speech outlining a new approach—what Reagan called "a new realism." Affirming his commitment to the Camp David Accords, which imagined a five-year transition period to full autonomy for West Bank and Gaza Palestinians, Reagan announced that the United States had a special role to play in bringing peace. He emphasized that the United States would support positions in negotiations anchored in commitments to Israeli security and Palestinian self-government. They included a complete Israeli settlement freeze and some ultimate framework for Palestinian self-government.

On the eve of Reagan's speech, David Landau—a future editor of both the *Jerusalem Post* and *Haaretz*—stated,

> When George Ball wrote [in 1977] of the need for the U.S. to "save Israel from itself," virtually the entire nation bayed in outrage. Indeed, Ambassador Lewis has spent the past five years assuring everyone here that Washington is neither willing nor able to heed Ball's advice. Yet . . . how many Israeli moderates, in their hearts, prayed for Washington to do just that: save Israel from itself?[74]

Yossi Sarid, an influential Labor Party member of Knesset and future leader of the dovish-liberal Meretz Party, supported Reagan's call for a settlement freeze and welcomed the Reagan Initiative as capable of ending "the dangerous deadlock in the region,"[75] while other doves described the plan as a "breakthrough."[76] Peace Now responded by calling for an immediate end to all settlement activities.[77]

Prime Minister Begin, on the other hand, is reported to have responded to the Reagan Initiative speech by declaring the day "the saddest of my life." He needn't have worried.[78] The announcement of the Reagan plan was quickly overshadowed by the Phalangist massacre of Palestinians in Beirut refugee camps (abetted by Defense Minister Ariel Sharon and the Israeli military) and by a truck bomb attack in Beirut that killed 241 marines, leading to American withdrawal from that country and an effective end to the Reagan Initiative.

With the U.S. retreat from mediation efforts, dovish demands for American pressure faded between 1983 and 1987. Although parties on the Left continued to appeal to Washington "to become more involved in saving the Israeli Government from itself,"[79] a wide-ranging meta-analysis of polling data published in 1985 showed that large majorities of Israelis were confident that traditional levels of U.S. aid and support for Israel would continue. Israelis simply did "not perceive their own country's actions as permanently impairing the US commitment." For example, in a 1983 poll only 10 percent believed that "US-Israeli relations would be 'severely' damaged if Israel refused to stop building settlements." Accordingly, the possible repercussions of Israeli policies on U.S. interests did not influence their positions on peace issues.[80] One dovish intellectual explained the crippling impact of America's unconditional support on Israel's ability to address its biggest problems:

> The situation will never be remedied as long as the country's leaders know that they may expect prodigious inflows of unilateral funds. Nor is Israel's political dependence on the US a good thing. The greater that dependence grows, the more likely Israel is to become embroiled in actions and circumstances not in line with its own interests, while the basic problem—namely, a solution to the Palestinian problem— remains unresolved.[81]

Extreme Israeli dependence on the United States created at least the theoretical possibility that a small U.S. adjustment in its policy could deliver a surprising and politically significant shock to the system. With the outbreak of the First Intifada in December 1987 and the emergence of President

George H. W. Bush's new activist foreign policy team in Washington, led by Secretary of State James Baker, that is exactly what happened.

The intifada spurred dovish politicians and commentators to speak out once more about the need for Israel to learn from its suffering and from the inevitability of American pressure that serious compromise with the Palestinians was required. In February 1988 *Maariv* journalist Moshe Zak, discussing U.S. secretary of state George Shultz's upcoming visit to Israel, took note of the upsurge of such sentiments among Israeli doves but warned them not to expect the help they yearned for from Washington: "Those among us who are opposed to the use of clubs to restore order in Judea and Samaria are longing for the whip of American pressure to force Israel to withdraw from those territories."[82] But, Zak predicted (accurately as it turned out), that "those who are longing for the whip of American pressure will be disappointed . . . when they learn that Shultz has no intention of using it."

Sarid was one of those dovish Israeli politicians to whom Zak was referring. Writing also in February 1988, Sarid predicted that the United States and the Soviet Union would respond to escalating protests and violence in the territories by imposing a solution.[83] "Pay Up Now" was the title of a long piece published by Amir Oren. The author noted that this same article title had been used in 1982 to forecast American demands on Israel. It turned out to be incorrect then, he noted, but he hoped that this time things would be different.[84]

President Bush entered the White House in January 1989 and was personally appalled by the intransigence of the Shamir government, its settlement policies, and its rough treatment of Palestinians protestors. Following a blistering meeting between Bush and Shamir in April,[85] Secretary of State James Baker delivered a speech to AIPAC. Baker told the Israel lobby that Israeli leaders had to "lay aside once and for all the unrealistic vision of a greater Israel," urging them to recognize the Palestinians as "neighbors who deserve political rights." This shift in the public face of American policy pushed the Israeli political system closer to producing a government capable of implementing a TSS than it had ever been or ever would be.[86]

Following Baker's speech to AIPAC, the organization mobilized 95 senators and 235 congressmen to sign a declaration of support for Israel.

Desperate to protect Baker and his peace initiative from attacks by Israeli ministers and the Israel lobby, some Israeli doves denounced AIPAC explicitly, identifying it as the taproot of Israel's political paralysis. Alon Pinkas in the Labor Party newspaper *Davar* described AIPAC as a "super-intelligent" guide dog, accustomed to "guessing in advance where the blind man [U.S. presidents and secretaries of state] intended to go. Whenever the blind man would make a mistake, the dog, knowing his owner's mind, would correct him at once." AIPAC effectively "defines Israel's interests." "This efficient and powerful organization," he wrote, "sows fear in Washington. Perhaps we, the Israelis, should also begin to fear it."[87]

In 1989 Yossi Beilin was a Labor politician close to Shimon Peres and a leader of Israeli doves. In response to Prime Minister Shamir's opposition to the Bush-Baker initiative and even while serving as deputy finance minister in the National Unity Government, Beilin called for the overthrow of the governing coalition. He warned that "if the U.S. does not have a formula which is acceptable to Egypt and the Palestinians and seeks only to placate the Likud—this will be a gross interference [by the United States] in Israel's internal affairs."[88] A month later Beilin was part of a delegation of dovish Israeli parliamentarians who visited Washington to persuade senators and congressmen to support American efforts to bring peace.[89]

Ariel Sharon, then a leading member of the cabinet, labeled Beilin's group "a commando of Jewish informers" seeking to elicit U.S. interference in Israeli affairs. Although its leader defended the delegation by saying it had advised American leaders "not to pressure Israel with aid now," the delegates obviously wanted to diminish Israel's sense that U.S. support was unconditional.[90]

In March 1991 as Secretary of State Baker was en route to Jerusalem, one Israeli journalist wrote him an open letter describing Israel as a "spoiled child." Quoting George Ball that "Israel must be saved from itself," the letter advised the Secretary that Israel would respond to economic pressure if coupled to a "practical" proposal as long as the administration did not "repeat the mistake of the Reagan administration by giving money . . . and not demanding influence in Israel in exchange for it."[91]

In September 1991 Yossi Sarid celebrated the "moment of truth" in U.S.-Israel relations that had finally arrived and likened Israel to an "arrogant beggar":

> Forbearance of the most altruistic and generous millionaire will get exhausted if an arrogant beggar whom he feeds at his table continues to misbehave, spit, break precious vessels, and violate all the rules of table etiquette. . . . Israel, through habituation and excess of pampering, not only got used to free lunches, but became convinced that the benefactor was pretty senile, big in stature, but small in intelligence, bending down in submission whenever somebody knocks his head.[92]

Yoel Marcus, a member of the *Haaretz* editorial board, described the Israeli government as living in a "paradise of fools" created by what was now being revealed as the "myth," reminiscent of the Protocols of the Elders of Zion, that thanks to the Israel lobby, America could be ruled by Israel. Marcus wrote that this myth used to frighten "quite a lot of American politicians, from Presidents to Congressmen," and that without it a "tiny" a state such as Israel would not have received the gigantic amounts of U.S. aid it had enjoyed. Now, however, things were changing. "Israel was being put on a spit and fried, like a steak, on a slow fire."[93]

Another dovish journalist, Boas Evron, writing at the same time, compared Israel to a "drunken hoodlum running amok, beating children and robbing the elderly" while the police, instead of arresting him, keep giving him "Stolichnaya and Chivas Regal": We are the drunkard. With all our rioting, our craziness, and our provocative (*chutzpadik*) settlements, the billions keep flowing to us just fine.[94] Doves, Evron continued, had always warned Israelis of the coming reckoning with the United States and the world, "but our warnings could not convince the Israelis, because they were always refuted by the continuing grants of American money."

In 1991 Israeli doves hoped that the decisive confrontation between the United States and Israel they had long imagined was about to arrive. In the aftermath of the American victory over Iraq in the Persian Gulf War, President Bush's approval ratings soared to 90 percent. With this cushion of political protection at home, Bush's policy in the Middle East was to establish American credibility with the Arab world, convene an Arab-Israeli peace conference, and move toward a comprehensive peace treaty, including a solution to the Palestinian problem.

A key element was to demonstrate American firmness against the expansive settlement policies of the Shamir-Sharon government in Israel. In defiance of most senators and congressmen, President Bush announced that the amount of any Israeli expenditures on settlements would be deducted from Israel's $10 billion request for loan guarantees. The Shamir government refused to comply, leading Bush to declare on July 1, 1991, "We're not giving one inch on the settlements question. . . . We're not going to change our position on settlements. So please, those in Israel, do what you can to see that the policy of settlement after settlement is not continued. It is counterproductive."[95]

Amid the vast array of unconditional deliveries of American economic, security, and diplomatic assistance to Israel, Bush's move amounted to a very small amount of money (about $400 million). Nevertheless, this was the most explicit and serious effort to use American aid to affect Israeli policy toward the West Bank and the Gaza Strip since 1967. AIPAC and other allied organizations responded by condemning both the president and the secretary of state. One thousand lobbyists flooded Congress seeking full satisfaction of Israeli requests via the foreign aid bill and a legislative decision to deny Bush's request that it defer consideration of the loan guarantee request for four months to enhance prospects for the Madrid Peace Conference.[96] Pricked by accusations of anti-Semitism and frustrated by the Israel lobby's mobilization against his policies, an angry President Bush called a news conference:

> I think the American people will support me. They know we support Israel. . . . [W]e're up against very strong and effective . . . groups that go up to the Hill. I heard today there were something like a thousand lobbyists on the Hill working the

other side of the question. We've got one lonely little guy down here doing it.[97]

The fierce battle in Washington over what had become Bush's request merely to defer discussion of this small reduction in loan guarantees was met in Israel by a risky attempt by doves to celebrate and encourage U.S. pressure on Israel. The diplomatic correspondent for *Haaretz* observed that the stakes of the encounter were fully understood by Yitzhak Shamir, the most hard-right prime minister in Israel's history. According to *Haaretz*'s diplomatic correspondent, Akiva Eldar, Shamir was willing to go to Madrid, as President Bush insisted, not only because of tight restrictions placed on the Palestinians but also because settlements would be unaffected by his formal participation. Unless Bush escalated pressure beyond the wrist slap of the loan guarantees, Shamir calculated that he and the Likud Party would benefit politically. Despite disquiet triggered by the prolonged intifada, his message in the upcoming election would be that "only Likud could manage to load [Israel] with both dollars and settlements at the same time, without the slightest undertaking to give up a single inch of territory." Eldar then hammered home the larger meaning of the confrontation:

> If the guarantees are given with no political strings attached (including the cessation of settlement), that would deal a death blow to the central argument of the Labor Party and the Israeli left. The $10 billion will prove that the right wing's policies do not harm the vital interests of Israel's citizens. On the contrary, they [will appear] as beneficial.[98]

With the approach of Israeli elections in June 1992, Bush did impose the restriction on loan guarantees. Israeli doves were ecstatic. They described Baker as "the sole leader of the Israeli opposition."[99] The doves' call for vigorous U.S. action to orchestrate political outcomes in Israel was justifiable and necessary, they reasoned, to counterbalance the consequences of the American-spun cocoon of virtually unconditional support. Tracing this dynamic to "the immense political mobilization . . . of the Jewish organizations and the Jewish lobbyists in the United States, mainly AIPAC," a leading Israeli sociologist, Baruch Kimmerling, asked "who intervenes, in favor of whom, when and with what effect?" He answered his question by noting that "every American deed and every American mistake is intervention in [Israel's] internal affairs" and that "unconditional aid" from the United States had been "the decisive factor in the tremendous growth of the right-wing camp."[100]

Israeli doves were pleased with the declared policies of Bush and Baker, worrying only that they might waver, that Washington might not be focused clearly enough on settlements to drive the necessary wedge between Likud and the majority of Israeli voters, or that Israel lobby influence in Congress might thwart administration efforts to contribute to the "long-term political education of the Israeli public."[101]

Despite these worries the Bush-Baker gambit worked, helping Yitzhak Rabin and the Labor Party eke out the narrowest of victories over Likud, mainly because just enough new immigrant voters in Israel switched from the Right to the Left and center.[102]

And yet in the end, it did not work. Shortly after Rabin took office the loan guarantees were approved in full, even though the Labor Party continued settlement construction.[103] President Bush lost his bid for reelection in 1992, due in part to efforts by the Israel lobby.[104] The Israeli Right rejoiced, even as the Left pleaded for "continued U.S. pressure on Israel" as "the most important condition for advancing the entire [peace] process."[105] In the face of mass right-wing protests and threats of civil war directed at a compromise solution, Ron Kislev called upon the United States to help the Labor government by exerting counterpressure on a scale much stronger than anything Israeli doves could mount.[106] Ze'ev Sternhell, a leading Israeli authority on fascism, was just as explicit. Several months into the Clinton presidency he called for "strong American pressure."[107]

But President Clinton and his notoriously passive secretary of state, Warren Christopher, ignored these pleas. American diplomacy shifted back to a publicly supportive, even fulsome, stance toward Israel rather than an evenhanded or confrontational role.[108] During Clinton's two terms U.S. aid to Israel remained high and steady even as settlement construction vastly expanded, contributing directly to the collapse of the Oslo process and the end of the Labor Party's ability to offer a realistic alternative to right-wing governments.

The miniconfrontation between the Bush-Baker team and the Shamir government was the last time a puncture in the cocoon of unconditional American support had a significant impact on Israeli politics and the trajectory of Israeli-Palestinian relations.

To be sure, Israeli doves also welcomed President George W. Bush's Annapolis commitment to the Road Map for Peace, though it produced nothing of substance. Next, they welcomed President Obama's effort to press Prime Minister Netanyahu in 2009 for a settlement moratorium. On cue but with less fervor and hope than in the past, Israeli doves and supporters responded to Obama's initial demand for an Israeli settlement freeze by clamoring for decisive American pressure.[109] One prominent Israeli journalist noted the blunt and consistent criticism that U.S. leaders were leveling against Netanyahu's stonewalling, quoting a senior American official as saying that "if Netanyahu doesn't realize that Washington has changed, that will be a very bad mistake on his part."[110] Calling for an extension of the "moratorium" on expanding settlements, Tzipi Livni, head of the opposition Kadima Party, warned that Netanyahu was jeopardizing Israeli strategic interests by saying no to every American proposal.[111] But no progress was made during the initial ten-month period of the U.S.-encouraged settlement freeze.

Obama could not stand up to Netanyahu's tactics, supported as they were by bitter opposition from the Israel lobby to the president's focus on settlements. In the fall of 2010 Obama backed down and decided never again to pay a political price at home for public criticism of Israel. The hopes of the Israeli peace camp were dashed once more. By abandoning his settlement freeze demand and then vetoing a February 2011 UN Security Council resolution critical of Israeli settlements, Obama, as described by Akiva Eldar, showed his "hypocrisy" and his "true colors."[112]

The analyses, warnings, hopes, and disappointments regarding U.S. policy toward Israel that I have surveyed are familiar to anyone who has engaged over the years with Israeli doves and their frustrations. In my own research trips to Israel—conducted on average every two to three years since 1973—I have listened over and over to Israeli proponents of trading the territories for peace plead with me for help to understand why American pressure on Israel had not come and when it would. Since 2010, expectations have all but vanished that Washington will exert significant pressure on Israeli governments. The most I have heard recently from my dovish interlocutors are forlorn descriptions of American intervention as "probably impossible, but still the only hope."

For the vast majority of Jewish Israelis, Zionism is still the legitimizing basis for Israeli policies and political appeals. But Zionism's legacy of the Iron Wall breeds distrust and territorial maximalism rather than inclinations to compromise from a position of strength. As a result, the Zionist political formula itself became a barrier to the achievement of a land-for-peace agreement. Against this historical and ideological background and shaped by Holocaustia's grip on Israeli political culture and psychology, American policies that subsidized right-wing, ultranationalist, and expansionist political appeals gave the coup de grâce to dovish forces in Israel and to their chances for mobilizing even a bare majority in parliament.

Between 1976 and 2017, Israeli politicians who favored concessions to achieve peace regularly told Israeli voters they were necessary because it would be impossible to defy the United States. Repeatedly, that argument was proven false. Partly as a result, politicians and parties who offered conciliatory approaches, warning of the need for short-term compromise to protect Israeli vital interests over the long run, suffered regular defeats and a steep decline in the proportion of the population willing to support them at the ballot box. Today, warnings of a crisis with the United States over Israel's policies toward Palestinians have lost all force. In July 2018, nearly 90 percent of Israeli Jews named the United States as their "most admired country." At a time when Israeli government policies toward peace, settlements, and the Palestinians were as hard-line as they had ever been, 62 percent of respondents believed that the "special relationship" between the United States and Israel was permanent. Eighty-four percent believed that the United

States would rescue Israel from any dire military or strategic threat it might face in the future.[113] Israelis have learned to be fully confident of American support, no matter what the policies of Israel's government. This is critical to understanding why, since 2009, no party committed to even a dimly plausible TSS has been a member of a governing coalition. Polls taken since 2012 consistently show that the proportion of Israelis identifying themselves as "Left" or "Moderate Left" has plummeted to below 15 percent, while the proportion identifying themselves as "Right" or "Moderate Right" is four times as great.[114] Following the victory of Likud and Netanyahu in Israel's 2019 Knesset election, Michael Oren, a Middle East studies expert and former Israeli ambassador to the United States, told the *New Yorker* that for all intents and purposes, "just about everybody" in Israel is "right wing."[115] Indeed, left-of-center politicians avoid even referring to themselves as such because of the pejorative connotation that the term "*smolani*" (leftist) has taken on in Israeli political discourse. It is therefore unsurprising that the dovish-liberal bloc has lost its ability to restrain government policy, win elections, or constitute a credible shadow government while in opposition.

The massive, indeed overwhelming support that successive American administrations gave to Israel, which crippled Israeli moderates and empowered Israeli maximalists, was sustained not by presidential preferences, cultural affinities between Israel and the United States, or prudent considerations of American national interest but instead by the calculations of American politicians facing a sophisticated, powerful, single-issue movement. The cocoon spun around Israeli democracy by this support helped make it impossible for Israelis to appreciate how massively and negatively their governments' policies would impact the status of their country and the prospects for its future. Israeli politicians who defied the electoral attractiveness of hard-line, triumphalist policies toward the Palestinians did so at their peril. For ambitious Israeli politicians, being both honest about the challenges the country faced and capable of achieving power proved impossible. Those who tried were defeated or driven from politics altogether. Rising stars whose careers originated within the Labor Party but who were stymied by their association with dovish positions include Yossi Beilin, Haim Ramon, Yossi Sarid, Shulamit Aloni, and Shlomo Ben-Ami.

Israel would have been somewhat more likely to have arrived at a TSS had it not been for the 1995 assassination of Prime Minister Yitzhak Rabin by a right-wing extremist. Rabin was a charismatic leader, a military hero, and a pragmatist who shook Yasser Arafat's hand after decades of swearing he would never negotiate with the PLO. On the other hand, Rabin never gave up his Jordanian, rather than Palestinian, orientation and never embraced the principle of an independent and viable Palestinian state.[116] Although his views may have been changing in the months before his death, his words and his policies (including settlement expansion) were consistently directed toward establishing a subservient Palestinian protectorate, with Arafat functioning as a bribable dictator and ruthless enforcer. Shimon Peres, who assumed the premiership after Rabin's assassination and was perhaps more committed than Rabin to a real political agreement with the Palestinians, continued his predecessor's policies and failed to defeat the Likud candidate in the May 1996 elections—Benjamin Netanyahu. Netanyahu was a harsh critic of the Oslo peace process and had implicitly associated himself with the attacks on Yitzhak Rabin as a traitor that led to Rabin's assassination. A key factor in Labor's defeat was Likud's exploitation of America's unwillingness to pressure Israel. This allowed Likud to shift Israeli attention from an opportunity to secure a historic peace to an exercise in extracting maximum advantage against the Palestinians. While unwilling to officially cancel the peace process, Netanyahu dedicated his government to Oslo's delegitimization, evading restraints placed on Israeli policies in the West Bank and the Gaza Strip, turning what had been designed as a "transitional" Palestinian authority into a mechanism for enhancing Israeli security, and preserving opportunities for expanded West Bank settlement.[117]

By the time Ehud Barak replaced Netanyahu as prime minister in 1999, the Oslo process had lost almost all its credibility among both Israelis and Palestinians. In a gamble to save his political career, Barak enlisted the United States in a scheme for suspending implementation of the Oslo Accords in favor of a high-stakes summit on his terms. With President Clinton personally acting as "Israel's lawyer" and against a background of massive settlement and road-building projects in the West Bank, Barak proposed an agreement featuring Israeli sovereignty over the Old City of Jerusalem and division of the West Bank into pieces separated by Israeli-ruled settlements and roads. His attempt to score a political victory by radically reducing the meaning of Palestinian self-determination severely miscarried. The July 2000 Camp David summit exploded in failure.[118] This ended serious negotiations and triggered the bloody Second Intifada (2000–2005), including heavy casualties among both Israelis and Palestinians and large-scale Israeli attacks on the Gaza Strip as well as Jenin and Ramallah. The Oslo process fell apart, leading to Israel's unilateral evacuation and blockade of the Gaza Strip in 2005 and a series of wars in Lebanon and Gaza.

During all this time the clout of the U.S. Israel lobby increased and further cocooned—arguably, atrophied—Israeli politics. At a symposium at the Hebrew University in 2010 on Israeli-Russian relations, Ephraim Halevy, head of Israel's foreign intelligence service, Mossad, from 1998 to 2002 and a consummate political insider, was one of the participants. The audience chuckled in agreement when Halevy said, "We don't think a power like Russia will do exactly what Israel wants it to do. We only expect that of the United States."[119] Not that Halevy saw this as a good thing. In an interview with another former Mossad operative, Joseph Alpher, Halevy observed that both Sharon and Netanyahu had believed that AIPAC was in such effective control of Washington's policies toward Israel that there was no real need for Israel to participate in any negotiations with Arabs that could lead to concessions. "We in practice nearly destroyed our regional capabilities because we rely on Washington. At the end of the day we have Congress, we have the White House, we have the media, we have AIPAC."[120]

The American-spun cocoon around Israel has vastly distorted Israeli perceptions and greatly reduced the country's ability to gauge the real effects of its policies. The cocoon ruined the careers of dovish politicians while enhancing the prospects of those catering to Israeli fantasies and fears. Opportunities for peace that might have been grasped were missed or destroyed. There is hardly a political analyst in Israel who can imagine how political parties genuinely committed to a negotiated TSS could ever form a government.

Chapter 4

Dead Solution Walking

Paradigms and Political Projects

A negotiated two-state solution (TSS) has failed as a policy option to resolve the Israeli-Palestinian conflict. But its failure is more profound than that. The TSS has also failed as a paradigm—an array of concepts, assumptions, agendas, questions, commitments, and beliefs associated with a partitionist approach to the "problem of Palestine." Understanding the rise of the TSS and the implications of its failure is crucial for developing more effective ways to think about the conflict and appreciating otherwise obscured paths toward a less violent and more equitable future.

Paradigms in politics and in science are functionally equivalent: they are shared beliefs strong enough to guide thinking about difficult problems for long periods of time. They are precious. They allow communities to form and their projects to advance, united by common vocabularies, aspirations, and tasks. They encourage both cooperation and competition among community members, which in turn foster dedication and hard work. Faith in paradigms does not ensure that projects built upon them will succeed, but projects whose foundations are doubted will struggle to survive.

Paradigms are as useful for preventing questions from being asked as they are for encouraging debates based on the shared assumptions that comprise them. The very meaning of an effective paradigm is that it makes some questions appear absurd, because posing them would contradict fundamental claims about the world that must be treated as true if the community's belief system is to remain intact. These intellectual closures are barriers to critical thinking, but they protect communities and projects from being sidetracked by cosmic questioning or nitpicking distractions. Questions that will not be or cannot be entertained in a community comprise what the mathematician turned neopositivist philosopher of science Imre Lakatos called its "negative heuristic." The problems that members of the community *are* encouraged to pose, goals that they are urged to pursue, and methods that they are authorized to use comprise what he terms the community's "positive heuristic."[1]

Activists within a social movement or political party also use unquestioned assumptions, overarching aspirations, and a shared frame of reference to argue productively, learn from one another's mistakes, build knowledge, accumulate confidence, and justify sacrifice. Crucially, sustained political projects and sustained scientific/scholarly projects both require privileged beliefs—claims about the world that both scholars and politicians publicly honor as presumptively true even if privately they may view them as problematic or unstable. Leaders of both types of projects must ensure that foundational assumptions are neither criticized nor questioned.

The Pathology and Promise of Paradigm Collapse

But what happens when the foundations of a political or scientific project *are* challenged and when evidence for their falsity mounts? What can we learn from the rise and fall of scientific paradigms about how those fully committed to the two-state paradigm can be expected to react as the project's basic assumptions are severely challenged?

Building directly on work by philosophers of science Karl Popper and Thomas Kuhn, Lakatos asked what made scientific progress possible when the paradigms, or "research programs" as he called them, guiding scientists are themselves exposed as fundamentally invalid. Lakatos's answer emphasizes long-term processes of political and scientific competition among rival communities, each guided by its own research program, that is, its own productive or dysfunctional paradigm.[2] As both Kuhn and Lakatos emphasize, because contending research programs are based on untestable assumptions and fundamentally incommensurate bodies of evidence, their findings cannot directly contradict or overthrow one another. Science progresses, however, as the communities working within these research programs either succeed or fail to attract sufficient resources, pose problems that adherents feel compelled to address, and generate answers consistent with basic assumptions. In a process that can be as much political as it is "evidence-based," research programs flourish, expand, stagnate, decay, get replaced, or replace others. This is how science progresses and knowledge accumulates.

Maintaining the integrity of a research or political community requires the sense or at least the promise of progress. Occasional failures of analysis, persuasion, mobilization, or prediction can be rationalized as errors of measurement or technique, but sustained contradictions of expectations are serious threats. The key to project survival is to respond to anomalies by ignoring them until their challenges can be explained or treated with authorized techniques and with basic assumptions still intact. Lakatos calls these instances "progressive problem shifts" in which anomalous observations or events become "exceptions that prove the rule," yielding new insights and provoking more interesting questions by extending the project's positive heuristic without contradicting its core assumptions, its negative heuristic.

But defense of a paradigm is often achieved in ways that are not progressive and indeed undermine its vitality and competitive position. If experimental or predictive failures are repeatedly excused by specifying new assumptions, the paradigm quickly becomes more complex but less coherent and useful. More and more work is required to make arguments that are less and less interesting or effective. A paradigm defended in this way, with numerous excuses and new ad hoc assumptions, narrows opportunities for success, discourages learning, and prevents discoveries. Less able to elicit excitement or satisfy curiosity, the project can become a doctrine of orthodoxy that relies less on empirical results and more on political clout to fend off competition. In Lakatosian terms, the project enters a "degenerative" phase.

To be sure, the first response of research and political communities to evidence that contradicts their negative heuristic should be to question its credibility or relevance or to ignore it as an "anomaly," unworthy of sustained attention. When contrary evidence becomes more difficult to deny or ignore, both scientists and politicians have shown extraordinary ingenuity. They have offered brilliant strategies and arguments to extend the life of projects even in the face of seemingly stark evidence of error and failure. In the eighteenth century, chemists explained combustion by the presence of phlogiston. When it was found that rusted metals or burned substances weighed more, not less, than they had prior to combustion, most chemists simply ignored the anomaly. Those who did ask why removing weightless phlogiston could increase the weight of burned material found imaginative ad hoc hypotheses that protected key assumptions. Perhaps, they maintained, phlogiston had buoyancy—a "negative weight"—that, when removed, increased the weight of the burned substance. Others hypothesized that disappearing phlogiston created air deposits that added more weight than was removed by its elimination. After decades of work, however, experimental chemists using increasingly accurate measurements and new theories about individual gases produced a consensus that combustion added mass from surrounding gases to burned materials rather than removed phlogiston from them. Only then were accumulating anomalies and the increasing complexity of phlogiston theory interpreted as having exposed the degenerative character of the phlogiston research program, leading to abandonment of the belief that phlogiston even existed.[3]

The same pattern is observed in the social sciences. In the middle decades of the twentieth century the "modernization paradigm" dominated social scientific approaches in sociology, economics, and political science. The presumptive truth of this research program and its associated political projects was that industrial technology would produce "modernity" in all "traditional" cultures and societies exposed to it in Asia, Africa, and Latin America. Modernization's fundamentally identical, irresistible, and revolutionary effects would mold those societies and their political systems to American and West European models. Despite their obvious predictive failures, modernization theorists stuck by their assumption of a fundamental incompatibility between "traditional" and "modern" norms and organizing principles. For decades they offered elaborate ad hoc subtheories and hypotheses to protect and save the paradigm. These included "breakdowns in modernization," "prismatism," "polynormativism," and "crises and sequences." Entire careers, projects, institutes, and subspecialties were built around these efforts to save modernization theory by protecting its hardcore belief from growing examples of its predictive failure. By the end of the twentieth century, however, little remained of the dichotomous ontology and technological determinism at the heart of the modernization paradigm or its expectation of convergence toward a single secular, rationalist, capitalist, and liberal democratic social order. What began as a series of progressive problem shifts eventually became a flood of excuses that burdened remaining modernization theorists with the frustration, anomie, and intellectual waywardness characteristic of a degenerative research program.

We are seldom surprised when political leaders use verbal gymnastics to interpret events as confirming long-standing beliefs or official doctrines. We are less accustomed to scientists displaying similar behavior with respect to paradigms that undergird *their* work. Both in politics and in science, project leaders and rank-and-file supporters shield core assumptions from contrary evidence. Consequently, both scientific and political projects maintain institutional dominance far longer than could be justified by their ability to explain or change the world. When science does change, it owes as much to politics and interests as it does to evidence. That is why Thomas Kuhn's theory of scientific revolutions, which explains the overthrow of previously hegemonic ideas in the natural sciences and the discontinuities surrounding that process, borrowed its key concept—revolution—not from natural science itself but instead from political science. As Kuhn writes (and as Lakatos would agree), "As in political revolution, so in paradigm change—there is no standard higher than the assent of the relevant community."[4]

No successful system of belief can contain within itself the means to quickly recognize when its time has passed or equip itself with procedures to discard outdated assumptions when they become obstacles rather than routes to progress. Even when naturalized ways of looking at the world are exposed as false, suitable alternatives may be unavailable and certainly will be difficult to identify. For those whose lives, reputations, and peace of mind are linked to the collapsing project, even plausible claims of rivals will seem silly, fantastical, transparently self-serving, and even immoral. As consensus cracks, disorganized, confused, and even extravagant ideas will appear. In these periods, the struggle to build new communities based on new assumptions about what is commonsensical and what is important to investigate will be driven as much by politics as by evidence, as much by emotion as by interest, and as much by rhetoric as by insight. It is precisely from within this ferment of thinking that more effective research programs and paradigms arise.

The Rise and Decline of the TSS Paradigm

Paradigm Ascendant

The TSS is not simply a scenario for achieving a stable peace between Israel and the Palestinians and, more broadly, between Israel and its Middle Eastern neighbors. It became a highly consequential political and analytic project. To understand its rise and decline as well as its continuing impact, we must consider it both as a political program, with activists and politicians who hitch their ambitions to it, and as a paradigm or research program for analysts, scholars, and journalists who want to understand the Israeli-Palestinian conflict and identify paths toward its melioration.

In Lakatosian terms, the TSS project scored tremendous successes in its rise to prominence and then dominance in the last decades of the twentieth century. The idea of resolving the "problem of Palestine" through the creation of two states, one Arab and one Jewish, first emerged during the British mandate period (1920–1948). The idea gained the imprimatur of the international community after a majority on the United Nations (UN) Special Committee on Palestine recommended it in 1947. Thereafter two-thirds of the UN General Assembly supported the recommendation. Though belief in the idea of peaceful relations between two national states in Palestine faded after 1948, it was, to quote Charles Dickens's *A Tale of Two Cities*, "recalled to life" after the 1967 war.

When the TSS reemerged after 1967, it was not a paradigmatic organizer of public debate but rather a marginal idea propounded by avant-garde Israeli, Palestinian, and international peacemakers. The key to peace, they argued, would be the trade of most or all the territories captured by Israel in the 1967 conflict for recognition of Israel and peaceful relations between Israel and a Palestinian state located in the West Bank (including Arab Jerusalem, al-Quds) and the Gaza Strip. Remaining problems in Israeli-Arab relations would then be handled through normal diplomatic and political processes of competition and negotiation.[5]

The idea gained momentum over subsequent decades among Palestinians and Israeli Jews and in the international community. The principle of trading land for peace, security, and recognition—although not the idea of a Palestinian state—was enshrined in the November 1967 UN Security Council Resolution 242 and affirmed in Resolution 338 following the Arab-Israeli war of 1973.

In the 1990s the establishment of a Palestinian state west of the Jordan River became the dominant way of thinking about the purpose of peace negotiations. Both the Oslo process and repeated diplomatic efforts that followed the failed Camp David summit of 2000 were guided by explicit commitments to a TSS as the key element in a final status agreement.

The Lakatosian "hard core," or "negative heuristic," of the TSS research program can be summarized as follows:

- Israel can withdraw from enough of the territory occupied in 1967 to make this land-for-peace deal possible;
- A land-for-peace deal can be arrived at through negotiations;
- Geographical partition of Palestine/the Land of Israel, can be the basis for long-term acceptance by Palestinians and Israelis of a new and peaceful political status quo;
- The Arab and Muslim worlds and the wider international community will use this agreement as a legitimizing framework for the presence of a Jewish state in the Middle East.

A growing number of institutions, communities, and countries were pleased to accept these claims as true or came to fear that they were becoming true. In line with its paradigmatic status, most of the world eventually saw the Arab-Israeli conflict as a struggle over the TSS.

The paradigm had a positive heuristic as well: a set of predictions and questions worth answering about how to achieve (or prevent) achievement of the two-state vision. These shaped the data-gathering and analytic problems to be solved and the tasks of organization, mobilization, and persuasion to be undertaken by researchers, opinion leaders, activists, politicians, and diplomats. This agenda for thinking and for work attracted talent and resources, which ensured a constant flow of important questions to be solved and tasks to be performed—"progressive problem shifts," as Lakatos would say, "normal science" in Kuhnian language. For its enthusiasts the TSS paradigm as a political project offered focused, satisfying activity capable of building confidence, converting former doubters or opponents, and attracting resources to achieve future success.

In the first twenty years of the occupation, most Israelis advocating territorial compromise did so based on the idea of an arrangement with Jordan. A key element in their position was the Allon Plan (named after Yigal Allon, the Labor Party leader and hero of the 1948 war who initially advanced it). In its various versions, the plan entailed transfer of the central mountainous areas of the West Bank to Palestinian control, either as autonomous entities within Israel's overall control or as ruled by Jordan as part of a peace treaty with the Hashemite Kingdom. Consistent with the principle, but not the boundaries suggested by Allon, was King Hussein's 1972 offer of the Hashemite Kingdom Plan, involving a peace agreement with Israel featuring Jordanian rule of the West Bank and the Gaza Strip. The Camp David Accords of 1978 were also based on Allon Plan thinking. As described in Chapter 1, they imagined Jordan as the Palestinian representative in negotiations with Israel. Efforts by Prime Minister Shimon Peres and King Hussein in 1985 to achieve a bilateral peace were also based on the Allon Plan.

From their marginal position on the Israeli political spectrum in the late 1960s, the 1970s, and the early 1980s, proponents of the TSS argued against relying on Jordan and advanced instead images of an independent

Palestinian state in the West Bank and Gaza. Their arguments gained credibility with the collapse of each effort to solve the Palestinian problem via Jordan. Seven months after the eruption of the First Intifada in December 1987, Jordan revoked its 1950 annexation of the West Bank, abandoning its claim to sovereignty over the area. This was a major victory for the two-state project. Two-staters had not only rejected Jordan as a viable interlocutor for resolution of the Palestinian problem and predicted the need to negotiate directly with Palestinian representatives, including the Palestine Liberation Organization (PLO), but also had judged impossible another form of the Jordanian option, advanced by many on the Israeli Right. Under the slogan "Jordan is Palestine," Prime Minister Yitzhak Shamir, Ariel Sharon, and others had called for an end to the Hashemite Kingdom and for it to be replaced by a Palestinian state on the East Bank of the Jordan River. This idea had no support among Palestinians, and following the First Intifada it largely disappeared, even within Israeli political space.

From the 1970s through the 1990s, a series of remarkable analytic and political victories advanced the TSS project. One important success was the correct prediction that both Palestinian and Israeli Jewish opinion would move toward acceptance of the TSS as a minimally satisfying compromise capable of meeting, or seeming to meet, each side's minimal requirements. A few factors indicated this victory:

- An increasing number of Palestinian and Israeli activists and politicians were willing to speak publicly in favor of some sort of TSS.
- Legal barriers in Israel to meeting with PLO representatives were removed.
- PLO resolutions opened the door to negotiations toward a two-state outcome.
- The PLO formally declared its support in 1988 of a Palestinian state existing nonbelligerently alongside the State of Israel.

Inaugurated in 1993, the Oslo process, although not explicitly based on a two-state outcome, was generally understood to be guided by that idea.[6] It was supported by public opinion surveys in the 1990s that showed solid majorities among both Palestinians and Israelis in favor of the TSS. The TSS program called for a Palestinian state with enough territory and territorial continuity in the West Bank and the Gaza Strip to make it politically viable. This meant attracting sufficient support among Palestinians and Arabs generally to achieve something like an end-of-conflict peace agreement with Israel.

This goal and the analysis that supported it led two-staters to mobilize early against settlements in the occupied territories. Most settlements in the late 1960s and early to mid-1970s were built under Labor government auspices. They were small and were rationalized either as being located within territory that Israel would keep as part of an Allon Plan–style territorial compromise or as temporary bargaining chips. After 1977, settlements were established in accordance with Likud government plans explicitly committed to preventing a TSS. These settlements provoked more widespread protests. Activists within the TSS movement correctly predicted that the unintended consequences of Labor government settlements and the burgeoning growth of the Likud settlements would be the creation of vested economic interests, infrastructure, security positions, legal precedents, political attachments, ideological commitments, and psychological expectations, which would drastically reduce prospects for negotiating and implementing a land-for-peace agreement.

In response to these threats, the TSS campaign was sustained and wide-ranging. Eventually it was as active in North America and Europe as it was in Israel and among Palestinians. The campaign yielded academic, journalistic, and political activities that shaped fields of study; established or enlivened numerous careers; produced think tanks; focused the attention of intelligence communities and policy analysts; and spawned dozens of academic and political projects. Some of these efforts sought to increase goodwill between Jews and Arabs or to organize back-channel talks between elites—so-called track-two diplomacy. Others studied prolonged ethnopolitical conflicts in search of ways to measure ripening and identify productive if adverse stalemates. As one of its key elements, meant to attract Israeli Jewish support, the project highlighted "the demographic problem"—the threat to Israel's Jewish majority and to Zionist principles posed by the absorption of Palestinian populations in the West Bank and Gaza.

Two-stater forecasts were confirmed when debate in Israel shifted from whether to annex the occupied territories as formal parts of the State of Israel to the implications of their gradual but undeclared incorporation by creeping processes of de facto annexation. In the early 1980s the two-state research program popularized the concept of the point of no return. Although it had appeared in warnings issued by prescient analysts soon after the 1967 war, it was made famous by the Israeli geographer, journalist, and researcher Meron Benvenisti, who described the situation in the West Bank as "five minutes to midnight."[7] Benvenisti first used this phrase in 1982. "Within thirty-six months," he declared, "there will be some 100,000 Jewish inhabitants of the West Bank. If this occurs it will become impossible for any Israeli government to relinquish control."[8] In February 1983, he warned that failure to implement the Reagan Initiative to advance a land-for-peace agreement between Israel and Jordan (representing the Palestinians) would mean that Israel's annexation of the territories would soon reach the point of no return.

Benvenisti took the 100,000 settlers threshold from plans developed by fervent annexationists within the Likud government and experts within the World Zionist Organization who were charged with planning and rapidly expanding Jewish settlement in the occupied territories.[9] These plans were part of explicit government efforts to ensure permanent incorporation of the occupied territories into Israel that began in 1977 with the election victory of Menachem Begin's Likud Party. Begin named his agriculture minister, Ariel Sharon, as chair of the Interministerial Committee on Settlement and charged him to carry out as comprehensive and as rapid a buildup of Jewish settlements in the occupied territories as possible.[10] Despite the frenetic pace of land expropriation and settlement construction, well-informed observers such as the *Haaretz* newspaper's chief correspondent for West Bank affairs Yehuda Litani found it "hard to believe settlement expansion can stop eventual partition."[11] In these years, those in charge of settlement planning as an enterprise precisely to prevent Israeli withdrawal were also dubious that it could succeed. In October 1980, the leader of the planning unit of the World Zionist Organization's Land Settlement Division and author of the 1978 "100,000 plan" was reportedly "afraid time might run out before his plan could be implemented."[12]

But facts on the ground gave credence to the idea that soon efforts to stop Israel's permanent incorporation of the territories, or at least the West Bank, would be futile. The idea quickly came to dominate debate over the future of the occupied territories. Benvenisti's writings and interviews received widespread attention and featured complex phrasings of his position on whether irreversibility had been absolutely attained, whether a turning point toward eventual irreversibility had been reached, or whether the forces working toward annexation now outweighed those working toward withdrawal.[13]

Benvenisti's data and analysis terrified proponents of territorial compromise, frantic that it would soon be too late to stop the annexationist juggernaut. In April 1982 Shmuel Toledano, a Labor Party moderate and Arab affairs adviser to the prime minister from 1966 to 1977, predicted that as a result of Likud government policies "within a few years, if anyone were to suggest giving up any part of the territories, it would be regarded as no different than that of giving up part of the Negev or the Galilee."[14] Yehuda Litani had scoffed in 1980 at the notion that settlements could determine the fate of the West Bank but soon changed his mind. In February 1983 he concluded that within just seven weeks negotiating initiatives for a territorial compromise could become irrelevant.[15]

The following month the famed author and journalist Amos Elon wrote that "for all practical purposes [Judea, Samaria, and Gaza] have already been annexed to the State of Israel, perhaps irrevocably."[16] In 1983 Peace Now distributed a fifteen-page pamphlet warning that settlement of 100,000 Jews on the West Bank would lead inevitably to annexation, something looming ahead within the next five or even three years.

Palestinians shared the same concerns. In February 1983 Bethlehem mayor Elias Freij believed that "the Palestinians have only two months left to prevent the Israeli takeover of the West Bank and Gaza Strip from becoming an accomplished fact," though a month later he thought that perhaps it would be another year before there would be "nothing left to talk about."[17] Under the circumstances, he appealed directly to the PLO to move swiftly toward negotiations with Israel before 100,000 Jews had established themselves in the West Bank, a state of affairs that would make it "impossible to turn the clock backwards . . . where no solution can be found and it will simply be too late."[18]

King Hussein of Jordan agreed and spoke regularly of an approaching point of no return. In January 1983 he described Israel as "about to complete the last stages of swallowing up the land, including Jerusalem."[19] In an interview a year later he was asked how much time was left "before there will be nothing left to negotiate about." "Not much time, sir," he responded, "not much time."[20] Despite their worries that acknowledgment of a point of no return would back them into a corner, PLO leaders also expressed deepening fears that annexation was very close to being a fact.[21]

A U.S. State Department spokesman in August 1983 sharpened the sense of a decisive change in the landscape of political possibility. The spokesman said that while a freeze on settlement activity was desirable, the idea of dismantling West Bank settlements in the context of a peace agreement was no longer "practicable."[22]

The idea of a critical point that was approaching but had not yet been passed spurred TSS advocates to mobilize, hoping that decisive and immediate action might yet avert catastrophe. The image of a closing window of opportunity for peace served the TSS project in two important ways. Analytically, it focused attention on the systematic but often purposely obscured strategies of Likud governments and their allies to implement settlement plans, subsidies, and infrastructure projects in ways that would tie the hands of future governments. It also helped explain what often seemed like a chaotic, random rush to build settlements, "grab hilltops," engineer large-scale transfers of land to state control, and subsidize settlers. Politically, the "point of no return" specter enabled leaders of the Israeli peace movement to mobilize funds, fuel demonstrations, and increase public support for a quick change in government by warning that the chances for or even the very possibility of peace were disappearing with every settlement and every settler.

But this analytic sword had two edges. Leading Likud government officials, including Ariel Sharon, minister of housing and construction David Levy, and Eliyahu Ben-Elissar, chairman of the Knesset Foreign Affairs and Defense Committee, greeted Benvenisti's arguments enthusiastically as "scientific" confirmation of their strategy's success to incorporate the territories into Israel by settling them.[23] In mid-1984 the editors of the leading settler journal, *Nekuda*, proclaimed that "by the end of the summer there would be 50,000 Jews living in Judea, Samaria, and the Gaza district . . . enough in terms of creating settlements and political facts, to guarantee the hold of the Jewish people on the heart of the Land of Israel for generations to come."[24]

As the impression spread that the process of annexation might indeed have become irreversible, leaders of the dovish camp stopped hailing Benvenisti as a prophet and began denouncing him as a demoralizing Cassandra, a traitor to peace, a disguised enthusiast for a Greater Land of Israel, or a political ignoramus who had been fooled into thinking that anything in politics could be irreversible. In 1982, former Israeli foreign minister and leading dove Abba Eban had pointed to Benvenisti's "point of no return" warnings to motivate antiannexationist efforts but within two years changed course. Fearing that belief in the irreversibility of settlements would scuttle efforts to end the occupation, Eban and most advocates of territorial compromise rejected the idea either because the settlement enterprise was said to be too puny to matter in the long run or because infrastructure and demography could not themselves produce enduring political realities. According to Eban, Benvenisti and those who hailed his findings suffered from a psychological disorder that included "an almost fetishistic attachment to roads." Eban wished that Benvenisti would "go see the roads in Algeria and in Kenya. The world is full of road systems, built from Roman times onward, and the architects of those systems have long since vanished."[25]

The apex of the two-state project—its single biggest analytic victory and political opportunity—came after the intifada. This sustained mostly nonviolent mass uprising by West Bank and Gaza Palestinians began in December 1987 and lasted for years, despite a brutal and expensive crackdown by Israel. One result was the return of the Labor Party to power in 1992 and the launching of what became the Oslo peace process. Even Benvenisti himself, who had closed his West Bank Data Project in 1989 amid what seemed to be the inexorable march of de facto annexation, wondered fleetingly if the Palestinian intifada had opened the possibility for a TSS.[26]

A key part of the Oslo process was an informal agreement in 1995 between Israeli and Palestinian leaders to create a Palestinian state in the West

Bank and the Gaza Strip as the cornerstone of a negotiated settlement. The understanding was reached by Labor minister Yossi Beilin, a close confidant of Shimon Peres, and PLO leader Mahmoud Abbas (Abu Mazen). Abu Mazen, who was appointed prime minister of the Palestinian Authority (PA) by Yasser Arafat, himself became president shortly before Arafat's death. The Beilin-Abu Mazen Agreement, covering borders, settlements, and Jerusalem, was central to Oslo, but little progress was made toward its implementation in the two years before Yitzhak Rabin's assassination. At the Camp David summit in 2000 when Israeli prime minister Ehud Barak effectively renounced it, the Oslo process ended. From 1995 until its collapse, the Oslo process produced a weak PA in the West Bank and Gaza, brief periods of satisfying economic interaction, no significant withdrawals of Israeli authority beyond the archipelago of Area A towns and cities, 145,000 more settlers in the West Bank, and intermittent spasms of unprecedentedly bloody violence between Palestinians and Israelis.[27]

Paradigm Crisis

In the aftermath of Oslo, champions of the TSS project had to explain its failure in ways that would leave its hard-core assumptions intact. Its defenders responded by finding excuses for failure by stipulating a variety of conditions that had previously not been said to be necessary for achieving a TSS.[28] Israeli leaders such as Benjamin Netanyahu, it was now said, would have to be replaced, along with their policies of sabotaging the goal of two states, while paying lip service to the principle of a painful territorial compromise. Israeli governments would have to be bolder and more genuine in their embrace of a real partnership with Palestinians than either Rabin or his Labor Party successors (Peres and Barak). The American president, or successive presidents, would need to be fully, consistently, and skillfully engaged in the negotiating process. The constant and steep increase in the number of settlements established in Arab areas would have to end, and both Israel and the Palestinians would have to stop the bloody cycles of targeted assassinations, suicide bombings, and massive retaliation.

This long list of daunting requirements made success for the TSS seem increasingly unrealistic if not altogether fanciful. This was especially so following the bloody Second Intifada. Israeli Jewish opinion radicalized, Ariel Sharon rose to the premiership, and Israel emerged as a key ally of Washington's neoconservative-led war on terror. In 2002 Israel briefly reoccupied Palestinian cities in the West Bank and isolated and destroyed Arafat's compound in Ramallah. In 2005 Israel withdrew settlers and military bases from the Gaza Strip, setting the stage in 2006 for an election there that brought the anti-Oslo Islamic Resistance Movement (Hamas) to power.

Since then and despite an attempt in 2008 by a tottering government in Israel headed by Ehud Olmert to resume the Oslo process, Israeli-Palestinian relations and prospects for productive negotiations have continued to deteriorate. The PA, widely perceived as corrupt and as a tool of Israel, lost support among West Bank Arabs, while Palestinian attacks on Israeli territory from Gaza triggered increasingly punishing Israeli attacks on the denizens of that region. Diplomatic and political initiatives were discouraged or thwarted by these spasms of violence and destruction, by the right wing's solid grip on power in Israel, by constantly growing numbers of West Bank settlers, and by the burdens imposed on West Bank Arabs by the separation barrier and close to 150 checkpoints. All of these deepened Palestinian fear, hatred, and despair while inducing hopelessness within the Israeli peace camp.

Since 2006 the analytic machinery of the TSS project has stultified, revealing the project's degeneration as a research program and its collapse as a paradigm for guiding thought and action. Like phlogiston scientists or modernization theorists confronting a long series of incorrect predictions, TSS advocates have struggled to convince others and even themselves of the validity of their traditional arguments. However, with so many unlikely if not impossible conditions now identified as necessary for success, claims that had been repeated since the mid-1980s came to appear as dogma, catechism, or worn-out proverbs rather than reasoned or evidence-based analysis. They prompt sighs and eye rolls rather than elicit interest or excitement from target audiences.

The desperate straits in which defenders of the two-state paradigm now find themselves are apparent from the palpable inadequacy of their arguments on key topics: settlements, demography, the attraction of Mizrahi Jews to the TSS banner, and the role of the United States in the peace process.

SETTLEMENTS

In the mid-1980s TSS advocates argued against irreversibility claims by asserting that the settlement enterprise had exhausted itself without changing demographic or political realities. At that time, with fewer than 50,000 settlers in the West Bank, the argument was plausible. But the number of West Bank settlers passed the 100,000 mark in 1993—the original point of no return identified in the early 1980s by both proponents and opponents of the settlement movement. In 2001 the number of West Bank settlers (outside expanded East Jerusalem) hit 200,000. Eight years later there were 300,000, and by 2018 there were over 400,000, with 200,000 more across the Green Line in expanded East Jerusalem. In 2019 1 out of every 11 Israeli Jews lived in territory occupied in 1967.

Two-state advocates have responded to the steeply rising and seemingly unstoppable upward curve of settlement in three ways:

- Accepting the permanence of multiple Israeli settlement blocs, including within East Jerusalem and its environs;
- Promoting land swaps to compensate Palestinians with (barren) land adjacent to the Gaza Strip and the southern West Bank; and
- Devising elaborate plans for tunnels and bypass roads to preserve "transportational continuity" as a substitute for the "territorial contiguity" that the archipelago of Palestinian districts could no longer have.

Despite these concessions and the steep increase in the complexity of their plans, two-staters have been unable to keep pace with the continuing expansion of settlements. Concentration on the settlement blocs has meant ignoring the fact that more than 170,000 Israeli settlers live in more than one hundred settlements outside their boundaries.[29] Nor have two-staters been able to cope with the administrative and legal arrangements that Israel has implemented, largely superseding international laws governing belligerent occupation that partly constrained Israeli behavior in the occupation's first decades. Since at least 2009, it has simply been impossible to detail the contours and prerogatives of a Palestinian state in ways consistent with the minimum stated requirements of both Israeli and Palestinian leaders.

Shaul Arieli has been foremost among two-staters in trying to reconcile his continued pursuit of a TSS with changing realities. A retired colonel with command experience in the Gaza Strip, Arieli was a negotiator with the Palestinians and has been a key figure in TSS organizations such as the Geneva Initiative and Commanders for Israel's Security. Arieli was intimately involved in planning the route of the separation barrier and is widely recognized as an expert on the history and details of proposals to demarcate borders between Jews and Palestinians in the West Bank. He has offered numerous blueprints of how Israeli withdrawal could be achieved and a Palestinian state could be created, despite the enormous expansion of settlements. In a detailed 2013 study titled *Why Settlements Have Not Killed the TSS*, Arieli used language that, except for its understated tone, could easily be mistaken for two-stater arguments made thirty years earlier:

> An increasing number of people, from various political perspectives, are asserting that it is becoming geographically unviable to create a separation between Israel and the West Bank, if it has not become so already. The reason given is that Israeli settlement construction has reached a point that it is no longer possible to create a border between Jewish and Palestinian population centres.[30]

Even those, Arieli said, "who believe and hope for a two-state solution to the conflict . . . express concerns that there is a window of opportunity for implementing this which will soon close." As an example he pointed to a recent statement by British foreign secretary William Hague that "if progress on negotiations is not made next year, then the TSS could become impossible to achieve."[31]

Arieli acknowledged that settlements "complicated the issue of drawing a border and undermines confidence in Israel's intentions." Still, he claimed, it was imperative "to challenge the claim that the possibility for creating a border has almost closed." He admitted that more than 60,000 Israelis lived in West Bank settlements located outside the blocs he imagined as annexable to Israel. But most of these settlements were small, he emphasized. The growth of the settlements as a whole had slowed. The settler population was heavily ultraorthodox and would therefore be ready to move when told to do so by their rabbis. By removing subsidies, many settlers would be encouraged to leave voluntarily. Geographically, Arieli concluded, "drawing a border remains entirely possible" because the Jewish population was just 12 percent of the population of the West Bank, meaning that the settlements "have not achieved Jewish dominance across the territory."[32]

Arieli's 2013 conclusion, that the "real difficulty in implementing the idea of partition is not physical but political," was a commonplace observation in the early 1980s.[33] Four years later after the failure of John Kerry's intensive diplomatic initiative to save the TSS, Donald Trump's victory in the United States, and Netanyahu's continued domination of Israeli politics, the political winds seemed even less favorable than they were in 2013. Nonetheless, in a 2017 *Haaretz* opinion piece, Arieli still insisted that the struggle for two states should not be abandoned and that the success of the settlement enterprise was overblown. What had changed was his tone. It was no longer clinical and understated; it was extravagant, frustrated, and desperate:

> The facts speak for themselves. The interpretation of the facts is another matter. You can always argue about it, but overdosing on fantasy pills and sliding into hallucinatory messianic trips aren't recipes for longevity. Israel would be better off overcoming the addiction and preparing for a TSS.[34]

In a subsequent interview, Arieli confronted the fact that even by his reckoning, 150,000 Israeli settlers would have to be evacuated to enable implementation of even a minimalist Palestinian state. He described that task as "doable," even as the political prerequisites he had identified in 2013 for that to happen seemed considerably less attainable than they had been four years earlier. The prerequisites were Israeli election of a government committed to giving up the West Bank, an end to Palestinian infighting, a Palestinian willingness to accept extensive "border adjustments," and a belief among disillusioned Palestinians and Israelis that "a solution is workable."[35]

Few observers quarrel with Arieli's basic point. Incorporation of the West Bank into Israel and the disappearance of plausible opportunities for a Palestinian state in that territory are political questions with geographical, demographic, and infrastructural dimensions, not practical questions with political dimensions. But once incorporation has occurred, the character of the political questions that are crucial also changes. Arieli's arid counsel in the spring of 2013 reflected the intellectual and political dead end of the TSS. "Ultimately," he said, "it's about having the political courage to say, 'Now is the time for the two-state solution.'"[36] It might better be said that political courage is about saying "Then was the time for the TSS; now is the time for something different."

DEMOGRAPHY

Over decades of struggle, two-state advocates have put special emphasis on the demographic problem as an argument for changing the Israeli political equation in their favor. By exploiting and even deepening Jewish Israeli fears of and distaste for Arabs and by emphasizing their supreme commitment to a Jewish democratic state, two-state advocates have consistently warned that de facto annexation would bring a demographic catastrophe: a State of Israel that contained a large and eventually a majority Arab population. Adding so many Arabs to the state would mean either permanent civil conflict, violence, and terrorism (the Lebanonization or Belfastization of Israel) or democratization that would bring Arabs to power and thereby end the country as a Jewish state.

The TSS project invested heavily in the demographic argument not only because it appealed to popular prejudices but also because it could

recast compromise as being inspired by strong nationalist and specifically Zionist commitments. Some months after becoming prime minister
in 1992 while secret negotiations to start the Oslo process were under
way, Yitzhak Rabin offered a characteristically blunt version of the demographic argument for trading land for peace. Referring to the region
all Israelis know as densely populated with Arabs, he commented that
"it would be good if Gaza would be swallowed up by the sea, but that's
impossible."[37]

In some ways, however, the doves' use of the demographic argument
boomeranged. Decades of occupation increased Palestinian resistance, including terrorism, heightening anti-Arab and even racist sentiments among
Israeli Jews. Especially after the Second Intifada, demographic arguments
helped reinforce fears, stereotypes, and hatreds. Ultimately this undermined readiness to compromise that might have existed among sectors of
the Jewish population not already firmly in the peace camp.

In addition, it became clear that forming a government coalition based
on anything other than a right-wing religious alliance would require a large
Arab vote and the cooperation if not participation of Arab members of
Knesset. By using the demographic argument, the Israeli peace camp alien-
ated that key segment of the population, thereby suppressing its turnout in
elections.[38] Meanwhile, supporters of Likud and other right-wing parties
felt reassured by fraudulent but widely believed claims that official statistics
greatly exaggerated both the size of the Arab population and projections of
its future growth.[39]

The net result of incorporation of the West Bank into Israeli life and
the presence there of an enormous, feared, and hated Arab population was
mass Israeli Jewish support for the construction of the separation barrier
and associated checkpoints and restrictions. These have confined Palestinians in the West Bank to scores of ghettoized enclaves, thereby minimizing
contact between West Bank Palestinians and Jews. This has also blunted the
demographic argument, since more Israeli Jews have come to believe that
rule of the West Bank does not automatically mean more exposure to the
Arabs who live there or a state that is or feels less Jewish than it would be
without the West Bank.

MIZRAHIM

Another argument in the political quiver of two-state advocates has been that Mizrahim (Israeli Jews who came from or whose ancestors came from Muslim countries) will eventually respond to their material interests by abandoning Likud and its allies. Their voting record of strong support for Likud and right-wing religious parties was chalked up to historical, cultural, and social-psychological factors, including infamous anti-Mizrahi outbursts by leading Labor politicians in 1981. Things would change dramatically, so went the argument, if only Mizrahi politicians delivered a clear message that directly connected massive expenditures on settlements to their community's socioeconomic difficulties. When Amir Peretz led the Labor Party in 2006 he ran on this platform, giving this theory its clearest test.

Peretz was born in Morocco. He was a wounded veteran and a charismatic politician who began as the mayor of Sderot, a poor development town, and became secretary-general of the Histadrut (Israel's powerful association of trade unions). He was well known for his dovish views and his belief that money spent on settlements should instead be used to solve social problems. In 2006 he became leader of the Labor Party and the first serious Mizrahi candidate for prime minister. Although there is evidence that Peretz increased the percentage of Mizrahim voting for Labor, that vote still did not exceed 30 percent, and the Labor Party went down in defeat. Since then, the great mass of Mizrahi votes have gone consistently to Likud or to a traditional Likud coalition partner, the explicitly Mizrahi-religious party Shas.

Shas's continued success is instructive. It is the only major party that explicitly appeals to Mizrahi identity and traditional Mizrahi resentments (against both Ashkenazim and Arabs) while emphasizing a grassroots commitment to improving the living conditions of its (mostly poor) constituents. Two-state advocates have been disappointed and surprised for decades that Mizrahi voters for Likud and Shas are not swayed by platforms to shift settlement and occupation-related resources to socioeconomic programs. But as Danny Gutwein has argued, neoliberal policies that shrank Israel's welfare state made Mizrahi voters more reliant than ever on government subsidies to the settlements.[40] Indeed, more than half the population of one of the largest settlements in the West Bank, Maale Adumim, is Mizrahi. In addition, Gutwein argues, polarization between Jews and Arabs, including extremely restricted access for Palestinians to the Israeli labor market, accentuates the value of Jewishness to lower-class Israeli Jews and solidifies their material interest in a continuing relationship of hostility. The sequence featured in the traditional argument offered to Mizrahi voters by the peace camp—first end settlements so that funds can be spent in slums—is often heard as telegraphing that the doves' real agenda is to solve the Palestinian problem, not help poor Israeli Jews. Repeated failures at the ballot box have shown that it is not a winning slogan.

THE UNITED STATES

As discussed in Chapter 3, the peace camp in Israel depended on the United States to follow its interests and thereby save Israel from itself. But the yearning for effective American pressure toward a TSS was never satisfied. Despite a few tantalizing episodes suggesting that sustained and focused U.S. pressure on Israel could work, the peace process became a carousel of failure instead of a path to resolution. Another sign of the degeneration of the two-state project—its inability to offer inspiring or enlightening guidance for its supporters—is the continued invocation of the United States as a decisive part of the solution. In April 2014 when Secretary of State John Kerry's last peace initiative was approaching its widely predicted collapse, the Canadian Israeli analyst Bernard Avishai, a stalwart champion of the TSS, wondered if it was at all realistic to imagine the Barack Obama administration, or any American government, with the will to do what had to be done. According to Avishai, that meant "offering an American plan for Israeli-Palestinian peace and rallying the world to it, while challenging, or even shattering, Netanyahu's fragile coalition."[41] The following year Avishai was more explicit. In Israel, "a majority for change can be built . . . but not in the absence of pressure from Washington," meaning at least U.S. support for UN resolutions condemning settlements and support for sanctions against Israel for continuing to expand them.[42]

Three years later in the wake of the Obama administration's failure to heed his advice, Avishai was still clinging to a TSS, now recast as a

"confederation" between two states. Admitting that "talk of confederation
. . . sounds wistful in the current environment, with Donald Trump in the
White House, Likud in power, and Hamas in Gaza," Avishai nevertheless
cited "American leverage" as being decisive in creating economic conditions in the West Bank and Gaza that might eventually create opportunities
for a confederation between two states. That he could offer no interest-
based rationale or precedent for U.S. action of this kind only emphasizes
how not only wistful but also essentially whimsical the two-state argument
had become.[43]

In a December 2017 discussion among European, American, Israeli,
and Palestinian experts about whether the TSS was "over," most participants agreed that it could no longer be salvaged. In their contributions, TSS
advocates could do no better than place their forlorn hopes on a change
in U.S. policy.[44] However, with David Friedman, a fervent supporter of Israeli settlement throughout the West Bank, as ambassador to Israel, with
Mike Pompeo, who has refused to declare U.S. opposition to Israel's annexation of the West Bank, as secretary of state, and with Jared Kushner,
who rejects the significance of Palestinian political aspirations, in charge of
American diplomacy on the issue, it has been difficult to find evidence of
serious Washington interest in a viable TSS.[45] As of this writing, the Trump
administration has made clear its abandonment of the TSS. Nonetheless,
it still rides the peace process merry-go-round with diplomatic consulta-
tions, leaks, and promises of the "deal of the century." The Trump-Kushner
plan, however, seems less like a bargain between Israel and Palestinians,
supported by the United States, and more like an agreement between Israel
and the United States to enshrine the one-state reality at the expense of the
Palestinians.

Sociologist Gershon Shafir is among the most outstanding scholars and
observers of Israel and the Israeli-Palestinian conflict. Before coming to the
United States, where he earned his doctorate, he worked as a journalist in
Israel. In 2017 he published the book *A Half Century of Occupation* that
reviewed the history of Israel's rule of the Palestinian territories captured
in 1967. He questioned whether the TSS he yearned for was still feasible
and concluded that it was but only barely. An end to American policies that

have enabled Israeli annexationism was one of the requirements he identified as necessary. However, his lengthy list of the improbable subconditions
required to meet just that one requirement reveals more clearly than his official conclusion the extremely narrow empirical base on which two-staters
argue their case:

> For the United States to take either a legal or political route
> to withdraw its blanket foreign policy protection for Israel
> would require the continued decline of both the Evangelicals'
> and the neocons' influence, the politicization of the Ameri-
> can Jewish community's silent majority, the rise of a new and
> more liberal Jewish leadership, [and] a redefinition of the
> United States' broader interests in the Middle East, as well
> as a new administration that would revive an emphasis on
> the US national interest at the expense of special interests.[46]

Paradigm Collapse

Since the Second Intifada, a question and a metaphor have come to dominate public discussion of the TSS. The question that hangs above its advocates like a sword of Damocles is whether de facto annexation has rendered
the project impossible or so implausible that the entire paradigm of separat-
ing the West Bank from Israel as the route to peace must be abandoned. The
prevailing metaphor is death. Has the TSS "died?"[47] Is it "on life-support,"
is it "dying but not dead," or is it "dead but not buried?"[48] Or is it "dead as a
dodo"? Did the United States give the TSS "the kiss of death" when it recognized Jerusalem as Israel's capital? Or was that act its "death knell?"[49] "There
is no doubt . . . the TSS is definitely in trouble, if not on its deathbed."[50] Or
is it in a "death spiral."[51] Should it be "allowed to die a natural death?" Is it
"dead," or is it "long dead and decomposing"? Or perhaps it should be considered "almost completely dead, and . . . closer to death every day."[52] Is it
"in trouble but not dead?"[53] Did the TSS die, or was it "put to death?" Can
we see signs of possible life or only the "reflexive twitching" a dead body can

sometimes exhibit.[54] Should we say it "isn't dead" but "it is dying"—that is "stuck, but not dead"?[55] If it is dying, "perhaps the TSS can be rescued and resuscitated."[56] A major 2013 symposium in the Jewish periodical *Moment* magazine was titled "Is the Two State Solution Dead?" Instructively, four years later the *New York Times* published a long article with the same title and effectively the same analysis.[57]

From an analytic as well as a psychological perspective, it seems profoundly correct to imagine the TSS as something that has died, is dying, could die, or is dead. For the organism involved death *is* a final end, even though, for those who care, such finality can be difficult to recognize or accept. With denial can come grief, anger, and confusion. Something very similar is true of paradigms and of those who have lived by and within them. The collapse of a paradigm is a wrenching, even traumatic, experience for a scientist or a political activist to contemplate, let alone accept, as acceptance means that cherished beliefs, idealized objectives, and naturalized categories of thought have become sources of distortion and error rather than insight and accomplishment.

In any event, most two-staters have abandoned efforts to describe realistic paths to their goal. The peace movement in Israel—what is known as the Zionist Left—has all but disappeared from the political landscape.[58] With Palestinians insisting on territorial contiguity and equivalent land swaps while refusing to accept the demand to endorse Zionism by recognizing Israel as the national state of the Jewish people, with no Israeli government in sight even favoring a genuine TSS, and with no recent history of or prospect for productive diplomatic activity, defenders of the two-state project have retreated to the paradigm equivalent of the castle keep. Forced to treat their negative heuristic as a hypothesis, they can do little more than try to remain persuaded of the continued feasibility of the TSS. Increasingly these efforts rely on dramatic declarations of faith in its eventual realization and insistence that alternatives to the TSS are sufficiently catastrophic to make it impossible (for moral and emotional but not empirical reasons) to believe otherwise.

To be sure, there are two-staters who no longer believe that dividing the land into two states is possible without disguising it as something else or blurring the picture of the future they imagine so as to avoid having to confront partition's unattainability. Accordingly, they suggest futures featuring two states operating, via intricate networks of administrative and geographical responsibilities, in or over the entire land between the sea and the river. For example, Oren Yiftachel and collaborators associated with Israel/Palestine Creative Regional Initiatives (IPCRI) have argued for thinking about how to construct "two states in one space" as a version of "confederation."[59] Others have advanced concepts such as "parallel states";[60] "two states in one space";[61] "one country, two states";[62] two national homes in one state;[63] an "interspersed nation-state";[64] an "Israel-Palestine Union" with distinctions between citizenship and residency;[65] or "post/decolonial cohabitation."[66] Some of the ideas in these formulations may become important as the one-state reality discussed in the concluding chapter evolves. However, none of these pretty pictures are attached to strategies for surmounting the political obstacles blocking other two-state initiatives or attracting interest in negotiations toward such an objective.

The elaboration of increasingly complex schemes to avoid implications of contrary evidence and the reliance on existential, faith-based, or value-based imperatives are typical of collapsing research programs and failed political projects. In some extremely complicated way, phlogiston scientists ended up arguing that phlogiston exists, and somehow its contribution to combustion will be measured and documented. In some way, argued modernization theorists, technological change will lead to the rationalization and democratization of societies, and eventually some theory, however complex, will be fashioned to explain how and when that will occur. In some way, two-staters have argued, achievement of a TSS via negotiations will be achieved, and somehow the international system and the Israeli political process will align to produce leaders with the determination and authority to implement a TSS fully enough to satisfy Palestinian elites.

These attempts to square the circle reflect a desperation in two-state thinking on full display by the Geneva Initiative, a two-state advocacy organization founded in 2003 to encourage bottom-up support for an agreement reached by nongovernment Israeli and Palestinian elites. In 2018 it launched the Two-State Index project to help preserve hope for the idea.

Each month two-state advocate experts, both Palestinians and Israelis, assess developments on four dimensions—the solvability of core issues, the political and public arena, the diplomatic and legal arena, and reality on the ground—that they consider relevant to the TSS. The index, which ranges between 0 and 10, goes up if the month's developments are judged positively and goes down if they are judged negatively. What is most instructive, however, about the index is not that it went down during its first four months, from 5.60 to 5.38, or that it had dropped to 5.36 by April 2019 but rather that it was purposely constructed to inflate impressions of the TSS's availability. The architects of the index neither discuss nor justify their crucial decision—to calibrate what was by all accounts a fairly desperate situation in April 2018 as just above 5, in other words, closer to achievement than to impossibility. Absent evidence of intercoder reliability for the judgments that flow into the ratings and without showing that if applied historically Two-State Index criteria would establish current ratings as appropriate, the effort is best understood as a public relations strategy to insulate the TSS by statistical fiat from evidence of its demise.[67]

One could expect more convincing defenses of the two-state paradigm in scholarly books devoted to that object. In recent years, a number of high-powered researchers who are also TSS advocates have authored monographs on the precarious status of the TSS. Each presents evidence of its possible obsolescence and admits growing difficulties but urges continuation of the struggle to bring about a TSS. Contradicting their conclusions, however, are the terms of their arguments, most of their evidence, and the strained language with which their conclusions are formulated. These authors may have come to praise the two-state paradigm, as it were, but they bury it instead.

In 2010 Menachem Klein, professor of political science at Bar-Ilan University, published *The Shift*.[68] Klein does an excellent job of documenting the conflict's transformation from that imagined by the two-state paradigm—a "territorial" struggle between separate national projects for control of space adequate to survive—into an "ethnic" struggle within a single political framework brought about by "the difficulties of arriving at a TSS." Klein characterizes them as "seemingly insurmountable." Klein describes public opinion among both Israeli Jews and Palestinian Arabs that a mutually agreeable TSS is unrealistic if not illusory; he takes as a "given" the apparent "irreversibility" of the settlement enterprise, and he emphasizes the entrenching effects of ongoing Israeli colonialist practices.[69] In these respects Klein dooms all efforts to turn the "de facto single state that currently exists" into a two-state future.[70]

And yet, in the last two pages of the book Klein reverses course. "Today's reality is not necessarily that of tomorrow." Ignoring the implication of that declaration—that the single democratic state he describes as an impossibility today might not be so tomorrow—Klein offers a cri de couer that although "the road toward two states living side by side seems to have grown longer, and the cost of reaching such a settlement may well be higher than it was just ten years ago . . . there is a consensus that Israeli rule in its current form cannot and must not last." Thus, Klein resorts to the logically empty claim that something "must" happen because the alternatives are too unpleasant, and so it will happen, all the while invoking a simple cost-benefit model of Israeli policy toward the West Bank that his entire analysis was dedicated to invalidating. The book ends with the author's declaration of faith in the ultimate rationality of Israelis and therefore in the "inevitability" of "a two-state accommodation."[71]

A similar non sequitur appears as the conclusion to Avi Shilon's detailed 2017 volume *The Left-Wing's Sorrow: The Crisis of the Peace Camp; The Untold Story*. The book is a political biography of Yossi Beilin, a minister and deputy minister in government during the 1990s with close ties to Shimon Peres. Beilin was the leader of the Israeli peace camp for a while and of the dovish-liberal Meretz Party. He aspired to the premiership so as to save his liberal Zionist vision of Israel by signing a two-state agreement with the Palestinians. Shilon shows how decades of neoliberalism eviscerated sources of political solidarity for democratic socialists and dovish liberals in Israel, such as Beilin, even as a right-wing backlash to the violence of the Second Intifada destroyed the public basis for a government capable of territorial compromise. Beilin left political life, according to Shilon, "knowing that from the perspective of history his political path—dividing the country in an agreement with the Palestinians—had been victorious as an idea, but had failed from the point of view of its ability to be implemented in time."[72] Despite his assertion of the impossibility of the TSS, Shilon ends by imagining that President Trump might bring peace based on a nonliberal version of a TSS. This strange hope, Shilon admits, is not based on evidence but rather on an "exaggeration of [my] optimism," which is "simply the only way to end a biography of Yossi Beilin."[73]

The target of Asher Susser's 2012 book *Israel, Jordan, and Palestine: The Two State Imperative* is the one-state solution.[74] Susser describes as "devastating" the argument against the one-state solution that there is no discernible path to achieving it.[75] Notably, he ignores this criterion when it comes to the TSS. The ostensible imperative in the book is achievement of a TSS, but in fact Susser not only fails to describe how he thinks it can be achieved but actually declares that it *cannot* be and never could be. "The Palestinian state that the Israelis were willing to endorse was never a fully sovereign and independent member of the family of nations, but an emasculated, demilitarized, and supervised entity, with Israeli control of its airspace and possibly of its borders."[76] For Susser, the real imperative is not to achieve a TSS but instead to preserve the image of the possibility of a TSS so as to prevent the emergence of one state.[77]

In 2016 Joseph Alpher, a former Mossad official with a history of back-channel involvement in TSS negotiations, wrote an analysis very similar to Susser's in *No End of Conflict: Rethinking Israel-Palestine*.[78] Like Susser, Alpher categorizes himself as a "security dove" and characterizes a one-state outcome as a kind of infinite catastrophe—either "Lebanon on steroids"[79] or a binational, non-Zionist country from which masses of Jews would emigrate.[80] Unlike Susser, however, Alpher rejects the idea that Jordan might someday solve Israel's problem by taking responsibility for West Bank Arabs.[81] Characterizing "the Oslo final-status paradigm" as having "exhausted itself prior to 2013,"[82] Alpher makes clear that his sympathies lie with the "Blue-White Future" movement, dedicated to resolving the Israeli-Palestinian conflict "on the basis of a 'two states for two peoples' solution."[83] But after exploring five different options for initiating new peace negotiations toward that objective, he judges them all as unlikely "to be broached, much less implemented, by any of the major involved parties in the second decade of the twenty-first century."[84] Although declaring the need for "a new innovative framework," Alpher fails to advance one, concluding instead with an endorsement of limited unilateral measures that would reduce the scope of Israeli control over the West Bank and its vulnerability to developments there. Tellingly, these measures are recommended not because Alpher can imagine how they might lead to a mutually satisfying Israeli-Palestinian agreement or because they are implied by a new and coherent framework for thinking about a replacement for the TSS paradigm but simply because they are the only things he believes can be done.[85] They *might* slow down the slide toward the catastrophe of one state,[86] and at least theoretically, they could contribute to "keeping a comprehensive solution alive."[87]

Finally, I return to Gershon Shafir's widely read 2017 book *A Half Century of Occupation*, which asks whether the "endless interregnum" of Israel's occupation "has made Israel's rule of the West Bank permanent and a TSS impossible."[88] As is the case in so many efforts to defend the feasibility of the TSS option, Shafir spends much of the book attacking the one-state solution and those who support it, fearing how growth in this support would affect TSS prospects. He presents what he describes as a "feasibility study from the perspective of the social sciences" of the claim that Israel has irreversibly absorbed the West Bank and that therefore the TSS should be classified as impossible. The answer, Shafir reports, is "no." Israeli absorption of the West Bank is not irreversible, and therefore the TSS is "not out of the question."[89]

Of course, to say that something is not impossible is an extremely modest claim, considering the vast number of things that do not contradict the laws of physics but are so implausible as to not be worth pursuing. Whatever the case, the difficulty of fulfilling the conditions that Shafir stipulates as necessary to realize a negotiated two-state-solution (discussed earlier in this chapter) means that the book is more likely to discourage readers from working toward a TSS than to give them actionable ideas to rescue it from oblivion.

Indeed, to take Shafir's advice and work for a TSS requires rejecting the core of his argument about the nature of Israel and the dynamics of Israeli-Palestinian relations. His fundamental claim is that the West Bank settlement enterprise is a malignancy whose origins lie in the deep character of

Zionism as a settler colonialist movement. That movement, he maintains, lacked the political maturity to restrain itself from repeating in the territories that it captured in 1967 what it had done in the portions of Palestine that it ruled before the Six-Day War.[90]

Shafir's erudite and convincing analysis of Zionism also stands in tension with the fierce denunciation of the Palestinian-led boycott, divestment, and sanctions (BDS) movement with which he concludes his book. Shafir condemns BDS for, as it were, "inconveniently" targeting all of Israel. To assist the liberal Zionist project in ways favored by Shafir, the BDS movement should target only Israeli occupation of the West Bank and its settlements there. This is a puzzling demand, since it directly contradicts his analysis of the settlement enterprise as an extension of what Israel is by its nature: an expansionist settler state. This critique of BDS also implies that what determines the fate of the Zionist project is not its own fundamental character but rather whether or not those whom Shafir characterizes as Zionism's most prominent victims, the Palestinians, will be willing to drastically reduce their own national and political ambitions so as to rescue a vision for Israel and Zionism that he and other two-staters still cherish. This is as far-fetched a possibility as can be imagined, akin to the Palestinian wish before 1948 that Zionism would abandon its raison d'être to ensure that justice was done for the Arab inhabitants of the land it had targeted as its own.

For many years the TSS paradigm guided creative analysis and effective political action by TSS advocates. It can no longer do so. The insights, forecasts, guidance, and confidence that the paradigm inspired have all but vanished. By insisting that the only alternative to the TSS is catastrophe, TSS diehards conflate necessity with feasibility. Warning passionately about the calamitous implications of abandoning hope in the TSS, they find themselves unable to provide reasons for that hope, whether for the emergence of an Israeli government committed to a two-state arrangement the Palestinians would accept or for the territorial contiguity they had long said was a requirement for a viable Palestinian state. In desperation, they devise

Rube Goldberg networks of tunnels, bridges, and land swaps to imagine a Palestinian state composed of dozens of islands in a territorial sea of Jewish settlements and sovereignty.

Antonio Gramsci described the period between the failure of an established order and the emergence of a new one as a "crisis [that] consists precisely in the fact that the old is dying and the new cannot be born; in this interregnum a great variety of morbid symptoms appear."[91] Lakatos terms this morbidity the "degeneration" of a research program. The "old"— the TSS as a paradigm for understanding and addressing the Israeli-Palestinian problem—has encountered anomalies that it has been unable to ignore or remove. The TSS paradigm at one time yielded brilliant and effective insights about political opportunities for Israelis and Palestinian elites and the nature of the conflict. But following decades of failed initiatives and amid the demise of politicians and parties identified as being sincerely committed to the TSS, its adherents can offer only a growing list of excuses for failure.

The next and final chapter mobilizes a key theme of this volume—the dominant influence of unintended consequences—to present a new way to think about the protracted Israeli-Palestinian conflict and a new basis for hope.

Chapter 5

The One-State Reality and Its Future

Two states for two peoples *was* a solution to the Israeli-Palestinian conflict, but it is not a solution today. For a few decades, the two-state solution (TSS) combined a pretty picture of the future with a plausible way to get there (negotiations to divide the country roughly along the pre-June 1967 borders). The picture remains, but the way to get there is gone. The TSS has become every bit the fantasy of an unattainable future that its advocates believe the "one-state solution" to be.

Though there is no "solution" in sight, there is a reality. There is today one state, the State of Israel, between the Mediterranean Sea and the Jordan River. It is an apparatus of power, recognized by the international community, whose policies and actions decisively affect the lives of everyone in the area. It collects taxes from West Bank and Gaza Palestinians and determines who enters and leaves those areas, who enjoys rights to property, and who can live, build, or even visit where.[1] In its current form, the state is no group's pretty picture. It was achieved by no one's carefully implemented plan. It is not a solution but an outcome—a one-state reality (OSR).

Palestinians of Gaza and of the West Bank are citizens of no other recognized state. As measured by the State of Israel's impact on the intimate details of their lives and indeed on whether they live at all, they are as much its inhabitants as black slaves were of the United States and as Africans in the Bantustans were of apartheid South Africa. The five-decade occupation of the West Bank and the twelve-year blockade of Gaza, combined with the exposure to state violence that these populations regularly endure, do not mark their *exclusion* from the Israeli state. Rather, they simply register the fact that Israel rules different populations in different regions in different ways. Though the Arab inhabitants of the West Bank and the Gaza Strip came within the ambit of the Israeli polity fifty-two rather than seventy-one years ago, the palpable fact is that they live within it.[2]

Officially, the Israeli government views lands west of the Jordan River but across the Green Line—the 1949 armistice line that separates Israel from territories occupied in 1967—as "disputed," which implies that from their perspective they are part of the country. Thus, when Israel's Central Bureau of Statistics reports the number of Israelis in the country, it counts every Israeli living west of the Jordan River, not just those living in the part of the country surrounded by the Green Line.

Most official Israeli maps feature no divisions between the sea and the river other than administrative boundaries of districts and regions.[3] Textbooks show lines surrounding the Gaza Strip and around Area A clusters and a slightly different shading for Area B clusters. But the only lines indicating a border between Israel and another sovereign country are those along its borders with Arab states—and these separate both Gaza and the West Bank from the Arab states.[4] A map accessed in December 2018 on Israel's Ministry of Foreign Affairs website was titled "Israel within Boundaries and Ceasefire Lines." The map labels the Gaza Strip as "under Palestinian jurisdiction" and the Oslo demarcated areas of "A" and "B" in the West Bank as characterized by Palestinian responsibility for "civil affairs." The country's international boundary includes both the Gaza Strip and the West Bank within the state.[5] All mail that enters or leaves the West Bank or the Gaza Strip does so via Israel. The undeclared OSR is also revealed in the ordinary language of public communications: images of the country used by Israeli ministries, weather maps, maps of annual average temperature and rainfall, maps of the topography of the "State of Israel," road maps, and iconic depictions of the country's borders used for tourism and other purposes.

These pictures of the country are not anomalies or errors. They are consistent with an OSR in which the state exercises different kinds of domination in different regions and prefers to blur all of these regions into one domain of power. Yet as we have seen, die-hard TSS advocates still warn of the imminent "catastrophe" of one state. Stubborn refusal to acknowledge that the warning of one state has already come true, whether catastrophic or not, reveals the deep attachment among Jewish two-state advocates to obsolete beliefs in a small Jewish and democratic Israel as well as their fear of living with Arabs and relying on alliances with them to build a democratic society.

Because of the presence of 430,000 non-Jewish non-Arabs (mostly families of non-Jewish immigrants from the former Soviet Union who came to Israel as relatives of Jews), the 6.5 million Arabs living in the land are currently a plurality but not a majority.[6] But even though Jews have only recently become a minority in the whole land, Israel as "Jewish and democratic" has always been a slogan, not an accurate caption for the country's political system. It always meant a polity controlled by Jews and for Jews but one that could front itself as a democracy with equal rights for all. However, no state whose policies toward half the people under its control include overwhelming rates of incarceration, heavy and constant surveillance, a strangulating system of pass laws and checkpoints, collective punishment, and bloody violence can convincingly claim the mantle of democracy.

Clearly, Arabs in different regions have different access to the Israeli political arena and experience the power of the Israeli state differently. One and a half million Arabs are citizens of Israel with full civil and political rights but second-class access to state resources and opportunities to exercise those rights. The 350,000 Palestinian Arabs who are permanent residents of Greater Jerusalem are citizens of the municipality they inhabit but not of the state. They have residency rights but severely restricted access to municipal resources. Two million inhabitants of the Gaza Strip live under Israeli state control in a ghetto sealed against anything but closely regulated minimal contact with the outside world. Their diet, health, exposure to violence, and life chances are almost entirely subject to Israeli government decisions. More than 2.7 million West Bank Arabs live in an archipelago of cities, towns, and villages. While not as tightly ghettoized as Gaza Palestinians, they are subject to a strict system of pass laws whose constantly changing and arbitrary requirements empower Israeli soldiers at nearly 150 checkpoints to summarily refuse exit from or entrance into their localities or lands.[7] Meanwhile, 620,000 Israelis living in the West Bank (including expanded East Jerusalem) inhabit their own archipelago of gated cities, towns, and villages. While subject to violent attacks by Arabs, they enjoy many legal immunities as well as the full political rights of first-class Israeli citizens.

Dov Weisglass, who helped Ariel Sharon engineer Israel's "disengagement" from Gaza while putting the peace negotiations in "formaldehyde," endorsed one Palestinian's characterization of the West Bank and the Gaza Strip as the "only prison in the world where the prisoners have to provide for themselves." Israel, wrote Weisglass,"has the authority of the sovereign in the territories—without the obligations."[8] In Gaza, Israel permits Hamas to absorb most of the day-to-day responsibilities for meager services provided to the population. In the West Bank (or in Israeli parlance "Judea and Samaria") the Palestinian Authority (PA) promotes the fiction that it is independent of Israel while working intimately with the Israeli security apparatus to protect the privileges of the thousands of families whose livelihoods directly depend on it. From Israel's point of view, the PA functions as a supervisory apparatus for tasks that the state prefers not to perform directly. The PA's impotence in relation to Israel was demonstrated with casual brutality in December 2018 when, without comment or legal justification, the Israeli military declared a multiday lockdown of the city of Ramallah—the PA's "seat of government." Indeed, the Israeli parliament often discusses legislation for different parts of the West Bank without any thought of consultation with the PA. Thus, the institution that most effectively claims a monopoly on the legitimate use of violence in the West Bank is the same state, Israel, that "governs," albeit in different ways, Gaza, the Galilee, the Negev, Jerusalem, and Tel Aviv.[9]

The idea that processes of "creeping annexation" would lead to the de facto incorporation of the West Bank and the Gaza Strip, along with their populations, has a long pedigree. It became a staple of debates over the future of the occupied territories in the late 1970s and early 1980s. Meron Benvenisti, whose writings on this idea were especially important, never

claimed that what he saw crystallizing was a "solution." It was simply a reality—a conflict-laden reality but a reality nonetheless. After more than fifty
years of Israeli rule, Benvenisti's predictions as well as the warnings of so
many dovish critics of Israeli policies have indeed materialized. The entire
area under Israel's rule has been transformed into a single if segmented
society and a single if nondemocratic state.

In 2005 Oren Yiftachel described the process not as "creeping annexation" but instead as "creeping apartheid."[10] Ariella Azoulay and Adi Ophir
analyzed this reality effectively in their 2012 treatment of the psychological
and political integration of the area between the sea and the river and of the
operation, across different zones and different populations, of interlocking
institutions and integrated control mechanisms.[11] That same year Adrian
Guelke's book *Politics in Deeply Divided Societies* featured Israel/Palestine
as one of its most prominent cases.[12] In 2018 an article in *Foreign Affairs* on
secessionism included the Palestinian struggle to separate from the State of
Israel.[13] According to legal anthropologists, Israeli courts can no longer distinguish between norms and precedents pertaining to the West Bank and
those used on the western side of the Green Line.[14] In 2017 a Hebrew University professor's book compared Lebanon and Israel as two "divided societies" produced by expanding states.[15] A poll at the end of 2015 reported
that 57 percent of Israeli teachers had never heard of the Green Line,[16]
which might explain a veteran journalist's 2018 report that Israeli students
were entirely ignorant of its existence.[17] Later in 2018 a leading Palestinian
candidate to replace Mahmoud Abbas called upon Palestinians to abandon
illusions about negotiations leading to a Palestinian state and instead "start
internalizing the notion of one state for two nations."[18] Simultaneously, an
Israeli national security think tank released a study focused heavily on the
dangers of the "One-State Situation" followed by another study warning of
increased support among Palestinian elites and opinion leaders for Israeli
annexation and a struggle focused on gaining equal rights in Israel.[19]

Circumstances today are vastly different than they were half a century ago, when negotiations toward a TSS were first suggested. Radically
different conditions require radically different strategies, and they are not
likely to come from leaders of organizations whose raison d'être has been

tied to the TSS and its core assumptions. With one state an undeclared but undeniable reality, where different populations within that state have different rights and differential access to the dominant political arena, negotiations between authoritative representatives of Jews and Arabs cannot be the path to positive change. Both peoples deserve opportunities for self-determination, but the struggle for peace *between* Jews and Arabs can no longer be separated from the struggle for equality *of* Jews and Arabs.

Many phlogiston chemists and Newtonian physicists could not acknowledge the exhaustion of their projects. Max Planck, a Nobel Prize winner in physics, famously remarked that science progressed "from funeral to funeral." Certainly, it will be difficult in the extreme for many TSS believers to accept that its usefulness as a paradigm has run its course.[20] Yael Tamir was a founder of Peace Now, a minister of immigration absorption and of education, the author of a well-known book on liberal Zionism, and a prominent two-state advocate. In 2017 she admitted that while she still had a pretty picture of a TSS in mind, she no longer had any idea how it could be achieved:

> I've sort of given up, I'm sorry, I've been in this business for many years and once a year I come to a meeting like this because I feel really blameworthy that I'm not doing something about it, and then I remind myself that I don't know what to do. So here is my confession. I think I know what the solution should be; I think we all know what the solution should be. I don't know how to get there.[21]

In desperation, two-staters unable to chart a plausible path forward still maintain that there is no alternative path. They correctly point to the absence of a coherent "one-state solution" paradigm. Despite decades of efforts, no detailed plan or political strategy has been devised for how such a future could be attained. But neither God nor history guarantees that the Israeli-Palestinian problem has a "solution." It is illogical to argue, as two-state advocates now commonly do, that since there is no one-state solution, there *must* be a TSS. To argue in this way conflates two meanings of "must" as something "acceptable" versus something "inevitable." Sadly, the world is not organized so that what is deemed acceptable is also necessarily inevitable—or even possible.

The One-State Reality as a Nascent Paradigm

One state is the reality on the ground. It is time to treat this reality, not this or that blueprint for a solution, as a new paradigm for thought and action. Doing so can sharpen the focus of scholarly analysis and channel the activity of the many liberal Zionists and TSS supporters who feel as lost and confused as Tamir as well as guide more effective action by one-state idealists. It is a shift in gestalt that is crucial, from a one- or two-state *solution* approach to a one-state *reality* perspective. Once we accept the OSR, the now boring questions that once seemed crucial to scholars and policy analysts—about the details of a two-state arrangement that might still work or about the implications of current events for the future of the peace process—appear as both irrelevant and uninteresting. From an OSR perspective, different and more interesting questions are posed about the political dynamics and unintended consequences of different forms of annexation and about what can be learned from the experience of deeply divided societies that evolved from states built originally by European settlers.

Politically, many events and developments take on radically different meaning when viewed through the OSR lens. Consider, for example, Israel's controversial "Basic Law: Israel as the Nation-State of the Jewish People," which removes Arabic's status as an official state language while declaring the state's Jewish-Zionist mission without mentioning democracy or equality for all citizens. From an OSR perspective, this Basic Law is not significant because it contradicts the TSS by insisting that only Jews have national rights in the Land of Israel. Instead, it is a sign of the instability of political formulas within the OSR, since with an Arab plurality in the country what was once "common sense" that did not need to be proclaimed now must be made into law. In January 2019, a poll of Israeli Jews showed a majority in favor of amending it to guarantee "democracy with equal rights to all citizens of the state."[22] As struggles to change develop in a country with a majority of non-Jews and a plurality of Arabs, the political function of the law will be exposed as a right-wing attempt to prevent Jews in the center and on the Left from allying with enough Arabs to win elections.

Likewise, from an OSR perspective, legislative proposals to impose Israeli law across the Green Line are not catastrophic barriers to separation but rather opportunities to argue for the broad and comprehensive application of the same laws to *all* people under the control of the same state. Under the reality of one state, equal citizenship for all is the only way to prevent a system of formalized apartheid.

Policies and laws hollowing out the political status of Arab citizens of Israel in the name of the "Jewishness" of the state can be opposed not because the "Jewishness" of the state can be preserved without discrimination but because they impede political alliances between Arabs and Jewish secularists and liberals.[23]

Proposals by two-state opponents to improve the living conditions of Palestinians and the development of ideas for doing so can be seen not as a sop to drain energy from the struggle for a separate state but instead as investments in the ability of Palestinians to secure their future as active and resourced inhabitants of the state in which they live.

"Vision statements" produced by Palestinians in Israel that imagine a state serving and protecting all its citizens become beacons of hope rather than defiant manifestos.[24] Instead of condemning Palestinian boycotts and "antinormalization" policies—Palestinian refusal to cooperate with Israelis except in the context of resisting occupation—as ornery and self-defeating, these stances can be seen as logical responses to the pathological consequences of an illusory peace process.[25] Once it is recognized that the primary struggle for the country's future is to transform the political arena that encompasses all Jews and Arabs under Israeli rule, then the rationale for Palestinians to cooperate with Israelis will become as compelling as it was three decades earlier, when intifada leaders were effective allies of Israelis working for the then plausible and now implausible TSS.

For two-staters, the boycott, divestment, and sanctions (BDS) movement is an infuriating distraction from the problem of engaging an Israeli government in negotiations. Launched in 2005 by Palestinian activists led by Omar Barghouti, BDS has become a global, strictly nonviolent struggle of economic and cultural protests and boycotts.[26] BDS challenges the TSS paradigm in fundamental ways. The TSS project is "solution" based, treating limits on Palestinian (and Jewish) rights as necessary compromises to achieve an agreement based on two states. It puts all its emphasis on the sovereign independence of those states, with almost no consideration of the rights and statuses of the populations they will govern. BDS, on the other hand, eschews any particular institutional arrangement (one state, two states, cantons, confederation, and so on). It is "process" based, focusing on realizing Palestinian rights to equality and nondiscrimination under international law and the laws of the state that governs them. Internationally, the TSS paradigm assumes Israel's reward will be acceptance as a legitimate member of the international community without having to abandon discriminatory elements of its Jewish-Zionist character. The "rights-based" critiques offered by BDS, however, raise questions about Israel's claim to legitimate membership in the international community, at least until it ends discrimination against non-Jews.

BDS's international appeal is an enormous problem for the two-state paradigm, but from an OSR perspective it is potentially an enormous resource for Israeli progressives. By focusing international opinion on problems of ethnically based discrimination and political inequality in all parts of the country, the appeal makes struggles for democratization, equality, and nonexclusivist national self-determination more salient for Israelis than they otherwise would be. As Palestinians become more fully integrated into institutions that have disproportionately served non-Arab populations and as inequality and discrimination become less a feature of the society and more of a bug, BDS critiques will become more specific and more akin to the norm-based criticisms to which all countries are routinely exposed.

Though President Donald Trump's decisions and policies are bemoaned by two-staters as tragic setbacks to the peace process, they appear differently from an OSR perspective. Two-staters condemned relocation of the American embassy to Jerusalem because it contradicted their image of a political-territorial division of the city with al-Quds as the capital of Palestine and Yerushalayim the capital of Israel. But note that the embassy is to be located in West Jerusalem in the portion of the city that Israel already controlled before the 1967 war. When two-staters objected to the American embassy's presence in West Jerusalem, they were tacitly admitting that for all intents and purposes Jerusalem has already become one city. If they further accepted that for all intents and purposes all of the Land of Israel/Palestine has already been incorporated into one state, then this one city, Jerusalem, would be the capital for all who live in that state. The apparent but still unofficial renunciation of the TSS by the Trump White House and the sympathy that administration officials have expressed for Israeli annexationist moves are deemed tragic abandonment of hallowed principles of American diplomacy by the peace process industry. But although Trump policies and plans appear to include no political rights for Palestinians, they may at least move the debate from contemplation of the impossibility of two states in the future to posing questions about the nature of one state that exists in the present.

The hugely expanded metropolis that is now the city of Jerusalem will figure prominently in discussion of these questions and as a kind of political laboratory. A Palestinian poll in 2015 reported that 52 percent of Arabs living in East Jerusalem "would prefer to be citizens of Israel with equal rights—compared with just 42 percent who would opt to be citizens of a Palestinian state."[27] In 2018, the mayoral election in Jerusalem was extremely close. The right-wing and ultranationalist candidate, Moshe Lion, won the runoff against the liberal, secular-oriented Ofer Berkovich by fewer than 4,000 votes—only 0.7 percent of the votes cast. For the first time a Palestinian Arab party registered a significant showing, attracting 3,000 votes for its mayoral candidate, Ramadan Dabash, in the first round of voting. Five months before the election a survey showed that 22 percent of eligible Palestinian residents of the city (who are citizens of the municipality but not the state) intended to vote. Had even a relatively small percentage of those who said they intended to vote actually participated in the runoff, the outcome would have been radically different, much to the benefit of the city's Arabs and liberal Jews.

Why did that not occur? Faced with abysmal services in their neighborhoods, Arab Jerusalemites have been increasingly dissatisfied with the results of municipal election boycotts. For them, pragmatic imperatives to act within the reality of an administratively united city have come to outweigh the theoretical defense of the claim that eastern sections of the city are only temporarily occupied by Israel. Two-staters find this calculation intolerable, and consequently the PA and its supporters heavily pressured and even threatened violence against the Arabs of Jerusalem.[28] The protection of one strut in the collapsing edifice of the TSS came at the cost of an opportunity to demonstrate the discrimination-reducing and life-enhancing potential of a Jewish-Arab political alliance.

Once it is accepted that the entire West Bank is part of the State of Israel, there is no reason for progressives—those committed to democracy and equal rights for all people ruled by the same government—to fret over how the expansion of a settlement or the establishment of new settlements is closing the door to the TSS. It is already closed. More Jews in the West Bank mean fewer in the Galilee or the Negev and therefore more opportunities for Arabs in those regions to feel secure in their demographic and cultural prominence. Instead of frantic struggles to chase the two-state mirage with technological fixes to the impossibly intertwined map of Jewish and Arab localities or quixotic ideas for ever more complicated land swaps, efforts can go toward insistence on equal housing, schooling, and employment opportunities for all inhabitants of Israel. Demands for the return of expropriated lands or proper compensation could be combined with alternative opportunities for Arabs as well as Jews to live and not just work in the settlements as they do in other Israeli localities.[29]

Two-stater solutionists struggle to offer ever more carefully calibrated ideas for unrealizable compromises; one-stater solutionists grope after equally fruitless plans to transform the country into a single shared state through negotiations between Jewish and Arab representatives. The OSR paradigm, however, puts the focus squarely on politics, not negotiations, and on immediate issues, not blueprints for the future: reducing political inequality, highlighting and mitigating social and economic discrimination, and insisting on equal protection of all citizens' lives and property. Inspiration can be drawn from sustained struggles by Zochrot (Memory) to teach Israeli Jews about the Nakba, by Breaking the Silence's campaign to expose the Israeli military's unequal treatment of West Bank Arabs and Jews, and by the defense of Palestinian villages in the West Bank against demolition by Ta'ayush, Rabbis for Human Rights, and the Center for Jewish Nonviolence, which work in coordination with grassroots Palestinian organizations, international solidarity groups, and progressive Jewish groups in the United States such as If Not Now and Jewish Voice for Peace.

Potentiating these efforts among left-liberal and moderate Jews, non-Jewish non-Arabs, and Arabs will be what Marxists used to call an "objective alliance," meaning one based on shared interests, not coordinated action. But as some political interests converge across ethnic lines, organized alliances will develop as well both in Jerusalem and in the larger Israeli political arena—including the West Bank and ultimately Gaza. They may arise first in mixed regions or municipalities and involve court cases, public protests, private ventures, or struggles to extend citizenship and suffrage. They may form within political movements and parties or between parties. They may become important in elections for the Knesset or in coalition negotiations. The pace of change is likely to be slow but will accelerate as both Arabs and Jews realize that neither will be able to ignore the other. Arabs will have to take a long enough view to perceive the democratization of the Israeli state—in whose grasp they now live—as the vehicle for their liberation. Jews will have to accept Arabs as political partners and honor the role they have played and will play in the democratization of Israel and in the return of their society to values of peace, tolerance, and freedom.

For Jews, this will require abandoning shrill warnings of Arab threats to Jewish demographic superiority. Appeals to the statist tradition within Zionism that Jews—and Jews alone—should wield political power over Jews will also have to be discarded in favor of equally authentic but less prominent Zionist ideals of a proud, secure, and thriving Jewish community in the Land of Israel living in peace and equality with its neighbors.[30] Many in Israel's peace camp have long been uncomfortable with the chauvinistic and pejorative connotations of anti-Arab arguments but have used them to attract support for the TSS by exploiting and even fanning Jewish hatred and fear of Arabs. The TSS is based on the separation of Arabs from Jews—"We here; them there," as Ehud Barak put it. In the OSR, however, encouraging Jews and Arabs to think they can only be safe or live contentedly apart from one another has had radically unprogressive implications. In the OSR, such beliefs cannot and do not increase prospects for equality or for the two peoples to fulfill dreams of self-determination. Intergroup fear and hostility only serve the purposes of those Jews who prefer de facto domination to democracy and those Arabs who prefer the elimination of Jews from the country to building a shared future.

A forecast of Jewish-Arab political alliances will certainly provoke skepticism. With so much fear and bloodshed, with so many contradictory Arab and Jewish dreams, and with so many political projects on both sides schooling their followers to believe that the ethnonational cleavage trumps all others, why should we expect joint interests to be perceived, let alone pursued?

There is cause for optimism in the overlooked reality that neither Arabs nor Jews will ever act or vote as a bloc. Ideological, cultural, ethnic, political, and economic divides within Jewish Israel have been so deep, and so many Jews share so much more with many Palestinians than they do with many or most Jews, that demography simply cannot be extrapolated into political destiny. Even in the "Jewish state" narrowly defined, Arabs have come to play a not insignificant role in Israeli politics. The Yitzhak Rabin government of 1992, which started the Oslo process, was formed and functioned only thanks to support from outside the coalition by Arab parliamentarians. In a highly partisan but successful 2007 campaign to make Shimon Peres president of Israel, a full-page newspaper advertisement chose to feature endorsements of him by both Jewish and Arab political personalities.[31] Arabs and Jews share membership in most political parties. In recent years Arab Knesset deputies have taken their seats representing not only majority-Arab parties, such as Rakah, the Communist Party, and left-center mostly Jewish parties, such as Meretz and the Zionist Union, but also centrist parties such as Kadima and Kulanu and even the right-wing parties of Likud and Yisrael Beiteinu. In the 2015 elections for the Knesset the Arab-organized and -led Joint List, which included Rakah, received the third-largest number of votes. In the April 2019 elections the constituent elements of that list split into two lists, but their joint vote total was larger than that of all but two of the other lists. The political reality of the importance of the Arab vote was reflected in polls and commentary in 2019 that almost uniformly included the Arab parties in references to the strength of the center-left bloc or prospects for a center-left government.[32]

It is also worth noting how dynamic Israeli public opinion on separate state or annexationist options has been.[33] Immediately after the 1967 war, an Israeli public opinion survey found that 10 percent of Israeli Jews favored allowing Palestinians to establish a state of their own.[34] In 1974, 20 percent agreed that there was "a need to set up a Palestinian state on the West Bank and Gaza Strip."[35] In the early 1980s, pollsters found on average that 25 percent of Jewish Israelis were willing to accept a Palestinian state in the context of a comprehensive peace, even though only 5 percent chose it as their preferred option in a 1984 survey.[36] Yet, within twelve years a majority of Israelis supported creation of a Palestinian state next to Israel.[37] In January 2018, a typical poll showed that 52 percent of Palestinians and 47 percent of Israeli Jews favored a TSS, but when details of an agreement close to what had recently been discussed were included in the question, the percentages in favor dropped to 40 percent of Palestinians and 35 percent of Jews.[38] At the end of 2018 pollsters with more experience than any other studying Israeli opinion about the future of the territories commented that the "peace issue" had "disappeared almost completely from the Israeli public discourse."[39] Tzipi Livni, who defected from Likud to embrace the TSS and sought to advance its prospects as foreign minister under Prime Minister Ehud Olmert from 2006 to 2009, resigned from politics rather than suffer certain defeat for her Hatnuah party in 2019. "The word peace," she said, had become "a vulgarity in Israel."[40] In the run-up to Israel's April 2019 Knesset elections, only three parties explicitly supported the TSS.[41]

Israeli public opinion has been equally dynamic in its support for (or opposition to) annexation, with or without the immediate grant of citizenship to Arabs. In 1979, 53 percent of Jewish Israelis favored the extension of Israeli law throughout the West Bank and the Gaza Strip.[42] From 1983 to 1985, polling showed 64–74 percent in favor of annexation, though a 1984 poll showed that only 5 percent favored annexation with citizenship accorded to the areas' Palestinian inhabitants.[43] Three years later just prior to the First Intifada, 25 percent favored annexation of the West Bank and Gaza, with 22 percent of those favoring full citizenship for their Arab inhabitants. In 1988 the same percentage favored annexation, while 15 percent favored full citizenship along with it.[44] As the intifada continued, support for annexation dropped to 5 percent by 1990.[45] Yet a December 2014 survey found that "about half the Jewish population of Israel favored annexing the territories as a one-state solution."[46] In early 2017 following President Trump's remark that he would welcome either a one-state or a TSS, polls showed 25 percent Jewish support for one state of equal citizenship for all.[47] In a separate poll, 37 percent of Israelis favored annexation of "large parts of the territories," with 24.5 percent favoring equal rights for Arab inhabitants of annexed areas.[48] Five months later after much talk by government leaders of imposing Israeli law in the West Bank and after Knesset passage of legislation extending Israeli legal protection to lands expropriated for West Bank settlements, 44 percent of Israeli Jews agreed that "the time has come to officially annex all the territories conquered in the [1967] war."[49] This would include, of course, the Gaza Strip. A subsequent poll in July 2018 found that 56 percent of Israeli Jews considered it a mistake to have disengaged from the Gaza Strip.[50] A March 2019 *Haaretz* poll found that 28 percent of Israelis opposed any form of annexation, 27 percent favored full annexation (11 percent with and 16 percent without political rights for Palestinians), and 15 percent favored partial annexation. A 30 percent plurality said they didn't know—a marked increase in this category reflecting growing fluidity of Israeli public opinion on this question.[51] In May 2019 Michael Oren, speaking as a politician who had moved rightward, said that to be credible as a right-of-center candidate and therefore to be relevant in Israeli politics, it had become necessary to support some form of annexation.[52]

Generally, Israeli public opinion has been responsive to government leaders' changing positions. For example, majority support for negotiations with the Palestine Liberation Organization (PLO) did not emerge in Israel until 1992, when Prime Minister Yitzhak Rabin announced that they were already under way. In the OSR context, future possibilities can be gleaned from endorsements by Israeli politicians, especially on the Right, of a future that would include equal citizenship for Jews and Arabs. President Reuven Rivlin was a stalwart Likud parliamentarian for eighteen years, including five years as Speaker of the Knesset. Chosen as president of Israel in 2014, Rivlin is a direct ideological descendant of Vladimir Jabotinsky, who was as staunch a liberal as he was a nationalist. In 1940, Jabotinsky endorsed a draft of the future Zionist state's constitution that guaranteed full and equal civic and political rights to Arabs.[53] In keeping with this strand of Jabotinsky's thinking, President Rivlin has repeatedly spoken in favor of an Israel that encompasses all of the Land of Israel west of the Jordan River within which Arabs and Jews would enjoy equal political rights. In 2017 he strongly opposed legislation for the West Bank that would apply different laws to Arabs and Jews. "I believe," he told a large right-wing gathering in Jerusalem,

> that all of Zion is ours and that the sovereignty of the State of Israel should be applied to every single piece of the Land. The imposition of sovereignty over a territory begins with the grant of equal citizenship to all who inhabit the territory, without exception.[54]

Explicit presentation by the head of state of a democratic vision of Israel through the entire country points to a broad repertoire of possibilities harbored within the OSR.

The imperative for those committed to a more progressive future is to fight for the inclusivist principles Rivlin has articulated by promoting categories of analysis that expose the insufficiency of prevailing theories and highlighting alternatives to ethnonationalist appeals.

Many Palestinian activists and scholars have responded to the OSR in precisely this way. Without categorically rejecting the possibility of a TSS, Sam Bahour has called for the Palestinian struggle to shift from being organized around "peace" to being organized around "equality."[55] In this context, Palestinians see the BDS movement as a crucial and effective element in efforts

> to cause a paradigm shift in thinking about the conflict from being composed of two national groups seeking territorial separation to being a single colonial structure that can best be dismantled by creating a democratic state for all of its citizens. In other words, it is a struggle for equal rights for all, Israelis and Palestinians, not statehood *per se*.[56]

Commenting on the revival among Palestinians of the settler colonial paradigm, Nadim Rouhana observes that "the new Palestinian struggle is being increasingly defined not around statehood, but around reclaiming the homeland and living in it with the human dignity that only equal citizenship can deliver."[57] In 2018 Diane Buttu, a longtime adviser to Yasser Arafat and the PA, declared that it was time to accept the impossibility of a TSS and struggle instead "for equal rights in a single state."[58] Nadia Hijab has advocated a "rights-based not solution-based" struggle, with "focus on the occupation and/or on the rights of Palestinian citizens of Israel and/or on the rights of Palestinian refugees."[59]

Politics will make strange bedfellows in these discursive and practical struggles. For example, Jewish progressives who accept the OSR will find allies among settlers and Jewish maximalists who share ambitions for Arabs and Jews to live together under the same government and laws. They may both believe that the governing authority should protect Arabs as well as Jews against vigilantism, terrorism, and discriminatory treatment. They may not agree on the exact measures or schedule for the equalization of Jewish and Arab rights, but democratic politics usually entails cooperation on the basis of partial agreement. Right-wing Israeli annexationists, many left-wing opponents of the occupation, and many West Bank Palestinians already call for the dissolution of the PA. In December 2018, an escalating dispute between the Israeli Agriculture Ministry and the PA hurt Palestinian and Israeli farmers, and both opposed it. As the OSR is recognized and embraced, political struggles will continue to feature Jews mobilizing Jews and Arabs mobilizing Arabs but will also feature Jews mobilizing Arabs and Arabs mobilizing Jews. Such campaigns might occur around any number of issues, including fair housing (which would raise Jewish property values while increasing life opportunities for Arabs), religious observance, the extension of Arab suffrage (which will benefit some Jewish groups while disadvantaging others), national service responsibilities, sanitation and health, ecological concerns, or investment schemes.

These struggles will not directly resolve the Israeli-Palestinian conflict or even be based on any solution to it. Nor will they require or entail the disappearance of powerful Jewish and Palestinian ethnonational identities. The logic rather is that the unintended second- and third-order effects of such struggles in the OSR will eventually create better problems in the future than the ones that Israeli Jews and Palestinian Arabs face today. Such strategies require a shift in thinking from how to get "there" to how to get somewhere better than "here." They also require considerably more sophistication about how politics works.

We typically imagine that political life is driven by pursuit of what people want and by calculations about how to defend against or adapt to threats. Imagined in this way, politics has clear winners and losers. Indeed, politics is filled with this kind of competition. But the political world has so many uncertainties and complex interdependencies—so many moving parts—that the end result of so much individual striving is usually unintended and even unimagined outcomes.

It is demanding but exciting to consider a shift in attention, away from blueprints for peacemaking and toward a more improvisational politics that exploits transformations emerging out of unanticipated events and unintended consequences. This shift would expand the time frame for imagining better futures—from months and years to decades and generations. And it would entail recognition that these better futures will not emerge because of the systematic implementation of anyone's plan. Transformation of Israel's occupation of the West Bank and Gaza into a single fragmented state took fifty years, several wars, two intifadas, revolutions in the Middle East, dramatic demographic developments, and radical change in Israeli politics. It will likely take just as much time and equally momentous events to transform that state into a democracy.

Some might find this time-scaling of the problem discouraging. Certainly the potential for catastrophic warfare in the Middle East suggests a horrific alternative to disjointed and evolutionary processes. Historically, however, the mass incorporation of excluded others into gendered, ethnocratic, or racial democracies has been slow, jagged, and commonly associated with war. Women's suffrage movements in Europe and America took fifty to a hundred years to come to fruition. Success was due in part to partisan calculations of advantage by men who had long resisted sharing political power with women and by the transformative effects of World War I.[60] In the 1860s, the Union Army occupied the Confederacy not because Abraham Lincoln intended to remake the United States into a multiracial democracy but because he insisted that the country be ruled by one state, not two. It took more than a century of world wars, depression, cultural change, and an expanded scope of federal government to move America from Jim Crow to the still imperfect but considerably more democratic multiracial state of the early twenty-first century. Britain annexed Ireland in 1801. Nearly 30 years passed before any Irish Catholics achieved the right to vote, 70 years before they became a powerful force in British politics, and 120 years (including industrialization, manhood suffrage, and a world war) before a TSS emerged. The South African Native National Congress was formed in 1912, but it took 80 years, the effects of two world wars, and a revolution in international political culture for blacks to achieve political equality in South Africa.

This kind of change, and the time it takes to achieve, can be observed in Israel itself. It took 18 years, from 1948 to 1966, to free Arab citizens of the country from rule by a military government (though they remained effectively controlled by a system of civilian agencies and security services for decades more). Following their mass immigration in the 1950s, Jews from Middle Eastern countries were discriminated against and relegated to what seemed a permanent place in Israel's political periphery by the Labor Party's Ashkenazic (European/American) elite. Along with the consequences of the 1967 war, the right-wing's mobilization of Mizrahi resentment powered the Likud (also dominated by Ashkenazic politicians) to victory in the 1977 "earthquake," resulting in a fundamental realignment of Israeli politics. After 1967, it took 20 years just for the ideas of negotiation with the PLO or two states for two peoples to move from the fringe of Israeli public opinion to the mainstream. It would be 25 years more before the failure of that plan began to produce new thinking about alternatives.

The Cunning of History and the Promise of the Future

In this book we have repeatedly seen political programs and projects transformed by the law of unintended consequences. Zionism's desperate strategy of the Iron Wall compelled Arabs to moderate their demands, but its partial success had unintended consequences. It inflated Jewish-Israeli demands and encouraged an intransigent maximalism that destroyed possibilities for the historic compromise it was designed to bring about. Likewise, the ascendance of Holocaustia in Israeli political culture was the unintended result of competition among rival collective memories. The perspective on the Holocaust that became hegemonic in Israel undermined peace with the Arabs because it sharpened fears, suspicions, and hatreds and made "compromise" a dirty word. Effective mobilization by the Israel lobby in America, fueled in part by the Holocaustia worldview, produced U.S. policies of unrestrained generosity toward Israel. The unintended consequence of the lobby's superabundant influence destroyed prospects for political moderation in Israel, shunted the politics of the Jewish state into rejectionism, sealed the destruction of the TSS, and brought more Palestinian Arabs than Jews within the compass of Israeli state power.

The project of the Israeli Right has been partially successful. The forcible integration of the West Bank and the Gaza Strip has made it impossible to engineer a TSS. But the Palestinians have not disappeared and continue to resist. Nor has the question of their future been removed from the center of Israeli consciousness and politics. One consequence of this partial success, including reliance on the fears and hatreds of Israeli Jews (rather than on their ideological commitment) to prevent territorial compromise, has been to deprive both the Left and the Right of a solution to the conflict. While lacking a plan for achieving it, frustrated two-staters still cherish their vision of the future. By contrast, most Likud leaders and others in Israel's national camp lack even a desired destination for the future, so of course they cannot devise a plan for getting there.

Instead, most of the TSS's traditional opponents have gravitated toward policies to "manage the conflict."[61] In Israeli military parlance this strategy is known as "mowing the lawn." It refers to regular use of major military operations, roundups of leaders, and economic sanctions to degrade Palestinian social, political, and military infrastructure. This is not Iron Wall-style "violent pedagogy" designed to produce malleable, peace-seeking adversaries. It is systematic brutality used against incorrigible foes to prevent threats to Israel's dominant position. Advocates of conflict management rely on the continued effectiveness of the PA for helping to maintain current security and often advise unilateral Israeli reduction of control over certain densely populated Palestinian areas. Politically and diplomatically, however, "managing the conflict" means

- Maintaining public perceptions of Palestinians and their allies as terrorists or as too extreme or unreliable to be partners for peace;
- Avoiding decisive and explicit measures to change or clarify the status of the territories;
- Expressing an official willingness to resume two-state negotiations while scuttling them with actions and demands that ensure their failure;
- Inuring Israeli Jews to the brutality of operations against Arabs in Lebanon, Gaza, and the West Bank;
- Reducing Palestinian mobilization and violence with policies of mass incarceration, ghettoization, strict controls on movement, and collective punishment;
- Enforcing limits on the PA and Hamas to keep Palestinians divided and to aid in surveillance and control; and
- Using unconditional U.S. support to defend Israel against transnational efforts to consign it to international pariah status.

These policies keep the growing Palestinian population under tremendous pressure. In any political system, the longer and more forcefully severely discontented populations are denied stabilizing accommodations, the more likely such "constrained volatility" is to produce unmanageable explosions. [62] Thus, the unintended consequence of the partial success of de facto annexation—that it has made Israel's separation from the territories impossible but has not reduced the hostility of their Palestinian populations—makes campaigns of nonviolent, semiviolent, and violent resistance all but inevitable.

The Israeli response will be bloody and destructive, with casualties in the tens of thousands. Simply to thwart protests along the fence surrounding the Gaza Strip, the Israeli military killed 271 Gaza Palestinians and shot or gassed more than 20,000 others in the year beginning with the first "Great March of Return" demonstration on March 30, 2018.[63] Targeting Arabs in both the West Bank and Gaza, Israel has used housing demolitions, deportation, collective punishment, bombing raids, drone attacks, clandestine killings, and abductions. As violence grows, so will the occasions when extreme and disproportionate Israeli responses are filmed and broadcast to billions of people.

In this context the surplus of Holocaustia thinking in Israel is likely to have unintended and ironic consequences. Israeli Jews have watched and will watch the suffering and seemingly endless punishment of helpless, hungry, and stateless people. Primed by Holocaustia to react powerfully to such images, many will identify with Palestinian victims rather than with Israeli persecutors and oppressors. In this way, the interpretation of the Holocaust as a human rights object lesson, earlier marginalized by the interpretation of the Holocaust as a template for Jewish life, can gain traction.

Outraged defenders of Holocaustia have labeled use of Nazi crimes as a moral yardstick for judging Israel as "Holocaust inversion" and denounced it as anti-Semitism and as more dangerous than Holocaust denial.[64] The targets of their wrath have mainly been Europeans and Muslims who compare Israel to Nazi Germany, but precisely because of Holocaustia's hold on Israelis it is impossible to prevent them from doing the same thing. An outstanding example of Holocaust inversion of this sort occurred during

Israel's Holocaust Remembrance Day ceremonies in 2016, when Deputy Chief of Staff Yair Golan warned that the murder of a helpless Palestinian prisoner by an Israeli soldier and widespread praise for his action required the nation to remember the most important lessons of the Holocaust:

> If there is something that frightens me about the memory of the Holocaust, it is seeing the abhorrent processes that took place in Europe, and Germany in particular, some 70, 80 or 90 years ago, and finding manifestations of these processes here among us in 2016.[65]

Although condemned for his remarks by the prime minister and the education and culture minister, Golan's statement illustrates that the Holocaustia template is not guaranteed a permanent hold on Israeli political culture.[66]

Given the density of hyperlinks to the Holocaust that fill Israeli minds and hearts, the prominence of this kind of comparison is guaranteed to increase. Instead of breeding fear, suspicion, and hatred, the memory of the Holocaust as a moral object lesson can lead Israeli Jews to recognize Palestinian suffering and even identify with it. Many are already repelled by actions against Palestinians they cannot help but associate with Nazi persecution of Jews. Unavoidably, they will be drawn to view struggles to protect Palestinian rights as righteous and even heroic.[67] When the famed Israeli journalist Ari Shavit was a young reservist guarding Palestinian prisoners in Gaza during the First Intifada, he wrote that he could not keep himself from seeing the prisoners as Jews and himself and other soldiers as Germans.[68] A photograph of soldiers at a checkpoint compelling an Arab to play the violin conjures images of Jews forced to entertain concentration camp guards. Incidents of soldiers forcing Arabs to eat dirt, beat themselves, or sing songs of praise for Israeli Army units inevitably produce memories of Jews forced by jeering Nazis to humiliate themselves. Palestinian "terrorists" caught or killed in tunnels burrowed underground from Gaza parallel Jewish "bandits" dragged by Nazi soldiers from sewers leading out of the Warsaw Ghetto. Israel's use of Palestinian authorities in Gaza to distribute the limited amounts of electricity and food allowed into the strip are reminders of

German uses of Judenräte (Jewish Councils) to distribute food and work in the ghettos. Slogans such as "Arabs out" and "Death to the Arabs," scrawled on walls and chanted at rallies and sporting events, mimic Nazi slogans and German behavior in minds attuned to Holocaustia. Violence and vigilantism against Arabs and against Jews perceived as Arab sympathizers by organizations such as Price-Tag, the proudly racist Beitar football club La Familia, and the race traitor-oriented Lehava (Flame) movement cannot help but trigger images of Nazi persecution of Jews in the last years of the Weimar Republic.[69]

The unintended consequences of the Israel lobby's extravagant success may also create the potential for dramatic change. The lobby's hammerlock on U.S. policy crippled Israeli moderates, accelerated de facto annexation, and transformed the peace process into a merry-go-round of failure. In every U.S. administration from Jimmy Carter through Barack Obama, American diplomatic initiatives cycled through four phases: slight prodding of Israel toward compromise, lobby mobilization against U.S. pressure on Israel, collapse of the peace process, and politically apologetic expansion of American guarantees and aid. In this way, each cycle produced ever higher obstacles to the success of future initiatives.[70]

One result of the right-wing lurch in Israeli life and the collapse of the TSS—both associated with U.S. policies enforced by the lobby—has been to damage Israel's traditional alliance with American liberals, large segments of the Democratic Party, and growing numbers of American Jews, especially young nonorthodox Jews. Outraged at President Trump, the vast majority of American Jews view him as a frightening and infuriating threat. Yet, in October 2018 he enjoyed a 69 percent approval rating among Israelis. In December 2018 Eric Goldstein, president of the New York Jewish Welfare Federation, told Israel's Ministry of Diaspora Affairs that previously generous donors say they "feel like throwing up" when they consider Israel's brutal policies toward migrants and Palestinians and that "every day donors tell the Federation that they don't want their funds invested in Israel."[71]

The slogan of ending the "occupation" has never resonated deeply with Americans, who associate that term with the peaceful and democratizing occupations of postwar Germany and Japan. But most Americans treat equal rights for all as self-evident truth. That will help campaigns seeking American support to democratize Israel by extending rights all its non-Jewish inhabitants. Sympathy among American progressives for the BDS movement, one of whose core demands is political equality for Arabs in Israel, has already induced change in the positions of candidates vying for the Democratic Party's presidential nomination.[72] When liberals and the Democratic Party regain power in Washington, U.S. policy toward Israel will likely start to shift from toleration of the status quo camouflaged by diplomatic blather about a TSS to the application of traditional American values, including the fundamental democratic principle of one person, one vote. Relying as heavily as it does on right-wing evangelicals, the insider influence of savvy operators, and superwealthy donors and as distant as it has become from the concerns of masses of voters, the lobby's influence over the U.S. government could fall sharply. Once Washington and the punditocracy acknowledge the impossibility of a negotiated separation between Israel and the Palestinians, attention will shift, as it already has in many respects, to Israel's behavior toward the Arabs it rules and to its denial of their civil and political rights.[73]

Taking a long-term view of the problem and exploiting the unintended consequences of projects designed for other purposes can restore confidence to those struggling to improve conditions for all who live in what some call Palestine and others call the Land of Israel. There is certainly much to be done and much to learn, including about the thinking of settlers and other supporters of Israeli rule of the territories, for they worry and think as much about the future as do progressives. Even if groups disagree about the ultimate purposes, they can work toward at least overlapping if not shared goals in the near term. For example, most right-wing annexationists want to avoid the stigma of apartheid and at least be seen as honoring democratic principles. This rationale for politicians on the Right to publicly endorse equality and democracy creates openings to shift Israeli political discourse. Without doubt most of what is said by right-wing proponents about the future is no more sincere than Prime Minister Benjamin Netanyahu's declaration of allegiance to the TSS in 2009. Most annexationist talk about democracy is also a double discourse. But while disingenuous support for a TSS postpones progressive mobilization for democracy by making it appear to undermine chances for peace, disingenuous support for democracy to justify annexation opens the door for Jews and Arabs to demand equality by turning the one state they inhabit into a state where all are ruled by the same laws.

Accordingly, it is important to note how unrealistic if not utterly fantastical most right-wing plans are for a positive future. These include transforming West Bank Palestinians into Jordanian expatriates living in Israel; inducing Egypt to accept responsibility for ruling Gaza and relocating its refugees to the Sinai; annexing the sparsely populated portions of the West Bank and granting citizenship to their inhabitants, with temporary self-rule to Arabs in most cities and towns; or changing Palestinian cities into autonomous but not independent tribal emirates in the West Bank and Gaza while formally annexing the rural areas.[74] Codicils attached to their proposals typically condition Arab citizenship on years of good behavior, loyalty oaths, and/or knowledge of Hebrew, with exclusions based on political views, refugee status, or past political activities.

In these proposals, the theoretical existence of legal avenues to full citizenship for Arabs shields apartheid-like arrangements of domination from international criticism while signaling worried Israelis that most West Bank and Gaza Palestinians would never qualify for the status. But the right wing's reliance on such provisions creates opportunities in the OSR once the TSS is set aside. If implemented, annexation or the extension of Israeli law, however conditioned and restricted, will eventually produce unintended and unimagined consequences. When President Lincoln issued the Emancipation Proclamation on January 1, 1863, for example, its terms belied the grandeur of its name. It emancipated only enslaved people living in some areas that were still under Confederate rule. Even those whose status was affected by it were not granted citizenship but only an end to involuntary servitude. It took a constitutional amendment to make them citizens and many decades of struggle against Jim Crow before most (but still not all) black citizens could enjoy real voting rights. In democracies the arc of history is long, but it does bend toward integration of formerly despised and excluded populations.

Indeed, many right-wingers prefer not to talk of the future, hoping that the Arab problem will disappear but not knowing or wanting to say how. However, one leader of that camp, Tzipi Hotovely, recognizing the political dynamism of the OSR, has stressed that if the "national camp" and the religious Right do not offer genuine programs for the future and practical solutions to the Arab problem, then the public discourse in Israel will be entirely dominated by the Left and their media allies.[75] Thus, some on the Right, in addition to President Rivlin, have made sincere proposals for annexation of all the territories *with* the grant of citizenship to all their Arab inhabitants. Occasionally, these ideas are advanced as religious or moral imperatives. But other advocates argue that these portions of the Land of Israel can only be completely incorporated into Israel if their populations are also completely incorporated. They express faith that the Jewish people will win the demographic contest by natural increase or by immigration.[76]

Consider the proposal of Uri Elitzur, a founder of the Jewish fundamentalist movement Gush Emunim, an activist and leader of various ultranationalist and religious parties, and long a confidant of Prime Minister Netanyahu. In 2009 as part of a symposium on solutions to the question of the Arabs of Judea, Samaria, and Gaza, Elitzur published a detailed article insisting that the "taboo" on discussion of the only real solution to the problem—annexation, with full citizenship for Arab inhabitants—had to be broken. Looking thirty years ahead, Elitzur argued that the only alternatives would be two states, which would mean an irreparable split in the Jewish people and endless bloodshed or a continuation of the status quo that—as a permanent arrangement—would be apartheid. He rejected various formulas popular on the Right, such as administrative autonomy, the Arab franchise in Jordanian elections, the establishment of cantons, and the pretense, forever, that the status quo was only temporary. He saw these as doomed attempts to camouflage the reality of masses of people living under Israeli rule but without Israeli citizenship. What would happen to such an apartheid state, he wrote, "is what happened to South Africa."[77]

A year later Hotoveley, former defense minister Moshe Arens, and Rabbi Hanan Porat, the best known of all the historic founders of Gush Emunim, endorsed the idea of "annexation with citizenship," although they stressed that it would take a generation to implement. While at that moment Hotoveley was talking only about the West Bank, the future of Gaza was very much on her mind. Israel, she argued, could pursue more ruthless measures in Gaza after annexation than the international community would tolerate as long as Israel is perceived as an occupier and not a legitimate state authority.[78]

The annexationist camp and progressives who accept the OSR both view the entire land as one space, even if they do not agree on whether the "Jewish" or "democratic" character of the state should prevail. If it is one space, the Right has a forceful argument that it is hypocritical for the dovish Left to treat Israel within the Green Line as legitimate while across the line it is not. If, say, annexationists, mass expulsions of Arabs, wholesale expropriation of land, and Jewish settlement in Arab areas to secure Israel's rule of territories acquired in 1948 were legitimate, then settlement and absorption of the West Bank and Gaza, with less harsh measures, can also be seen as legitimate.[79] If TSS advocates must come to terms with that jarring point, right-wingers will be forced to accept that just as the powerless Arab minority of the 1950s expanded to become a large and significant force in Israeli politics today, so too will any system of limits on democratic freedoms within an enlarged and self-described democratic polity ultimately fail.

An unequivocal declaration is not about to occur, but events march undeniably toward substantive annexation. Annexationists may think that the addition of nearly 5 million Arabs will not fundamentally change the state. It will. Although equal citizenship will not quickly be granted to most Arab inhabitants, annexation would create a political arena rich with possibilities. It would transform politics from a zero-sum struggle between Israeli Jews and Palestinian Arabs to more complicated competition among different Palestinian and Jewish groups searching for political allies and power within and across the boundaries of their national communities.

Expanding citizenship and suffrage for all will take decades of struggle. Nonetheless, leaving aside the potential for catastrophic war to produce drastically different outcomes, the democratization of the state will occur, not least because substantial numbers of Jews will find it in their interest to join with Arabs in the struggle for adult suffrage. Mixed governments that arise from a citizenry composed of millions of Jews, millions of Arabs, and hundreds of thousands of non-Jewish non-Arabs, all divided into religious, nonreligious, ideological, regional, and economic factions, will face enormous challenges—but with the likely enthusiastic support of the international community, there will be new ways forward as well. On the tactical level, the present imperative is to focus analysis and action on specific opportunities to advance equality and lessen or end discrimination, which means not opposing annexation per se but rather shaping it. It means treating Arabs and Jews as having equal political rights regardless of where, in relation to the Green Line, they live. It also means replacing appeals to Jewish demographic fears with encouragement of Palestinian-Jewish alliances, including integrating the masses of Arab Jerusalemites into the struggle for control of the Jerusalem municipality. In general, it means building long-term capacities for joint struggle instead of agonizing over how the peace process can be relaunched and whether the TSS is dead or not.

It is too soon to speak of one state as a solution rather than as a difficult but dynamic reality. But it is time to trade the festering problems of systematic yet unacknowledged domination for a better set of problems associated with learning to live with others as equals. In the end, it is only by thinking seriously about how to honor both democratic principles and the equal legitimacy of Jewish and Palestinian aspirations that Israeli, Palestinian, American, and European leaders can inject new life into a land too long stalked by death and bereft of hope.

Notes

Chapter 1

1. Neil Caplan, *Palestine Jewry and the Arab Question, 1917–1925* (London: Routledge, 1978), p. 113.

2. Charles D. Smith, *Palestine and the Arab-Israeli Conflict* (New York: St. Martin's, 1988), p. 80.

3. For details and documentation of these episodes, see Avi Raz, *The Bride and the Dowry: Israel, Jordan, and the Palestinians in the Aftermath of the June 1967 War* (New Haven, CT: Yale University Press, 2012); Elie Podeh, *Chances for Peace: Missed Opportunities in the Arab-Israeli Conflict* (Austin: University of Texas Press, 2015), pp. 88–106; Dan Bavly, *Dreams and Missed Opportunities, 1967–1973* [Hebrew] (Jerusalem: Carmel, 2002).

4. According to the Central Intelligence Agency's chief of mission in Amman, Israel only pretended interest in King Hussein's offer to decrease pressure from the United States "without conceding anything to the Jordanians." Quoted in Podeh, *Chances for Peace*, p. 91.

5. Ibid., p. 97.

6. Ibid., p. 121.

7. Statement to the Knesset by Prime Minister Meir, March 16, 1972, https://mfa.gov.il/MFA/ForeignPolicy/MFADocuments/Yearbook1/Pages/37%20Statement%20to%20the%20Knesset%20by%20Prime%20Minister%20Meir.aspx; Charles D. Smith, *Palestine and the Arab-Israeli Conflict* (Boston: Bedford/St. Martin's, 2013) pp. 319–21.

8. Nathan Thrall, *The Only Language They Understand: Forcing Compromise in Israel and Palestine* (New York: Metropolitan Books, 2017), pp. 44–45. The term "national authority" was subsequently used in the Oslo Accords by the PLO and Israel to describe the interim Palestinian entity established by those accords in the Gaza Strip and parts of the West Bank.

9. Helena Cobban, *The Palestinian Liberation Organisation: People, Power and Politics* (Cambridge: Cambridge University Press, 1984), p. 17.

10. For a comprehensive treatment, see Seth Ansizka, *Preventing Palestine: A Political History from Camp David to Oslo* (Princeton, NJ: Princeton University Press, 2018).

11. For detailed analysis of this shift, see Ian S. Lustick, *Unsettled States, Disputed Lands: Britain and Ireland, France and Algeria, Israel and the West Bank/Gaza* (Ithaca, NY: Cornell University Press, 1993), pp. 352–84.

12. For harsh criticism of Arafat's leadership and diplomatic skills, see, e.g., Rashid Khalidi, *The Iron Cage: The Story of the Palestinian Struggle for Statehood* (Boston: Beacon, 2006).

13. "Israel's Mass Incarceration of Palestinians," Institute for Middle East Understanding, https://imeu.org/article/israels-mass-incarceration-of-palestinians.

14. Ian S. Lustick, "Kill the Autonomy Talks," *Foreign Policy*, no. 41 (Winter 1980–1981): 21–43; Rashid Khalidi *Brokers of Deceit: How the U.S. Has Undermined Peace in the Middle East* (Boston: Beacon, 2013), pp. 13–37.

15. See Ian S. Lustick, "Zionist Ideology and Its Discontents: A Research Note," *Israel Studies Forum* 19, no. 1 (Fall 2003): pp. 98–103.

16. The idea that Palestine could not be emptied of its Arab population was Ben-Gurion's view, at least until the 1937 Peel Commission recommendations that included the forcible transfer of hundreds of thousands of Arabs from the territory designated for the Jewish state to the territory designated for the Arab State. See Ian S. Lustick and Matthew Berkman, "Zionist Theories of Peace in the Pre-State Era: Legacies of Dissimulation and Israel's Arab Minority," in *Israel and Its Palestinian Citizens: Ethnic Privileges in the Jewish State*, ed. Nadim N. Rouhana and Sahar S. Huneidi's (Cambridge: Cambridge University Press, 2017), p. 64n21.

17. Ibid., pp. 39–72.

18. *The Jewish Case: Before the Anglo-American Committee of Inquiry on Palestine as Presented by the Jewish Agency for Palestine, Statements & Memoranda* (Jerusalem: Jewish Agency for Palestine, 1947), p. 72.

19. Ibid., p. 73.

20. Ibid., p. 74.

21. Zionist institutions themselves evolved largely in response to the challenges they posed. See Gershon Shafir, *Land, Labor, and the Origins of the Israeli-Palestinian Conflict, 1882–1914* (Cambridge: Cambridge University Press, 1989); Gur Alroey, "The Servants of the Settlement or Vulgar Tyrants? A Hundred Years of the Hashomer Association: A Historical Perspective"

[Hebrew], *Cathedra—for the History of Eretz Israel and Its Yishuv*, no. 133 (April 2009): 77–104.

22. Benny Morris, "Thus Were the Zionist Documents Overhauled," *Haaretz*, February 4, 1994. See also Anita Shapira, *Land and Power: The Zionist Resort to Force, 1881–1948* (New York: Oxford University Press, 1992), p. 26.

23. Translations of the original Russian version of Jabotinsky's essay differ in many details (e.g., use of the term "native" vs. "indigenous"). Passages quoted here are based on a translation circulated by the World Zionist Organization titled "An Iron Wall (We and the Arabs)," with slight differences based on direct examination of Hebrew versions and the Russian original. See *Zionism: Background Papers for an Evaluation*, Kit no. 4 (Jerusalem: Youth and Hechalutz Department of the World Zionist Organization, 1969).

24. Ibid.

25. Moshe Dayan highlighted this convergence in his famous disquisition on Arthur Ruppin, a Zionist founder who abandoned his accommodationist views. See Moshe Dayan, "A Soldier Reflects on Peace Hopes," in *The Israel-Arab Reader*, 3rd ed., ed. Walter Laqueur, pp. 434–45 (New York: Bantam, 1976).

26. For details on these policies and practices, see Benny Morris, *Israel's Border Wars: 1949–1956* (New York: Oxford University Press, 1993).

27. Meron Rapoport, "Was 1967 a Victory Too Far for Israel?," *Eurozine*, June 8 2007, https://www.eurozine.com/was-1967-a-victory-too-far-for-israel/?pdf.

28. On these points see Riad Ashkar, "The Syrian and Egyptian Campaigns," *Journal of Palestine Studies* 3 (1974): 15–33; Chaim Herzog, *The Arab-Israeli Wars* (New York: Vintage, 1982), pp. 315–16. For an early and illuminating explanation of Arab strategy in both the War of Attrition and the Ramadan/Yom Kippur War, see Hassanain Heykal, "The Strategy of the War of Attrition," excerpts from articles published in *Al Ahram* March 27, April 11, and April 25, 1969, reprinted in *The Israel-Arab Reader*, pp. 414–27.

29. Speech to the Knesset, October 3, 1994, Voice of Israel Radio, transcribed by the Foreign Broadcast Information Service, *Daily Report: Near East and South Asia*, October 4, 1994.

Chapter 2

1. Marissa Newman, "IDF Chief Cites Holocaust to Justify Haredi Service," *Times of Israel*, March 2, 2014.

2. "President Rivlin Addresses Official Ceremony Marking the Commencement of Israel's Holocaust Memorial Day," President of the State of Israel

Reuven (Ruvi) Rivlin, April 15, 2015, http://archive.president.gov.il/English /ThePresident/Speeches/Pages/news_150415_01.aspx.

3. Peter Hirschberg, "Netanyahu: It's 1938 and Iran Is Germany; Ahmadinejad Is Preparing Another Holocaust," *Haaretz*, November 14, 2006.

4. "PM Netanyahu Addresses the Jewish Agency Board of Governors," *MFA Newsletter*, February 18, 2013.

5. Amos Elon, *The Israelis: Founders and Sons* (New York: Bantam Books, 1972), pp. 259–60.

6. The quotation in the subheading is from my interview with a Yad Vashem educator, June 2014.

7. Chaim Schatzker, "The Holocaust in Textbooks—A Comparative Analysis," in *The Historiography of the Holocaust Period: Proceedings of the Fifth Yad Vashem International Historical Conference, Jerusalem, March 1983*, ed. Yisrael Gutman and Gideon Greif (Jerusalem: Yad Vashem, 1988), p. 468.

8. See Doron Bar, "Holocaust Commemoration in Israel During the 1950s: The Holocaust Cellar on Mount Zion," *Jewish Social Studies* 12, no. 1 (Fall 2005): 16–38; Don-Yehiya, "Memory and Political Culture: Israeli Society and the Holocaust," in *Studies in Contemporary Jewry*, Vol. 9, ed. Ezra Mendelsohn (Oxford: Oxford University Press, 1993), pp. 140–41.

9. Hannah Arendt, *The Origins of Totalitarianism* (New York: Harcourt Books, 1994), pp. 275–90. The book was first published in 1948.

10. Peter Novick, *The Holocaust in American Life* (Boston: Houghton Mariner, 2000), p. 70.

11. On the prominence of this trope and metaphor, see, e.g., Yisrael Gutman, "Jewish Resistance—Questions and Assessments," in *The Historiography of the Holocaust Period*, pp. 641–77 (Jerusalem: Yad Vashem, 1988); Saul Friedlander, "The Shoah Between Memory and History," *Jewish Quarterly* 37, no. 1 (1990): 5–11, esp. p. 6.

12. For somewhat different treatments of the Ben-Gurion-Dinur relationship, see Uri Ram, "Zionist Historiography and the Invention of Modern Jewish Nationhood: The Case of Ben Zion Dinur," *History and Memory* 7, no. 1 (1995): 106; Roni Stauber, *The Holocaust in Israeli Public Debate in the 1950s* (London: Vallentine Mitchell, 2007), pp. 48–51; Idith Zertal, *Israel's Holocaust and the Politics of Nationhood* (New York: Cambridge University Press, 2005).

13. Ruth Firer, "The Treatment of the Holocaust in Textbooks: Israel," in *The Treatment of the Holocaust in Textbooks: The Federal Republic of Germany, Israel, the United States of America* (Boulder, CO: Social Science Monographs, 1987), p. 181.

14. Anita Shapira, "Whatever Became of 'Negating Exile'?," in *Israeli Identity in Transition*, ed. Anita Shapira (Westport, CT: Praeger, 2004), p. 86. The idea of correcting damage done to Israeli Jews' lack of empathy or identification with diaspora Jews was included in 1955 as an explicit tenet of the governing coalition's "Basic Principles." See also *Deepening Jewish Consciousness in Public Schools: Instructions and Curriculum* (Jerusalem: Ministry of Education, 1959); Julia Resnik, "'Sites of Memory' of the Holocaust: Shaping National Memory in the Education System in Israel," *Nations and Nationalism* 9, no. 2 (2003): 305–7.

15. Shabtai Teveth, *Ben-Gurion: The Burning Ground, 1886–1948* (Boston: Houghton Mifflin, 1987), pp. 850–54.

16. Dina Porat, "Ben-Gurion and the Holocaust," in *David Ben-Gurion: Politics and Leadership in Israel*, ed. Ronald W. Zweig (New York: Yad Izhak Ben Zvi, 1991), pp. 159, 162.

17. On the effective staging and exploitation of this episode, see Zertal, *Israel's Holocaust and the Politics of Nationhood*, pp. 46–50; Ian S. Lustick, "Four Constructions of the Holocaust in Israeli Political Culture," *Contemporary Jewry* 37 (April 2017): 141–42.

18. David Rising, "Germany Increases Reparations for Holocaust Survivors," *Times of Israel*, November 16, 2012.

19. Orna Kenan, *Between Memory and History: The Evolution of Israeli Historiography of the Holocaust, 1945–1961* (New York: Peter Lang, 2003), p. 40; Hanna Yablonka and Moshe Tlamim, "The Development of Holocaust Consciousness in Israel: The Nuremberg, Kapos, Kastner, and Eichmann Trials," *Israel Studies* 8, no. 3 (Fall 2003): 9; Nathan Eck, "Why Was Rescue Impossible," cited in David Bankier and Dan Mikhman, eds., *Holocaust Historiography in Context: Emergence, Challenges, Polemics and Achievements* (Jerusalem: Yad Vashem, 2008), p. 259; Meir Dworzecki, "Man and Society Facing the Holocaust," in Bankier and Mikhman, *Holocaust Historiography in Context*, p. 271. See also Philip Friedman, "Problems of Research," in Bankier and Mikhman, *Holocaust Historiography in Context*, p. 265.

20. This was a particularly sensitive matter in the aftermath of the infamous Kastner trial in 1955. Rudolf Kastner was a Labor Party official who, with support from Ben-Gurion, negotiated successfully with Eichmann and the Gestapo to save 1685 Hungarian Jews. To defend Kastner—and themselves—against charges of Nazi collaboration, the leaders of the Labor Party sued his accusers for libel. The government lost the case, and although the decision was eventually reversed, Kastner himself was assassinated. The trial raised sensitive and embarrassing questions about Ben-Gurion's own role in these matters. For details on the Kastner affair and its implications for Ben-Gurion, see Lustick,

"Four Constructions of the Holocaust in Israeli Political Culture," pp. 146–48, and a documentary film by Gaylen Ross, *Killing Kasztner: The Jew Who Dealt with Nazis* (GR Films, 2014).

21. Hannah Arendt, *Eichmann in Jerusalem* (New York: Penguin, 1963); Zertal, *Israel's Holocaust and the Politics of Nationhood*. See also Tom Segev, *The Seventh Million* (New York: Hill and Wang, 1993), p. 328; Yehiam Weitz, "The Holocaust on Trial: The Impact of the Kasztner and Eichmann Trials on Israeli Society," *Israel Studies* 1, no. 2 (Fall 1996): 14–15.

22. "The Trial of Adolf Eichmann: Sessions 6-7-8 (Part 3 of 10)," The Nizkor Project, http://www.nizkor.org/hweb/people/e/eichmann-adolf/transcripts /Sessions/Session-006-007-008-03.html.

23. "The Trial of Adolf Eichmann: Sessions 6-7-8 (Part 1 of 10)," The Nizkor Project, http://www.nizkor.org/hweb/people/e/eichmann-adolf/transcripts /Sessions/Session-006-007-008-01.html.

24. For this view, see Menachem Kasher, *The Great Era* [Hebrew] (Jerusalem: Torah Shlema, 1968), p. 32; Harold Fisch, *The Zionist Revolution: A New Perspective* (New York: St. Martin's, 1978), p. 85.

25. Ilan Gur-Ze'ev, "Defeating the Enemy Within: Exploring the Link Between Holocaust Education and the Arab/Israeli Conflict," *Religious Education* 95, no. 4 (Fall 2000): 393. Concerning the importance of the cultural trope of the *freier* in Israel, see Steven Fraiberg and Danny Kaplan, "Outsmarting the Nation, Together: Subversive Virtual Fraternity in the Israeli Men's Magazine *Blazer*," *Israel Studies Review* 30, no. 1 (Summer 2015): 42–65.

26. For detailed consideration of the relative decisiveness of these events in the transformation of Israeli collective memory concerning the Holocaust, see Anita Shapira, "The Holocaust: Private Memories, Public Memory," *Jewish Social Studies* 4, no. 2 (Winter 1998): 40–58.

27. Hanna Yablonka, "As Heard by the Witnesses, the Public, and the Judges: Three Variations on the Testimony in the Eichmann Trial," in *Holocaust Historiography in Context: Emergency, Challenges, Polemics and Achievements*, ed. David Bankier and Dan Michman (Yad Vashem: Jerusalem, 2008), p. 580.

28. Ibid., p. 571.

29. Ibid.

30. On the effects of the Eichmann trial, see Yechiel Klar, Noa Schori-Eyal, and Yonat Klar, "The 'Never Again' State of Israel: The Emergence of the Holocaust as a Core Feature of Israeli Identity and Its Four Incongruent Voices," *Journal of Social Issues* 69, no. 1 (2013): 132; Eliezer Don-Yehiya, "Memory and

Political Culture: Israeli Society and the Holocaust," *Studies in Contemporary Jewry* 9 (1993): 145, 149.

31. Robert C. Rowland, *The Rhetoric of Menachem Begin: The Myth of Redemption Through Return* (Lanham, MD: University Press of America, 1985), p. 60.

32. See note 20 above.

33. On the development of Holocaust consciousness among Mizrahim, see Hanna Yablonka, "Oriental Jewry and the Holocaust: A Tri-Generational Perspective," *Israel Studies* 14, no. 1 (Spring 2009): 94.

34. "Yossi Sarid, "Raised on the Holocaust," *Haaretz*, October 25, 2013.

35. Author notes, Safed, Israel, September 29, 1969. See Nurit Geertz, "The Few vs. the Many: Rhetorical Structure in the Election Speeches of Menachem Begin" [Hebrew], *Sifrei Siman Kriah* 16–17 (April 1981): 106–14. For Ben-Gurion's use of this trope, including descriptions of Nasser as a new Hitler, see Zertal, *Israel's Holocaust and the Politics of Nationhood*, p. 97; Yechiam Weitz, "Even Ben-Gurion Exploited the Holocaust When It Suited Him," *Haaretz*, October 31, 2013.

36. Rowland, *The Rhetoric of Menachem Begin*, p. 59.

37. Gerald Cromer, *A War of Words: Political Violence and Public Debate in Israel* (Milton Park: Frank Cass, 2004), p. 115.

38. Benny Morris, *Righteous Victims: A History of the Zionist-Arab Conflict, 1881–1998* (New York: Knopf, 1999), p. 512.

39. David Shipler, "Begin Defends Raid, Pledges to Thwart a New 'Holocaust,'" *New York Times*, June 10, 1981, p. 1. On Begin's identification of the Holocaust in every security challenge Israel faced, see Arye Naor, "Lessons of the Holocaust Versus Territories for Peace, 1967–2001," *Israel Studies* 8, no. 1 (Spring 2003): 136–41.

40. "PLO leaders 'Like Hitler and His Henchmen,' begin," *The Citizen* [Ottawa, Canada], August 5, 1982.

41. Naor, "Lessons of the Holocaust Versus Territories for Peace," pp. 130–52. Even left-wing and dovish figures are drawn to this rhetoric. Former foreign minister Abba Eban once referred to the boundaries that Israel held before the 1967 war as "Auschwitz borders"—a phrase repeated endlessly by right-wing Israeli politicians.

42. The resonance of these appeals with Jews in America was demonstrated in 2007 when 1,000 attendees flooded a Jewish studies conference at Queens College, New York, on the topic "Is It 1938 Again?" One of the editors of the volume recording and interpreting the results of the conference dubbed those

doubting the scale of threats to twenty-first-century Jews as "1938 deniers." David Schimel, "Cognitive Dissonance or Denial? Perhaps Both," in *The Jewish Condition: Challenges and Responses—1938-2008* (New Brunswick, NJ: Transaction Books, 2008), xiii–xv.

43. Yossi Sarid, "Raised on the Holocaust," *Haaretz*, October 25, 2013; Uri Avnery, "Trivializing the Holocaust," May 11, 2009, Antiwar.com, http://original.antiwar.com/avnery/2009/05/10/trivializing-the-holocaust/; Adi Ophir, "On Sanctifying the Holocaust," *Tikkun* 2, no. 1 (1987): 62; Ariel Rubinstein, "A Dozen Reasons Why Israel Should Do Away with Holocaust Memorial Day," *Haaretz*, April 16, 2015; Segev, *The Seventh Million*; Zertal, *Israel's Holocaust and the Politics of Nationhood*; Avraham Burg, *Victory Over Hitler* [Hebrew] (Tel Aviv: Yediot Acharonot, 2007); Moshe Zuckerman, *Holocaust in a Sealed Room: The "Shoah" in the Israeli Press During the Gulf War* [Hebrew] (Tel Aviv: Hotzat HaMachber, 1993).

44. *Achievements and Challenges: Annual Report 2017*, Yad Vashem, https://www.yadvashem.org/annual-report/2017.html.

45. National Library of Israel statistics for 2011, reported in Klar et al., "The 'Never Again' State of Israel," p. 127.

46. Jodi Rudoren, "Holocaust Told in One Word, Six Million Times," *New York Times*, January 25, 2014.

47. Jackie Feldman, *Above the Death Pits, Beneath the Flag: Youth Voyages to Poland and the Performance of Israeli National Identity* (New York: Berghahn Books, 2008), p. 202.

48. Ibid., pp. 204, 228.

49. Feldman, *Above the Death Pits*, pp. 17, 249. In Zionist parlance *masa* is a strenuous journey, a kind of political and spiritual pilgrimage. The journeys to the death camps are designed to re-create, for young Israelis, that same sense of danger, suffering, survival, and transcendent purpose associated with Zionist pioneers in Palestine. Repeatedly traumatized by guides following a strict schedule and script, the students experience emotional breakdowns. They return home from an anti-Semitism-drenched diaspora as witnesses responsible to deliver the message of the Holocaust to Jews and to protect the Jewish state from contemporary threats of annihilation. See Feldman, *Above the Death Pits*.

50. Yair Auron, "Jewish-Israeli Identity Among Israel's Future Teachers," *Jewish Political Studies Review* 9, nos. 1–2 (Spring 1997): 105–22.

51. Zuckerman, *Holocaust in a Sealed Room*.

52. As reported in Klar et al., "The 'Never Again' State of Israel," p. 127.

53. Study published in 2012 by Asher Arian, cited in Klar et al., "The 'Never Again' State of Israel," p. 125.

54. Amos Perlmutter, *The Life and Times of Menachem Begin* (Garden City, NY: Doubleday, 1987), p. 11.

55. "Israel Air Force Ceremony—F-15 Jets over Auschwitz," YouTube, April 20, 2009, https://www.youtube.com/watch?v=h1FHvsuMzAc.

56. Jodi Rudoren, "Proudly Bearing Elders' Scars, Their Skin Says 'Never Forget,'" *New York Times*, September 30, 2012.

57. Henriette Dahan-Kalev, "A Second Order Decision: Holocaust and Mizrahim," paper presented at the annual meeting of the Association for Israel Studies, Sde Boker, Israel, June 25, 2014.

58. In an interview with the author, one Yad Vashem educator said that this decision was meant to prevent unprofessional presentation of Holocaust material by teachers who lacked the necessary guidance to do so but did feel an urgent need to teach five-year-olds about the Holocaust.

59. Adi Ophir, *The Order of Evils: Toward an Ontology of Morals* (New York: Zone Books, 2005), p. 547.

60. Feldman, *Above the Death Pits*, p. 52.

61. Sandy Rashty, "Israelis' Tough Stance at Auschwitz," The Jewish Chronicle OnLine, January 30, 2014, http://www.thejc.com/news/uk-news/115241 /israelis%E2%80%99-tough-stance-auschwitz.

62. Or Kashti, "Education Ministry Bumps Professor from Post for Criticizing 'Superficial' Teaching of Holocaust," *Haaretz*, July 21, 2010.

63. Regarding the conflation of Arabs/Palestinians and Nazis in Israeli popular culture and in the collective imagination, see Burg, *Victory over Hitler*, pp. 129–31; Feldman, *Above the Death Pits*, p. 3; Morris, *Righteous Victims*, pp. 514–15. For explicit treatment of the use of the traditional biblical injunction to "wipe out the memory of Amalek" as applying to Arabs as it applies to Nazis, see Ilan Gur-Ze'ev, "Defeating the Enemy Within: Exploring the Link Between Holocaust Education and the Arab/Israeli Conflict," *Religious Education* 95, no. 4 (Fall 2000): 374–76.

64. Charles S. Maier, *The Unmasterable Past: History, Holocaust, and German National Identity* (Cambridge, MA: Harvard University Press, 1988).

65. See, e.g., Lesley Klaff, "Holocaust Inversion," *Israel Studies* 24, no. 2 (Summer 2019) : 73-90. For additional discussion of this point, see Chapter 5 .

Chapter 3

1. Text of Washington's Farewell Address, published as the appendix in Matthew Spalding and Patrick J. Garrity, *A Sacred Union of Citizens: George*

Washington's Farewell Address and the American Character (Lanham, MD: Rowman and Littlefield, 1996), pp. 184–85.

2. Elizabeth Stephens, *US Policy Towards Israel: The Role of Political Culture in Defining the 'Special Relationship'* (Brighton, UK: Sussex Academic Press, 2006), p. 253 (my emphasis).

3. Among the key sources used to arrive at this estimate are Eric Flexh and Theodore Sasson, "The New Philanthropy: American Jewish Giving to Israeli Organizations," Brandeis Institutional Repository, April 2012, http://bir .brandeis.edu/bitstream/handle/10192/39/TheNewPhilanthropy.pdf?sequence =1&isAllowed=y, and "United Jewish Appeal Federation of Jewish Philanthropies of NY Inc," ProPublica, https://projects.propublica.org/nonprofits /organizations/510172429.

4. Jeremy M. Sharp, *U.S. Foreign Aid to Israel,* Congressional Research Service, RL33222, April 10, 2018, https://fas.org/sgp/crs/mideast/RL33222.pdf.

5. *International Security and Development Cooperation Program,* Special Report No. 108, April 4, 1983 (Washington, DC: Bureau of Public Affairs, United States Department of State).

6. The list of these exemptions, dispensations, and privileges provided here is taken mainly from Clyde R. Mark's authoritative report on U.S. aid to Israel prepared for the Congressional Research Service, *Israel: U.S. Foreign Assistance,* Issue Brief for Congress (updated April 26, 2005). Mark was an analyst for the Congressional Research Service's Foreign Affairs, Defense, and Trade Division. See also Edward T. Pound, "A Close Look at U.S. Aid to Israel Reveals Deals That Push Cost Above Publicly Quoted Figures," *Wall Street Journal,* September 19, 1991; Amnon Cavari with Elan Nyer, *Trends in US Congressional Support for Israel,* Mideast Security and Policy Study No. 121 (Ramat Gan, Israel: Begin-Sadat Center for Strategic Studies, Bar Ilan University, June 2016), p. 16.

7. A letter questioning this aspect of Israel's aid package from eleven members of Congress was sent to Secretary of State John Kerry in February 2016. On the furious reaction to this letter from Israel's supporters in Congress, see Sarah Lazare, "Here's What Happens When a U.S. Senator Calls for Israel to be Held Accountable for Atrocities," AlterNet, April 4, 2016, http://www.alternet .org/grayzone-project/heres-what-happens-when-us-senator-calls-israel-be -held-accountable-atrocities.

8. "Relief for Israel Bond Holders," Jewish Telegraphic Agency, October 4, 1985, https://www.jta.org/1985/10/04/archive/relief-for-israel-bond-holders; Pound, "A Close Look at U.S. Aid to Israel."

9. "Joint Meeting & Joint Session Addresses Before Congress by Foreign Leaders & Dignitaries," History, Art & Archives, United States House

of Representatives, http://history.house.gov/Institution/Foreign-Leaders/Joint-Sessions/.

10. Ben Norton, "Over One Quarter of Netanyahu's Speech to Congress Consisted of Applause and Standing Ovations," Mondoweiss, March 4, 2015, http://mondoweiss.net/2015/03/netanyahus-consisted-standing/.

11. Cavari with Nyer, *Trends in US Congressional Support for Israel*, pp. 17–18. The rate and fulsomeness of these resolutions has only increased in recent years. See "U.S.-Israel Relations: Congress & the Middle East," Jewish Virtual Library, https://www.jewishvirtuallibrary.org/jsource/US-Israel/congtoc.html.

12. "S.Res.599—112th Congress (2011-2012)," Congress.gov, https://www.congress.gov/bill/112th-congress/senate-resolution/599/text.

13. "U.S.-Israel Relations: Congress & the Middle East." Approximately 2,200 Palestinians died, both civilians and combatants, compared with 71 Israelis.

14. Chris Coons and Marco Rubio, "Every Senator Agrees the U.N. Must Change," *Wall Street Journal*, May 2, 2017.

15. "5 Things You Need to Know About the U.S.-Israel Relationship Under President Obama," The White House, March 1, 2015, https://www.whitehouse.gov/blog/2015/03/01/5-things-you-need-know-about-us-israel-relationship-under-president-obama.

16. "Security Council—Quick Links," United Nations Library, http://research.un.org/en/docs/sc/quick.

17. On October 27, 2015, the United Nations General Assembly voted 191-2 to condemn the U.S. embargo against Cuba. Israel was the second vote in favor.

18. AIPAC is not coextensive with the Israel lobby. As I use the term, the "lobby" refers to a panoply of organizations, groups, and individuals (including Jews, Christians, and others) who advocate American policies favorable to the interests of Israel as perceived by those doing the advocating. Overwhelmingly, but not uniformly, these groups support the actions and policies of Israeli governments. Figures collected in 2009 show the annual lobbying budget of AIPAC as being nearly triple the combined amounts spent for that purpose by the next eight-largest (Jewish) organizations involved in Israel advocacy. Dov Waxman, "The Israel Lobbies: A Survey of the Pro-Israel Community in the United States," *Israel Studies Forum* 25, no. 1 (Summer 2010): 14.

19. Jeffrey Birnbaum, "Washington's Power 25: Which Pressure Groups Are Best at Manipulating the Laws We Live By? A Groundbreaking *Fortune* Survey Reveals Who Belongs to Lobbying's Elite and Why They Wield So Much Clout," *Fortune*, December 8, 1997.

20. Michael Massing, "Deal Breakers," The American Prospect, February 22, 2002, http://prospect.org/article/deal-breakers.

21. "AIPAC Delegates Rally to the Cause; Thousands Converge on Washington," Jewish Telegraphic Agency, May 25, 2005. See also "Hilary AIPAC 2005," YouTube, https://www.youtube.com/watch?v=iOdZwxx3J6g.

22. Yoav Karni, "A Reminder from AIPAC," Haaretz, March 22, 1991.

23. Connie Bruck, "Friends of Israel," New Yorker, September 1, 2014, p. 54.

24. For an AIPAC staffer's account of how a typical candidate with a tiny budget from a state sparsely populated by Jews (such as Idaho) can be snagged as an AIPAC supporter with a "bundled" donation of a mere $10,000, see Dan Fleshler, Transforming America's Israel Lobby: The Limits of Its Power and the Potential for Change (Washington, DC: Potomac Books, 2009), p. 43. Concerning the multiplication of the lobby's influence where Israel is unimportant to constituents and where few Jews live, see ibid., p. 46.

25. Charles R. Babcock, "Pro-Israel Political Activists Enforce 'Percy Factor,' Washington Post, August 7, 1986. Babcock was the author of a detailed series of four articles on the "special relationship" between Israel and the United States. The third of these, "Pro-Israel Lobbyists Target Sale of U.S. Arms to Arabs," focused on the techniques and effectiveness of the lobby in Congress. The article details the extraordinary success with which AIPAC used the Percy factor for "training" members of Congress—a conditioning so thorough that it sometimes was difficult to calibrate. See also "Senator Charles H. Percy, Interviewed by: Charles Stuart Kennedy," Association for Diplomatic Studies and Training Foreign Affairs Oral History Project, June 11, 1998, pp. 63–64, https://www.adst.org/OH%20TOCs/Percy,%20Charles%20H.toc.pdf.

26. "The Complete Unexpurgated AIPAC Tape," Washington Report on Middle East Affairs, December–January 1992–1993, pp. 13–16.

27. "'They Threw Me Under the Bus,'" Haaretz, November 21, 2010. For full documentation of the Rosen episode, see Philip Giuraldi, "AIPAC on Trial," The American Conservative, January 17, 2011, http://www.theamericanconservative.com/articles/aipac-on-trial/; Superior Court of the District of Columbia Civil Division, Rosen vs. American Israel Public Affairs Committee, Inc., et al., "Order Granting Defendants Motion for Summary Judgment," February 23, 2011, http://www.washingtonpost.com/wp-srv/politics/documents/OrderGRANTINGMSJ2-23-11.pdf.

28. "Netanyahu, Unaware of the Camera, Says 'America Can Easily Be Moved,'" YouTube, May 3, 2018, https://www.youtube.com/watch?v=lW8TxOwYte0. In this video recording Netanyahu speaks candidly in 2001

with settlers about why he was unconcerned with potential American opposition to his policies.

29. The interview was reproduced in "C1. Rep. Jim Moran (D-VA), Comments on the Influence of the Pro-Israel Lobby, Tikkun, May 2007," *Journal of Palestine Studies* 37, no. 1 (Autumn 2007): 205–7. *Tikkun Magazine* is a liberal Jewish journal.

30. Rebecca Leung, "Parting Shots from Fritz Hollings," CBS News, December 10, 2004, http://www.cbsnews.com/news/parting-shots-from-fritz-hollings/.

31. "Not So Gentle Rhetoric from the Gentleman from South Carolina," Jewish Telegraphic Agency, May 24, 2004.

32. Ibid. For testimony by other former legislators, see Charles McC. Mathias Jr., "Ethnic Politics and Foreign Policy," *Foreign Affairs* (Summer 1981): 975–98; Paul Findley, *They Dare to Speak Out: People and Institutions Confront Israel's Lobby* (Chicago: Lawrence Hill Books, 1985); James B. Abourezk, *Advise and Dissent: Memoirs of South Dakota and the U.S. Senate* (Chicago: Lawrence Hill Books, 1989). See also George W. Ball and Douglas B. Ball, *The Passionate Attachment: America's Involvement with Israel, 1947 to the Present* (New York: Norton, 1992); Pete McCloskey, "Congressman Pete McCloskey Speaks with Hesham Tillawi About AIPAC's Power," YouTube, October 5, 2012, https://www.youtube.com/watch?v=_5bw90MuFBw; John J. Mearsheimer and Stephen M. Walt, *The Israel Lobby and U.S. Foreign Policy* (New York: Farrar, Straus and Giroux, 2008); Grant F. Smith, *Big Israel: How Israel's Lobby Moves America* (Washington, DC: Institute for Research, Middle East Policy, 2016).

33. Mike Lofgren, *The Deep State: The Fall of the Constitution and the Rise of a Shadow Government* (New York: Viking, 2016), p. 209.

34. Ibid., p. 210.

35. Yossi Melman and Dan Raviv, *Friends in Deed: Inside the U.S.-Israel Alliance* (New York: Hyperion, 1994), p. 311.

36. M. J. Rosenberg, "The Think Tank AIPAC Built: The Washington Institute for Near East Policy," Political Correction, Media Matters Action Network, April 13, 2010, http://politicalcorrection.org/blog/201004130003.

37. "Global Programs," Onward Israel, https://onwardisrael.org/internship-programs/global-programs/.

38. *Everyone of Us, Together*, The Jewish Agency for Israel 2017 Performance Report, p. 17, http://lln-websites.com/pdf/Performance_Report/2017/mobile/index.html#p=1. The report lists eighty-one funders, all Jewish community organizations in the United States, except for three located in Canada and one in London.

39. "About The Israel Training Program," Hasbara Fellowships, http://www.hasbarafellowships.org/israelprogram.

40. "From Israel & Co. to itrek: New Name, Same Mission," itrek, September 5, 2018, https://itrek.org/2018/09/04/from-israel-co-to-itrek-new-name-same-mission-2/.

41. Leslie Komaiko, "Adam Milstein: Leading by Example," *Jewish Journal*, November 18, 2015, http://jewishjournal.com/tag/milstein-family-foundation-campus-allies-mission-to-israel/. The Milstein Foundation sponsors an international pro-Israel meme competition and gives $1 million per year in grants to a wide variety of Israel advocacy organizations and projects. "Who We Support," The Adam and Gila Milstein Family Foundation, https://www.milsteinff.org/who-we-support/.

42. Judy Maltz, "Anti-Terror Fantasy Camps Are Popping Up Throughout Israel and the West Bank—and Tourists Are Eating It Up," *Haaretz*, July 11, 2017, https://www.haaretz.com/israel-news/1.800375. Israel advocacy organizations such as the Zionist Organization of America, CAMERA (Committee for Accuracy in Middle East Reporting in America), and the David Project all mount heavily subsidized trips to Israel along with many other groups.

43. Melman and Raviv, *Friends in Deed*, p. 317.

44. Ben Norton, "AIPAC Taking All But 3 Freshmen Congresspeople to Israel in Effort to Sabotage Iran Deal," Mondoweiss, August 3, 2015, http://mondoweiss.net/2015/08/freshmen-congresspeople-sabotage/.

45. "Academic Exchange 2009–2018 Academic Delegations," Rabin Center, Academic Exchange, http://academicexchange.com/participants/.

46. According to the *Boston Globe* the trip was organized as part of a campaign in favor of legislation to combat public criticism of Israel expressed via boycotts of Israeli products and institutions. By Frank Phillips, "Antiboycott Groups Pay for State Officials' Israel Trips," *Boston Globe*, December 8, 2016, https://www.bostonglobe.com/metro/2016/12/07/antiboycott-groups-pay-for-state-officials-trips-israel/0IPW7On7xXhGJ05Qm8wEHL/story.html. For additional examples of junkets for state and municipal officials organized and paid for in whole or in part by Israel advocacy organizations, see "Rauner to Lead Israel Trip," *State Journal-Register*, October 17, 2017, http://www.sj-r.com/news/20171027/rauner-to-lead-israel-trip; Kate Zernike and Michael Barbaro, "Chris Christie Shows Fondness for Luxury Benefits When Others Pay the Bill," *New York Times*, February 2, 2015, https://www.nytimes.com/2015/02/03/nyregion/in-christies-career-a-fondness-forluxe-benefits-when-others-pay-the-bills.html; Eli Stokols, "Hickenlooper in Israel with Larry Mizel, Close Friends," April 10, 2013, KDVR, http://kdvr.com/2013/04/10/hickenlooper-in

-israel-with-larry-mizel-close-friends/; "Governor Eric Greitens to Lead Missouri Trade Mission to Israel," STL News, November 4, 2017, https://www .stl.news/governor-eric-greitens-missouri-trade-mission-israel/42721/; Edgar Walters, "Gov. Abbott Uses Casino Owner's Jet for Trip to Israel," *Fort Worth Star-Telegram*, January 19, 2016, http://www.star-telegram.com/news/state /texas/article55442970.html.

47. William Booth, "This Year's Oscar Swag Bag Includes a $55,000 Trip to Israel," *Washington Post*, February 11, 2016; Gabe Friedman, "What the $55,000 Israel Trip for Oscar Nominees Looks Like," Jewish Telegraphic Agency, February 10, 2016, http://jta.org/2016/02/10/arts-entertainment/what-the-oscar -nominees-55000-israel-trip-will-look-like.

48. Yuli Walzer, "Come All Bloggers: The Way to Market Israel Worldwide" [Hebrew], Ynetnews, September 1, 2015, http://www.ynet.co.il/articles/0,7340 ,L-4616209,00.html.

49. "Views of Europe Slide Sharply in Global Poll, While Views of China Improve," GlobeScan, May 10, 2012, https://globescan.com/images /images/pressreleases/bbc2012_country_ratings/2012_bbc_country%20rating %20final%20080512.pdf. The Pew Foundation reported in June 2017 that Israel and Russia were the only two countries in the world that preferred President Trump to President Obama. Pew Research Center, "Across 37 Nations Polled, Trump Gets Higher Marks Than Obama in Only Two Countries: Russia and Israel," Twitter, https://twitter.com/pewresearch/status/879509901428613120 /photo/1.

50. "Sharp Drop in World Views of US, UK: Global Poll." BBC World Service, July 4, 2017, pp. 30–31, https://globescan.com/images/images/press releases/bbc2017_country_ratings/BBC2017_Country_Ratings_Poll.pdf.

51. For vivid and detailed accounts of this episode, see Michael Massing, "The Storm over the Israel Lobby," *New York Review of Books*, June 8, 2006; Deborah Amos, "Paper on Israel Lobby Sparks Heated Debate," National Public Radio, April 21, 2006, https://www.npr.org/templates/story /story.php?storyId=5353855; Paige Austin, "Grabbing the Third Rail," *Mother Jones*, July 18, 2006; Richard Silverstein, "Walt-Mearsheimer Cancelled by Chicago Council on Global Affairs," Blogpost, August 10, 2007, https://www .richardsilverstein.com/2007/08/10/walt-mearsheimer-cancelled-by-chicago -council-on-global-affairs/; John Mearsheimer, "Israel and Academic Freedom," in *Who's Afraid of Academic Freedom?*, ed. Akeel Bilgrami and Jonathan R. Cole, pp. 262–75 (New York: Columbia University Press, 2015). For an "authors face their critics" roundtable, see "The War over Israel's Influence," *FP Roundtable* (July/August 2006): 57–66. For an excellent example

of campaigns of vilification and ostracism against those perceived by lobby-affiliated Israel advocates as threatening the boundaries they enforce on publicly acceptable discourse, see the successful effort to prevent Dartmouth College from naming as its dean of faculty someone who had four years earlier signed a statement of support for boycotting Israeli academic institutions implicated in the occupation in Colleen Flaherty, "Blacklisted for BDS?," *Inside Higher Ed*, May 23, 2017, https://www.insidehighered.com/news/2017/05/23/popular-native-american-studies-scholar-declines-deanship-dartmouth-amid-concerns. Groups such as Canary Mission, Campus Watch, and CAMERA have long invested great efforts in publicly scorning scholars, journalists, activists, and others as anti-Semitic for their criticisms of Israel or of the Israel lobby. The author has been among those subjected to this treatment by each of these organizations. See "Ian Lustick," Canary Mission, https://canarymission.org/professor/Ian_Lustick; search engine results for "Lustick" at Middle East Forum, https://www.meforum.org/search.php?cx=partner-pub-2951801646144412%3Ap24ltemdv6f&cof=FORID%3A9&ie=UTF-8&q=lustick&sa=Search; Dexter Van Zile, "Ian Lustick Needs a New Map (and Flare Gun)," CAMERA, March 28, 2013, http://www.camera.org/index.asp?x_context=2&x_outlet=33&x_article=2425.

52. For extensive documentation of lobby efforts from 2006 to 2015 to patrol and enforce limits to debate about Israel, see records kept at the website MuzzleWatch, http://muzzlewatch.com/. See also Jewish Voice for Peace, *Stifling Dissent: How Israel's Defenders Use False Charges of Anti-Semitism to Limit the Debate over Israel on Campus*, Fall 2015, http://stiflingdissent.org/; Sara Roy, "Reflections on the Israeli-Palestinian Conflict in U.S. Public Discourse: Legitimizing Dissent," *Journal of Palestine Studies* 39, no. 2 (Winter 2010): 23–38; Leslie Wagner, "Watching the Pro-Israeli Academic Watchers," *Jewish Political Studies Review* 23, no. 12 (November 15, 2010); *We Will Not Be Silenced: The Academic Repression of Israel's Critics*, ed. William I. Robinson and Maryam S. Griffin (Chico: AK Press, 2017). One contribution in this volume, by David Theo Goldberg and Saree Makdisi, was originally published as "The Trial of Israel's Campus Critics," *Tikkun Magazine* (September–October 2009), http://www.tikkun.org/article.php/sept_oct_09_goldberg_makdisi. For a response to this piece from one of the lobby's watchdogs that unintentionally corroborates their argument, see Tammi Rossman-Benjamin, "Campus Critics on Trial," *American Thinker*, November 1, 2009, http://www.americanthinker.com/articles/2009/11/campus_critics_on_trial.html; "Palestine and the Public Sphere," Eva Cheniavsky, ed., *South Atlantic Quarterly* 117: 1 (January 2018): 190–234.

53. Shai Franklin, "Road Testing Natan Sharansky's 3 D's of Anti-Semitism," *Huffington Post*, July 29, 2013, https://www.huffingtonpost.com/shai-franklin /road-testing-natan-sharanskys-criteria-for-anti-semitism-_b_3346143.html; Eric Marx, "Sharansky Article on Campus Tour Irks Hillel Leader," *Forward*, October 31, 2003, https://forward.com/news/6948/sharansky-article-on-campus -tour-irks-hillel-leade/; Robert Wiener, "Sharansky Sees Campuses as Jewish Battleground," *New Jersey Jewish News*, May 25, 2011, http://njjewishnews.com /article/5011/sharansky-sees-campuses-as-jewish=-battleground. For a portrayal of American campuses as a dangerous place for Jews based on Sharansky's characterization of them as "islands of anti-Semitism," see Harold Brackman, *Anti-Semitism on Campus: A Clear and Present Danger*, Report for the Simon Wisenthal Center, June 12, 2015.

54. Against fierce resistance by executive branch officials, the lobby forced the State Department to adopt an expansive "working definition" of anti-Semitism that enshrined much of Sharansky's language. One clever aspect of the "double standard" criterion is that any criticism of Israel can be classified as the result of a double standard by treating the object of criticism as belonging to a more general category than that intended by the critic. Israel's half-century occupation of Palestinian territory puts it in a small category of states promoted as Western democracies that rule large noncitizen populations by force of arms. When Israel is criticized for its harsh occupation policies toward Palestinians, the double-standard accusation is made because not all states that treat minorities harshly are being criticized as regularly. Such criticism is attacked as a double standard by identifying the relevant category as "all states," not as all Western-supported states ruling large noncitizen populations for half a century.

55. Eric Marx, "Sharansky Article on Campus Tour Irks Hillel Leader," *Forward*, October 31, 2003, https://forward.com/news/6948/sharansky-article-on -campus-tour-irks-hillel-leade/.

56. Israel on Campus Coalition, "2016–2017 Annual Report," https:// israelcc.org/wp-content/uploads/2017/09/2016-2017-Year-End-Report.pdf; see also https://israelcc.org/about-icc/. The ICC has been joined by another similar group, Students Supporting Israel, funded by the Adam Milstein Family Foundation; https://www.milsteinff.org/supported-organizations/students -supporting-israel-ssi/.

57. Peter Schmidt, "Bias Charges Divide Jewish Groups," *Chronicle of Higher Education*, April 22, 2012, https://www.chronicle.com/article/Bias -Charges-Divide-Jewish/131613. California campuses were a special focus of these accusations. In response, Stanford University's Research Group in Education and Jewish Studies interviewed students at six leading California campuses

and found no evidence that Jewish students felt intimidated. Those surveyed were reported to "dismiss claims that their campuses were either anti-Semitic or unsafe" but did consider debates over the Israel-Palestine conflict as being unnecessarily divisive and alienating. Ari Y. Kelman, Abiya Ahmed, Ilana Horwitz, Jeremiah Lockwood, Marva Shalev Marom, and Maja Zuckerman, *Safe and on the Sidelines: Jewish Students and the Israel-Palestine Conflict on Campus* Stanford Graduate School of Education (September 2017).

58. Robert Satloff, "Advice from a Parent: How to Navigate the Politics of Israel on the Campus," Washington Institute for Near East Policy, posted on Facebook, August 18, 2015, YouTube, https://www.youtube.com/watch?v=saT5jmKsib0. Much of the effort to prevent, disrupt, or punish speech or events on campuses deemed overly critical of Israel is conducted behind the scenes and is very difficult to document. An invaluable insider account, set in York University in Toronto, Canada, is Susan G. Drummond, *Unthinkable Thoughts: Academic Freedom and the One-State Model for Israel and Palestine* (Vancouver: UBC Press, 2013). See also Joan W. Scott, "Introduction to Academic Boycotts," *Academe* 2, no. 5 (September–October 2006): 35–38; Matthew Abraham, *Out of Bounds: Academic Freedom and the Question of Palestine* (New York: Bloomsbury, 2014).

59. The quote is from Morton Klein, president of the Zionist Organization of America. Nathan Guttman, "Secret Sheldon Adelson Summit Raises Up to $50M for Strident Anti-BDS Push," Forward, June 9, 2015, https://forward.com /news/israel/309676/secret-sheldon-adelson-summit-raises-up-to-50m-for -strident-anti-bds-push/.

60. In the 1970s the most popular publication for assisting Israel advocates on American campuses engaged substantive issues directly. See Benny Neuberger, *A Speakers' Manual of the Arab-Israel Conflict* (New York: n.p., 1970, 1971, 1975). By contrast, see the entirely brand- and spin-oriented works currently distributed, such as *Hasbara Handbook: Promoting Israel on Campus*, published by the World Union of Jewish Students in 2002 (supported by the Jewish Agency for Israel, among others); Frank Luntz, *The Israel Project's Global Dictionary* (n.p.: n.p., 2009), https://www.transcend.org /tms/wp-content/uploads/2014/07/sf-israel-projects-2009-global-language -dictionary.pdf.

61. Milstein, a close associate of Sheldon Adelson, has denied the report while acknowledging his funding of other similarly purposed organizations. Canary Mission still refuses to identify its funding sources. See "Pro-Israel Donor Adam Milstein Denies Report That He Funds Canary Mission," Jewish Telegraph Agency, August 27, 2018, https://www.jta.org/2018/08/27/news

-opinion/united-states/pro-israel-donor-adam-milstein-denies-report-funds
-canary-mission.

62. For lists of state legislation and executive orders against the BDS movement, see "Anti-Semitism: State Anti-BDS Legislation," Jewish Virtual Library, http://www.jewishvirtuallibrary.org/anti-bds-legislation; "Anti-Palestinian Legislation," Palestine Legal, https://palestinelegal.org/righttoboycott/.

63. Under Texas's anti-BDS law (subsequently overturned by the courts) an Arabic-speaking speech pathologist was fired by an Austin-area school district for refusing to sign an oath promising not to boycott Israel. Julian Gill, "Texas Speech Pathologist Fired by School District for Refusing to Sign Pro-Israel Oath," December 17, 2018, https://www.houstonchronicle.com/news /houston-texas/houston/article/Texas-speech-pathologist-fired-by-school -district-13472052.php.

64. According to the ranking member of the Pennsylvania House of Representatives committee responsible for considering anti-BDS legislation, few legislators believed that the proposal (later passed into law) was either warranted or constitutional, but that overwhelming and one-sided political pressure made its passage virtually inevitable. Author interview with Representative James Roebuck, July 15, 2015, Philadelphia.

65. Concerning the Anti-Israel Boycott Act, first introduced in the House in March 2017, see "H.R.1697—Israel Anti-Boycott Act," U.S. Congress, https://www.congress.gov/bill/115th-congress/house-bill/1697; Joshua Sharf, "Federal Anti-BDS Legislation—Common Sense and Constitutional," *The Hill*, August 14, 2017. For AIPAC's endorsement of the Combating BDS Act of 2017," see "The Combating BDS Act of 2017 (S. 170 and H.R.2856)," AIPAC, December 2017, https://www.aipac.org/learn/legislative-agenda/-media /052b78c518304d318f46385f1b172e2d.ashx. See also Ryan Grim and Alex Emmons, "Senators Working to Slip Israel Anti-Boycott Law Through in Lame Duck," The Intercept, December 4, 2018, https://theintercept.com/2018/12/04 /israel-anti-boycott-act-lame-duck/.

66. Hannan Adely, "U.S. Department of Education Reopens Case Against Rutgers Alleging Anti-Semitism," September 9, 2012, northjersey.com, https:// www.northjersey.com/story/news/education/2018/09/12/case-against-rutgers -university-alleging-atmosphere-anti-semitism-reopened/1276968002/.

67. Amy Kaplan, *Our American Israel: The Story of an Entangled Alliance* (Cambridge, MA: Harvard University Press, 2018).

68. For a sympathetic treatment of Israeli-American relations that yet portrays the two countries as being akin to a dysfunctional family, see Melman and Raviv, *Friends in Deed*, pp. 74–75.

69. Terry Karl, *The Paradox of Plenty: Oil Booms and Petro-States* (Berkeley: University of California Press, 1997), pp. 5–12.

70. See interview with Arthur Hertzberg, "Advice and Consent," *New Outlook* 19, no. 6 (September–October 1976): 6–11; Daniel Amit, "Piecing Together the Mideast Puzzle," *New Outlook* 19, no. 5 (July–August 1976): 24–31.

71. Nahum Goldmann, "Israel Facing a New Reality," *New Outlook* 17, no. 3 (March–April 1974): 7–18.

72. Naftali Ben-Moshe, "Peace or Strategic Depth: Who Should Beat His Breast?," *Al-Hamishmar*, November 27, 1973. See also Arie (Lova) Eliav, "The Times They Are a'Changing," *New Outlook* 19, no. 4 (June 1976): 18–20; Yeshiyahu Leibovitz, "Occupation and Terror," *New Outlook* 19, no. 6 (September–October 1976): 56–58, esp. 56.

73. "Elections, Weapons and Wars," *New Outlook* 19, no. 7 (November 1976): 3–4.

74. David Landau, "Lewis Must Answer for His Softness on Begin," *Jerusalem Post*, August 31, 1982. In 1990 Landau led a walkout of half the *Jerusalem Post*'s editorial board when that newspaper, under new ownership, shifted its editorial line sharply to the right. In 2003 he made waves with more graphic language than he used in 1982 to make the same point. At a private dinner in 2003 with Condoleezza Rice he told the secretary of state that Israel was a "a failed state" that needed to be "raped" by the United States in the form of "more vigorous U.S. intervention in the affairs of the Middle East." While Landau was severely criticized for his remarks and while Rice rejected his suggestion for forcible U.S. action, it was also reported that he "had been congratulated by several professors at the dinner who felt he 'articulated what many Israelis feel.'" Ezra HaLevi, "*Haaretz* Editor Asked US Secretary of State to 'Rape' Israel," Arutz Sheva, July 2, 2017, http://www.israelnationalnews.com/News/News.aspx/124729. On Lewis's pro-Begin sympathies, see also Melman and Raviv, *Friends in Deed*, p. 180.

75. Israel Defense Forces Radio, September 1, 1982, Broadcast transcribed by the Foreign Broadcast Information Service, *Daily Report: Middle East and Africa* 5, no. 171 (September 2, 1982): I3.

76. Jerusalem Domestic Television Service, September 1, 1982, Broadcast transcribed by the Foreign Broadcast Information Service, *Daily Report: Middle East and Africa* 5, no. 171 (September 2, 1982): I4.

77. Jerusalem Domestic Service, September 1, 1982, Radio broadcast transcribed by the Foreign Broadcast Information Service, *Daily Report: Middle East and Africa* 5, no. 171 (September 2, 1982): I4.

78. On the failure of the Reagan administration to follow through on Reagan's speech in any meaningful way, see Rashid Khalidi, *Brokers of Deceit: How the US Has Undermined Peace in the Middle East* (Boston: Beacon Press, 2013), pp. 16–28.

79. *Al-Hamishmar* (Mapam), as cited by Thomas L. Friedman, "America in the Mind of Israel," *New York Times Magazine*, May 25, 1986, p. 28.

80. Gloria H. Falk, "Israeli Public Opinion: Looking Toward a Palestinian Solution," *Middle East Journal* 39, no. 3 (Summer 1985): 265–66.

81. Gabriel Sheffer, "Global and Local Processes and the Weakening of Israeli Political Institutions," *Haaretz*, March 14, 1984.

82. Moshe Zak, "Fans of the Whip," *Maariv*, February 19, 1988.

83. Yossi Sarid, "The Imposed Solution, It Is Arriving," *Haaretz*, February 25, 1988. On the value of Palestinian resistance "because it takes us out of our dulled dependence on the myth of doing nothing because time is on our side," see Yoel Marcus, "It is Good That It Happened," *Haaretz*, February 12, 1988.

84. Amir Oren, "Pay-Up Now," *Davar*, February 19, 1988.

85. In a small group consultation in the Oval Office with the president and his top advisers that preceded this meeting, President Bush gave the author a jolting preview of the substance and tone of what he planned to say to Prime Minister Yitzhak Shamir. According to Melman and Raviv the meeting was "a case of hate at first sight. Never in the history of relations between the two countries was there such antipathy—true emotional dislike—between their heads of government." Melman and Raviv, *Friends in Deed*, p. 411.

86. See Nahum Barnea, "The First Day in the New and Difficult Life of Yitzhak Shamir," *Yediot Acharonot*, July 7, 1989; Ilan Kfir, "It's Not the Weather Forecast, It Is already Raining," *Hadashot*, May 25, 1990.

87. Alon Pinkas, "He Is Independent, So He Does Not Need Instructions," *Davar*, June 28, 1991, as translated and reproduced in *From the Hebrew Press* 3, no. 8 (August 1991): 11–12.

88. Wolf Blitzer, "U.S. Sources Say Baker May Send Envoys to Mideast," *Jerusalem Post*, October 8, 1989.

89. Michal Yudelman, "Peace Camp's Visit to U.S. Draws Wide Criticism," *Jerusalem Post*, May 6, 1991.

90. Oded Lifshitz, "Ironically, Sanctions Work," *Al-HaMishmar*, May 17, 1991.

91. Amnon Abramovitz, "Dear Secretary of State," *Maariv*, March 8, 1991.

92. Yossi Sarid, "Sharon's Fork," *Haaretz*, September 12, 1991.

93. Yoel Marcus, "They Destroyed Our Myth," *Haaretz*, October 11, 1991. For the extent to which Shamir was relying on the clout of the Israel lobby and a contemporary version of the anti-Semitic myth of Jewish power—the "Protocols of the Elders of Zion"—see Nahum Barnea, "The War Over the 'Protocols,'" *Yediot Acharonot*, September 13, 1991.

94. Boas Evron, "Gabi, the Message Has Been Understood," *Yediot Acharonot*, October 18, 1991.

95. Excerpts of Bush's remarks are in "Documents and Source Material," *Journal of Palestine Studies* (Autumn 1991): 185–86.

96. Five months earlier American Friends for Peace Now, an organization supportive of Israeli doves, announced a campaign to send 1,000 letters and telegrams to President Bush supporting his activist policies toward peace. The contrast here is unmistakable. For every letter or telegram that American Friends for Peace Now could hope to send to the president, AIPAC could send a lobbyist to Capitol Hill. Jonathan Jacoby, President, American Friends for Peace Now, "Dear Friend Letter," April 8, 1991.

97. "Excerpts from President Bush's News Session on Israeli Loan Guarantees," *New York Times*, September 12, 1991.

98. Akiva Eldar, "Guaranteeing the Continuation of the Occupation," *Haaretz*, September 5, 1991.

99. Daniel Ben-Simon, "Baker Is the Main Opposition," *Davar*, October 7, 1991.

100. Baruch Kimmerling, "The Counter-Revolution of 1992," *Haaretz*, March 13, 1992.

101. Eldar, "Guaranteeing the Continuation of the Occupation." See also Hillel Schenker, "We Must Continue the Struggle: An Interview with M. K. Shulamit Aloni," *Israel Horizons* (Spring 1992): pp. 7–10, esp. p. 9.

102. See Efraim Halevy, *Man in the Shadows* (New York: St. Martin's, 2006), p. 72. On the general strategy of a U.S. foreign policy based on dissociation from Israel's settlement policy as a way to productively divide the Israeli electorate, see Ian S. Lustick, "Israeli Politics and American Foreign Policy," *Foreign Affairs* 61, no. 2 (Winter 1982–1983): 379–99.

103. On April 1, 1992, the Senate passed a resolution by a vote of 99–1 calling on the president to extend loan guarantees to Israel, making no mention of settlements.

104. On the political price Bush paid for his defiance of the Israel lobby, see Glenn Frankel, "A Beautiful Friendship?," *Washington Post Magazine*, July 16, 2006. One Israeli commentator quipped that Yitzhak Shamir had even more

justification for celebrating Bush's defeat than did Saddam Hussein, since Bush had been unable to oust Hussein but did displace Shamir. Ran Kislev, "A Bit of Pressure, Please," *Haaretz*, November 9, 1991.

105. Ran Kislev, "A Bit of Pressure, Please."

106. Ibid.

107. Ze'ev Sternhell, "Strong American Pressure Is Necessary," *Haaretz*, March 5, 1993.

108. See Leon Hadar, "Clinton's Tilt," *Journal of Palestine Studies* 22, no. 4 (Summer 1993): 62–72.

109. See, e.g., David Com, "Why Now's Right for Obama to Go Bad Cop on Bibi," Congressional Quarterly, May 18, 2009, http://archive.peacenow.org /entries/archive6216.

110. Ben Caspit, "Building a Crisis," *Maariv*, June 7, 2009.

111. "Netanyahu's Refusal to Extend Settlement Freeze Is Hurting Israel," *Haaretz*, November 5, 2010, https://www.haaretz.com/1.5135661.

112. Akiva Eldar, "Thank You, Obama, for Showing the Israeli Left Your True Colors," *Haaretz*, February 21, 2011.

113. Chemi Shalev, "Israelis Support Equal Rights for Reform and Conservative Jews—But Want U.S. Jews to Keep Their Mouths Shut," *Haaretz*, July 4, 2018.

114. Asher Schechter, "Leftists Crushed, Israel's Right-Wing Starts Gnawing on Itself," *Haaretz*, December 16, 2016. See also Rory Jones, "Opinion Shift in Israel Fuels Dispute with U.S.," *Wall Street Journal*, December 31, 2016–January 1, 2017; Joseph Alpher, *No End of Conflict: Rethinking Israel-Palestine* (Lanham, MD: Rowman and Littlefield, 2016), pp. xii, 29.

115. Isaac Chotiner, "Michael Oren Cuts Short a Conversation about Israel," *New Yorker*, May 11, 2019, https://www.newyorker.com/news/q-and-a /michael-oren-hangs-up-on-a-call-about-israel.

116. See Yoram Peri's authoritative treatment of both the changes and limits in Rabin's thinking in *Yitzhak Rabin: The Rabin Memoirs* (Berkeley: University of California Press, 1996), pp. 35–62.

117. On the well-considered and systematically implemented strategy that Netanyahu used to destroy the Oslo process, see Ian S. Lustick, "Ending Protracted Conflicts: The Oslo Peace Process Between Political Partnership and Legality," *Cornell International Law Journal* (1997): 101–17.

118. See Aaron David Miller, "Israel's Lawyer," *Washington Post*, May 23, 2005. There is a vast and contentious literature on what happened at Camp David and who was to blame for the failure. For a brief analysis, the report of

Robert Malley, who was directly involved in the negotiations, is most reliable. Robert Malley and Hussein Agha, "Camp David: The Tragedy of Errors," *New York Review of Books,* August 9, 2001.

119. Author's notes, Hebrew University, Mt. Scopus Campus, Jerusalem, November 8, 2010.

120. Joseph Alpher, *Periphery: Israel's Search for Middle East Allies* (Lanham, MD: Rowan and Littlefield, 2015), p. 140.

Chapter 4

1. A heuristic is a rule for learning. See Imre Lakatos, "Falsification and the Methodology of Scientific Research Programmes," in *Criticism and the Growth of Knowledge,* ed. Imre Lakatos and Alan Musgrave (Cambridge: Cambridge University Press, 1970), pp. 133–38.

2. In their colloquial usage and in my treatment the terms "research program" and "paradigm" are interchangeable. I use the Lakatosian vocabulary associated with research programs to analyze the crisis encountered by the TSS paradigm because it is both richer and more precise than the language used by Thomas Kuhn in his discussion of the rise and decline of paradigms.

3. Despite its scientific flaws, phlogiston chemistry formed the basis of a thriving metallurgy industry in eighteenth-century Germany. For a discussion of how typical it is that scientists operating in new paradigms can offer exhilarating new perspectives, but yet not solve standard problems as well as those using the established ideas they will eventually displace, see Thomas S. Kuhn, *The Structure of Scientific Revolutions,* 2nd ed. (Chicago: University of Chicago Press, 1970), pp. 152–59.

4. Ibid., p. 94.

5. For early thinking in Israel and in the West Bank about establishing an independent Palestinian "entity" or state, see the London journal *New Middle East,* secretly funded by the Israeli Foreign Ministry from 1968 to 1973 and summarily closed when its editorial line strayed far from the government's: Avicenna, "Breaking the Circle," *New Middle East,* no. 4 (January 1969): 31–32; Averroes, "A Homeland, Not a Home," *New Middle East,* no. 10 (July 1969): 10; Uri Avnery, "Unofficial and Unrepresentative But . . . ," *New Middle East,* no. 12 (September 1969): 23–28; Aziz Shihadeh, "Must History Repeat Itself? The Palestinian Entity and Its Enemies," *New Middle East,* no. 28 (January 1971): 36–37; and a review by Nissim Rejwan of the 1971 book *No Peace Without a Free Palestinian State* by the West Bank Palestinian

intellectual Muhammed Abu Shilbaya, *New Middle East*, no. 39 (December 1971): 37–39. See also Ian Lustick, "What West Bank Arabs Think," *Jewish Frontier* (June 1970): 13–19.

6. Whether sincerely pursued or not, this was the overall framework within which Prime Minister Rabin authorized his foreign minister to begin the negotiations with the PLO that resulted in the Oslo agreements. See Avi Shilon, *The Left-Wing's Sorrow: The Crisis of the Peace Camp; The Untold Story* Hevel Modi'in: Kinneret, Zmora-Bitan, Dvir, 2017), p. 420.

7. Anthony Lewis, "Five Minutes to Midnight," *New York Times*, November 1, 1982.

8. "Summary of a Conversation with Meron Benvenisti" (mimeo), American Enterprise Institute, Washington, DC, October 27, 1983.

9. On the relationship between Benvenisti's analysis and that contained in Israeli government/Jewish Agency plans to advance Jewish settlement and Israeli incorporation of the West Bank, see Ian Lustick, "Israeli State-Building on the West Bank and the Gaza Strip: Theory and Practice," *International Organization* 41, no. 1 (Winter 1987): 151–71.

10. Ian Lustick, "Israel and the West Bank after Elon Moreh: The Mechanics of De Facto Annexation," *Middle East Journal* 35, no. 4 (Autumn 1981): 557–77.

11. Yehuda Litani, "Operation: 'The Fate of the Land of Israel,'" *Haaretz*, July 15, 1980.

12. Geoffrey Aronson, "And Quickly Grow the Settlements," *Middle East International*, no. 146 (March 27, 1981): 11.

13. Dozens of articles by Benvenisti or about his work and his sensational analyses and predictions appeared in major media outlets between December 1982 and February 1985. These included the *New York Times*, the *Washington Post*, the *New York Review of Books*, the *Christian Science Monitor, Maariv*, and *Haaretz*.

14. Shmuel Toledano, "Those Who Prophesy Doom Are Right," *Haaretz*, April 6, 1982. See also Yosef Goell, "Stumbling Blocks," *Jerusalem Post*, January 28, 1983.

15. "Quasi Faits Accomplis," *Haaretz*, January 14, 1983. See also remarks by Yehuda Litani and Dani Rubinstein in Goga Kogan, "Knowing the West Bank from the Inside," *Al-HaMishmar*, April 1, 1983.

16. "Stepping Up Annexation," *Haaretz*, February 26, 1983. See also Amos Elon, "The View from Mount Gerizim," *Haaretz*, February 4, 1983; Hirsh Goodman, "Questions of Democracy," *Jerusalem Post*, August 19, 1983; Lova Eliav, "Sever Israel's Twin," *New York Times*, October 13, 1983.

17. "International Peace Seminar Held in Jerusalem," *Jerusalem Post*, March 20, 1983.

18. Translated from *Ha'olam Hazeh,* March 16, 1983, in *Joint Publication Research Service Report: Near East and South Asia*, No. 83216, April 7, 1983. Similar observations and warnings were made by many Palestinian notables in the occupied territories.

19. Amman Domestic Service, January 10, 1983, speech transcribed by the Foreign Broadcast Information Service, *Daily Report: Middle East and Africa* 5, no. 007 (January 11, 1983): F7.

20. King Hussein interview with British Broadcasting Television, January 19, 1984, in *Jordan Times*, January 25, 1984, transcribed by the Foreign Broadcast Information Service, *Daily Report: Middle East and Africa* 5, no. 18 (January 26, 1984): F1, F5.

21. For comments by Yasser Arafat, see Land Day Speech in Damascus, Voice of the PLO, Baghdad, March 31, 1983, transcribed by the Foreign Broadcast Information Service, *Daily Report: Middle East and Africa* 5, no. 56 (March 22, 1983): A3; interview, Budapest Domestic Television Service, April 21, 1983, transcribed by the Foreign Broadcast Information Service, *Daily Report: Middle East and Africa* 5, no. 79 (April 22, 1983): A4. For comments by Farouk Qaddumi, see "Qaddumi on U.S. Pressure," Voice of the PLO, Baghdad, April 9, 1983, transcribed by by the Foreign Broadcast Information Service, *Daily Report: Middle East and Africa* 5, no. 70 (April 22, 1983): A5. For comments by Khalil al-Wazir, see "Al-Wazir on Ties with Jordan, U.S. Peace Plan," *Jordan Times*, March 21, 1983, transcribed by by the Foreign Broadcast Information Service, *Daily Report: Middle East and Africa* 5, no. 56 (March 22, 1983): A3.

22. For an angry reaction by a dovish Israeli journalist, see Tzvi Bar'el, "It Is Still Reversible," *Haaretz*, August 22, 1983.

23. See Aryeh Dayan, "The Last Option: Reactions," *Koteret Rashit* 68 (March 21, 1984): 18; Ariel Sharon, Israel Defense Forces broadcast, December 21, 1982, transcribed by the Foreign Broadcast Information Service, *Daily Report: Middle East and Africa 5, no. 246* (December 22, 1982): I3; "David Levi Interviewed on Syria Buildup Statement," *Yediot Acharonot*, November 25, 1983, transcribed by the Foreign Broadcast Information Service, *Daily Report: Middle East and Africa* 5, no. 229 (November 28, 1983): I5. For other delighted endorsements of Benvenisti's findings from settlement planners and right-wing officials and activists, see Minister of Communications Mordechai Tzippori, ITIM, October 24, 1983, in *Joint Publication Research Service Report: Near East and South Asia*, No. 84669, November 2, 1983; Ehud Olmert, *Harper's*

Magazine, December 1984, p. 47; Meir Ben-Gur, "Benvenisti's Lesson," *Maariv*, April 30, 1984.

24. "The End of an Era" [Hebrew], *Nekuda*, no. 75 (July 6, 1984): 6. To be sure, some settler activists remained concerned that de facto annexation was not quite so close to the point of no return as they wished it to be. For urgent appeals to expand settlements decisively before the opportunity to close the door on withdrawal was gone, see multiple articles and editorials in *Nekuda*, cited in Ian S. Lustick, *Unsettled States, Disputed Lands: Britain and Ireland, France and Algeria, Israel and the West Bank-Gaza* (Ithaca, NY: Cornell University Press, 1993), pp. 18, 463.

25. "From Israel: Keeping Israel Jewish," interview with Abba Eban, *Moment* 7 (June 1982): 26, 29. See also remarks by former Labor Party secretary-general Lova Eliav, quoted by Anthony Lewis in "Israel's West Bank Harvest," *New York Times*, July 22, 1984; A. Schweitzer, "The Illusion of Settlement," *Haaretz*, December 3, 1982; Aryeh Yaari, "The French Case," *Al-Hamishmar*, July 15, 1984; Raanan Weitz, "Facts on Paper in the West Bank," *Haaretz*, April 24, 1985; "The Prospects for the Peace Process," *New Outlook* 28, no. 7 (July 1985): 37–38; Yehoshaphat Harkabi, *The Arab-Israeli Conflict: Future Perspective* [pamphlet] (Tel Aviv: International Center for Peace in the Middle East, June 1985). For extended treatment of variations in hawkish and dovish responses to the argument in the 1980s that the settlements were irreversibly integrating the West Bank and Gaza into Israel, see Ian S. Lustick, *The "Irreversibility" of Israel's Annexation of the West Bank and Gaza Strip: A Critical Evaluation* (Alexandria, VA: Defense Technical Information Center, October 1985), http://www.dtic.mil/docs/citations/ADA161561.

26. Joel Brinkley, "Hard Facts Defeat Israeli Researcher," *New York Times*, October 22, 1989; recording of Meron Benvenisti Lecture, Van Leer Institute, Jerusalem, Israel, January 30, 1990, transcribed by the author.

27. Under the provisions of the Oslo Accords, the West Bank (apart from Israeli settlements) was to be divided into three zones during the transition to final status arrangements. Area A was composed of major cities where the PA was to have civil and primary security control; in Area B, composed of smaller towns and villages, security control was to be shared, while in Area C Israel would exercise exclusive control.

28. Lakatos explains that paradigms under pressure typically seek to protect their hard-core assumptions by adding "ceteris paribus assumptions," that is, by listing new conditions as necessary for predictions to be valid. Proliferation of such excuses usually means the research program has entered its

"degenerative phase." Lakatos, "Falsification and the Methodology of Scientific Research Programmes," pp. 154–59.

29. Yotam Berger, "How Many Settlers Really Live in the West Bank? Haaretz Investigation Reveals," *Haaretz*, June 15, 2017.

30. Shaul Arieli, *Why Settlements Have Not Killed the Two State Solution* (Bicom: Britain Israel Communications & Research Centre, January 7, 2013), p. 2. Arieli's analysis is used as an exemplar here because of his prominence, but other studies could be subjected to equivalent critiques such as David Makovsky, *Imagining the Border: Options for Resolving the Israeli-Palestinian Territorial Issue* (Washington, DC: Washington Institute for Near East Policy, 2011); Orni Petruschka and Gilead Sher, "Don't Believe the Hype: The Settlers Have Not Made the TSS Unachievable," *Fathom*, March 29, 2017, http://fathomjournal.org/dont-believe-the-hype-the-settlers-have-not-made-the-two-state-solution-unachievable/.

31. Arieli, *Why Settlements Have Not Killed the Two State Solution*, p. 3.

32. Ibid.

33. Ibid., p. 5. In his book on the problem of achieving partition, Arieli details arrangements and compromises to facilitate successful negotiations but never discusses how Israeli politicians capable of implementing his advice could come to power. Shaul Arieli, *A Border Between Us and You* [Hebrew] (Tel Aviv: Sifriat Aliyat Hagagg, 2013).

34. Shaul Arieli, "Settlement Movement Isn't Growing the Way You Thought It Was," *Haaretz*, March 5, 2017.

35. Dan Ephron, "The Battle to Capture Territory in the West Bank Ended Quickly. The Battle to Capture Israeli Hearts and Minds Took Much Longer," *Washington Post*, June 1, 2017. For a more recent and more desperate attempt to map settlements that will and will not be evacuated so as to preserve the idea of the possibility of a TSS, see Ori Mark, "You Lost," *Haaretz*, August 17, 2018. For an analysis of this effort pointing to the author's need to completely ignore the unacceptability of the shredded geography associated with this new picture of a Palestinian state, see Meron Rapaport, "In Advocating for a Palestinian State, *Haaretz* Forgets about the Palestinians," *+972 Magazine*, August 21, 2018, https://972mag.com/in-advocating-for-a-palestinian-state-haaretz-forgets-about-the-palestinians/137395/.

36. This was Arieli's conclusion to his contribution to the symposium "Is the Two State Solution Dead?," *Moment*, no. 3 (May–June 2013): 30. In the same symposium another two-stater, Dror Moreh, described his pessimism about future prospects for peace based on two states because "there is simply no will" to make it a reality (ibid., p. 35).

37. "Rabin: In the Golan Life Is More Secure Than in Tel-Aviv and Bat-Yam," interview with Moshe Vardi, *Yediot Acharonot*, September 4, 1992.

38. On the impossibility of the Israeli Left's success without an alliance with Arabs in Israel, see "The Zionist Left Needs to Understand That Change Is Impossible Without Us': An Interview with MK Ayman Odeh," *Fathom*, Summer 2017, http://fathomjournal.org/the-zionist-left-needs-to-understand -that-change-is-impossible-without-us-an-interview-with-mk-ayman-odeh/. Odeh's argument was corroborated by the results of the April 2019 election, as many observers commented. See, e.g., Raoul Wootliff, "Netanyahu Won, Everyone Else Lost: 5 Takeaways from the 2019 Elections," *Times of Israel*, April 10, 2019, https://www.timesofisrael.com/netanyahu-won-everyone-else-lost-5 -takeaways-from-the-2019-elections/; Mazal Mualem, "Israeli-Arabs Key to Returning the Center-Left to Power," Al-Monitor, May 8, 2019, https://www .al-monitor.com/pulse/originals/2019/05/israel-arab-parties-benny-gantz -demography-elections-meretz.html#ixzz5osEP6OU2.

39. For details on this controversy, see Ian S. Lustick, "What Counts Is the Counting: Statistical Manipulation as a Solution to Israel's 'Demographic Problem,'" *Middle East Journal* 67, no. 2 (Spring 2013): 185–205.

40. Danny Gutwein, "The Settlements and the Relationship Between Privatization and the Occupation," in *Normalizing Occupation: The Politics of Everyday Life in the West Bank Settlements*, ed. Marco Allegra, Ariel Handel and Erez Maggor, pp. 21–33 (Bloomington: Indiana University Press, 2017).

41. Bernard Avishai, "May 5, 2014: Israel's Independence Day, and Its Future," *New Yorker*, https://www.newyorker.com/news/news-desk/israels -independence-day-and-its-future.

42. Bernard Avishai, "The Trouble with Israel," *Harper's Magazine* (August 2015): 32.

43. Bernard Avishai, "Confederation: The One Possible Israel-Palestine Solution," *New York Review of Books*, February 2, 2018, http://www.nybooks .com/daily/2018/02/02/confederation-the-one-possible-israel-palestine -solution/.

44. Judy Dempsey, "Judy Asks: Is the TSS Over?," Judy Dempsey's Strategic Europe, Carnegie Europe, December 13, 2017, https://carnegieeurope.eu /strategiceurope/75000. See comments by Jonas Parello-Plesner, Shimon Stein, and Paul Taylor. For other often admittedly desperate invocations of a change in U.S. policy as necessary for achieving a TSS, see Paul Pillar, "Palestine and the New Peacemakers," *National Interest*, March 8, 2018, http://nationalinterest.org/blog /paul-pillar/palestine-the-new-peacemakers-20519; Mara Rudman and Brian Katulis, "A Practical Plan on the Israeli-Palestinian Front," Center for American

Progress, December 21, 2016, https://www.americanprogress.org/issues/security/reports/2016/12/21/295552/apracticalplanontheisraelipalestinianfront/; Daniel Kurtzer, "Waiting for Uncle Sam," *The Cairo Review of Global Affairs*, Fall 2017, https://www.thecairoreview.com/essays/waiting-for-uncle-sam/.

45. "Friedman Says Israel Shouldn't Have to Ask US Approval to Build in West Bank: Report," Middle East Eye, September 8, 2018, https://www.middleeasteye.net/news/friedman-says-israel-shouldnt-have-ask-us-approval-build-west-bank-report; Raphael Ahren, "As US appears to Back West Bank Annexations, Is Its Peace Plan Dead on Arrival?," *Times of Israel*, April 16, 2019, https://www.timesofisrael.com/as-us-appears-to-back-west-bank-annexations-is-its-peace-plan-dead-on-arrival/; Henry Storey, "Kushner's Peace Plan vs. Palestine's National Aspirations," *Foreign Brief*, April 15, 2019, https://foreignbrief.com/middle-east/kushners-peace-plan-vs-palestines-national-aspirations/#.

46. Gershon Shafir, *A Half Century of Occupation: Israel, Palestine, and the World's Most Intractable Conflict* (Berkeley: University of California Press, 2017), p. 164.

47. Jeff Halper, "The 'Two-State Solution' Only Ever Meant a Big Israel Ruling over a Palestinian Bantustan. Let It Go," *Haaretz*, January 18, 2018.

48. Interview with Robert Gates, CBS, *Face the Nation*, May 13, 2018, https://www.cbsnews.com/news/robert-gates-tells-face-the-nation-that-two-state-solution-between-israelis-palestinians-on-life-support/; Ilan Peleg, remarks at Association of Israel Studies Conference, Berkeley, California, June 26, 2018.

49. Quoted by Ben Norton, "Avi Shlaim on Liberal Zionism, the 'Dead' Two-State Solution, and Colonial Pizza," *Mondoweiss*, April 28, 2018; Husam Zomlot, "US Move 'Kiss of Death' to the Two-State Solution," Al Jazeera, December 8, 2017, https://www.aljazeera.com/news/2017/12/zomlot-move-kiss-death-state-solution-171208112719252.html; David M. Halbfinger, "As a 2-State Solution Loses Steam, a 1-State Plan Gains Traction," *New York Times*, January 5, 2018.

50. Daoud Kuttab, contribution to the *Moment* magazine symposium "Is the Two State Solution Dead?," p. 36.

51. Marc Lynch, "The New Arab Order: Power and Violence in Today's Middle East," *Foreign Affairs* 97, no. 5 (2018): 118.

52. Richard Falk, "Let the Two-State Solution Die a Natural Death," Mondoweiss.net, January 8, 2018; Yousef Munayer, "Thinking Outside the Two-State Box," *New Yorker*, September 20, 2013; Robert Wright, "The Two-State Solution on Its Deathbed," *The Atlantic*, April 4, 2012.

53. Harriet Sherwood, "Look Beyond the Oslo Accords, Say Architects of Middle East Peace Plan," *The Guardian*, April 24, 2012.

54. Gideon Levy, "The Real Radical Left," *Haaretz*, April 5, 2012.

55. Dani Seidmann, contribution to the *Moment* magazine symposium "Is the Two State Solution Dead?," p. 35; Barak Ravid, "Israel, Palestinians in Secret Talks to Restore PA Control of West Bank Cities," *Haaretz*, March 14, 2016, https://www.haaretz.com/israel-news/.premium-israel-palestinians-in-secret -talks-to-restore-pa-control-of-west-bank-cities-1.5417367.

56. Dror Moreh, contribution to the *Moment* magazine symposium "Is the Two State Solution Dead?," p. 35.

57. "Is the Two State Solution Dead?," *Moment*, no. 3 (May–June 2013): 29–37; Isabel Kershner, "Is 2-State Solution Dead?," *New York Times*, February 16, 2017.

58. In 2011 one of the founders and most effective leaders of the Peace Now movement in Israel, Tzali Reshef, told a Tel Aviv conference dedicated to analysis of its prospects that "firstly we have to be honest and admit our complete failure as a peace camp as a whole, both as political parties and as NGO's. We have lost our relevance in the Israeli discourse." "Conference for the Israeli Left: Your Opportunity to Have an Influence," YouTube, March 25, 2011, https://www.youtube.com/watch?v=KZWKMx97KuA. On the demise of the Israeli peace camp, see Tamar S. Hermann, *The Israeli Peace Movement: Shattered Dream* (Cambridge: Cambridge University Press, 2009).

59. A "confederation," as opposed to a "federation," is defined as an arrangement agreed upon between two states rather than an administrative or political arrangement implemented by a single state. Oren Yiftachel, "Between One and Two: Debating Confederation and One-State Solution for Israel/ Palestine," lecture delivered at Tel Aviv University, May 2012, SlideShare, https://www.slideshare.net/moshiklichtenstien/middle-eastreflectionsyiftachel -2013-between-one-and-two; Dan Goldenblatt and Laurie Laure Boutteau, eds., *Two States in One Space: A New Proposed Framework for Resolving the Israeli-Palestinian Conflict* (Jerusalem: Israel Palestine Creative Regional Initiatives, 2014), p. 10, https://www.ipcri.org/two-states-in-one-space.

60. *One Land, Two States: Israel and Palestine as Parallel States*, ed. Mark LeVine and Mathias Mossberg (Berkeley: University of California Press, 2014).

61. Goldenblatt and Boutteau, *Two States in One Space*.

62. Herbert C. Kelman, "A One-Country/Two-State Solution to the Israeli-Palestinian Conflict," *Middle East Policy* 18, no. 1 (Spring 2011): 27–41.

63. Ian S. Lustick, "The Balfour Declaration a Century and a Half Later: Accidentally Relevant," *Middle East Policy* 24, no. 4 (Winter 2017): 166–76.

64. Nathan Witkin, "The Interspersed Nation-State System: A Two-State/One-Land Solution for the Israeli-Palestinian Conflict," *Middle East Journal* 65, no. 1 (Winter 2011): 31–54.

65. Lev Grinberg, "Neither One nor Two: Reflections about a Shared Future in Israel-Palestine," in *Israel and Palestine: Alternative Perspectives on Statehood*, ed. John Ehrenberg and Yoav Peled, 279–304 (Lanham, MD: Rowman and Littlefield, 2016).

66. Teodora Todorova, "Reframing Bi-Nationalism in Palestine-Israel as a Process of Settler Decolonisation," *Antipode* 47, no. 5 (2015): 1381.

67. Geneva Initiative, http://www.geneva-accord.org/. For an account of the Two-State Index methodology, see "The Two-State Index: Makeup and Methodology," Geneva Initiative, https://index.genevainitiative.org/methodology. For monthly results, see "Archive," Geneva Initiative, https://index.genevainitiative.org/archive.

68. Menachem Klein, *The Shift: Israel-Palestine From Border Struggle to Ethnic Conflict* (New York: Columbia University Press, 2010).

69. Ibid., p. 4.

70. Ibid., p. 111.

71. Ibid., pp. 141–42.

72. Avi Shilon, *The Left-Wing's Sorrow: The Crisis of the Peace Camp; The Untold Story* [Hebrew] (Hevel Modi'in: Kinneret: Zmora-Bitan, 2017), p. 404.

73. Ibid., p. 429.

74. Asher Susser, *Israel, Jordan, and Palestine: The Two State Imperative* (Waltham, MA: Brandeis University Press, 2012).

75. Ibid., p. 198.

76. Ibid., 220. Toward the end of the book Susser refers to the TSS in the past tense. Although he holds out the possibility that if the proper unilateral steps are taken by Israel the basis for an agreement involving two states might someday emerge, the two states he has in mind are Israel and Jordan, not Israel and Palestine

77. Ibid., p. 198.

78. Joseph Alpher, *No End of Conflict: Rethinking Israel-Palestine* (Lanham, MD: Rowman and Littlefield, 2016).

79. Ibid., p. 140.

80. Ibid., p. 137.

81. Ibid., p. 138.

82. Ibid., p. 107

83. Ibid., p. 108. On the Blue-White movement, see Blue White Future, http://www.bluewhitefuture.org.il/english/.

84. Alpher, *No End of Conflict,* p. 117.

85. Ibid., p. 107.

86. Ibid., pp. 146–47.

87. Ibid., p. 107.

88. Shafir, *A Half Century of Occupation,* p. 12.

89. Ibid., pp. 6–7.

90. Ibid., pp. 53–54.

91. Antonio Gramsci, *Selections from the Prison Notebooks,* ed. Quintin Hoare and Geoffrey Nowell Smith (New York: International Publishers, 1971), p. 276.

Chapter 5

1. On Israeli collection of taxes arising from economic activity in the West Bank and the Gaza Strip, see "Economic Monitory Report to the Ad Hoc Liaison Committee," World Bank, April 19, 2016, http://documents.worldbank.org/curated/en/780371468179658043/pdf/104808-WP-v1-2nd-revision-PUBLIC-AHLC-report-April-19-2016.pdf; Mahmoud Elkhafif, Misyef Misyef, and Mutasim Elagraa, *Palestinian Fiscal Revenue Leakage to Israel Under the Paris Protocol on Economic Relations* (New York: United Nations Conference on Trade and Development, 2013), https://unctad.org/en/PublicationsLibrary/gdsapp2013d1_en.pdf. The Israeli military maintains a database of the entire population of the West Bank and the Gaza Strip. As in other domains, the Palestinian Authority operates as a data-gathering and administrative arm of the State of Israel. See COGAT (Coordination of Government Activities in the Territories), http://www.cogat.mod.gov.il/en/Pages/default.aspx. See also Peter Beinart, "Jewish Leaders Encase Israel's Actions in Gaza in Euphemism and Lies," If Americans Knew Blog, April 30, 2018, https://israelpalestinenews.org/peter-beinart-jewish-leaders-encase-israels-actions-in-gaza-in-euphemism-and-lies/.

2. In the Gaza Strip, Israel treats Hamas much as Palestinian prisoner organizations are tolerated in standard Israeli prisons. Inmate activity in prison yards is not wholly controlled by Israeli authorities but is nonetheless taking place within the Israeli state.

3. See a *Haaretz* editorial drawing attention to the maps and counting rules used by the Central Bureau of Statistics, "This is How Israel Inflates Its Jewish Majority," *Haaretz,* May 1, 2017.

4. "What Borders Does Israel Show in Maps in School Textbooks?," Quora, https://www.quora.com/What-borders-does-Israel-show-in-maps-in-school-textbooks.

5. "Israel within Boundaries and Ceasefire Lines," Israeli Minister of Foreign Affairs, February 1, 2006, http://www.mfa.gov.il/MFA/AboutIsrael/Maps/Pages/Israel%20within%20Boundaries%20and%20Ceasefire%20Lines%20-%20200.aspx.

6. There is dispute about the exact figures, but in March 2018 the Israeli military officially announced that there were more Arabs than Jews living between the sea and the river. Yotam Berger, "Figures Presented by Army Show More Arabs Than Jews Live in Israel, West Bank and Gaza," *Haaretz*, March 26, 2018, https://www.haaretz.com/israel-news/army-presents-figures-showing-arab-majority-in-israel-territories-1.5940676. Because 4 percent of Israel's population are non-Arab Christians and other ethnic minorities, Arabs are a plurality but not a majority in Palestine/the Land of Israel.

7. For details see Nasser Al-Qadi, *The Israeli Permit Regime: Realities and Challenges*, The Applied Research Institute—Jerusalem, 2018, https://www.arij.org/files/arijadmin/2018/permits1.pdf; Yael Berda, *Living Emergency: Israel's Permit Regime in the Occupied West Bank* (Stanford, CA: Stanford University Press, 2017); Cédric Parizot, "Viscous Spatialities: The Spaces of the Israeli Permit Regime of Access and Movement," *South Atlantic Quarterly* 117, no. 1 (January 2018): 21–42.

8. Dov Weisglass, "Oslo deal was good for the Jews," Ynetnews, August 21, 2012, https://www.ynetnews.com/articles/0,7340,L-4270970,00.html.

9. The most popular definition for a "state" among political scientists is one version or another of Max Weber's formulation that it is the institution that "upholds the claim to the monopoly of the legitimate use of physical force in the enforcement of its order."

10. Oren Yiftachel, "Neither Two States Nor One: The Disengagement and 'Creeping Apartheid' in Israel/Palestine," *Arab World Geographer* 8, no. 3 (2005) 125–29.

11. The book appeared originally in Hebrew. The English translation is Ariella Azoulay and Adi Ophir, *The One-State Condition: Occupation and Democracy in Israel/Palestine* (Stanford, CA: Stanford University Press, 2013).

12. Adrian Guelke, *Politics in Deeply Divided Societies* (Cambridge: Polity Press, 2012). On Israel, including the territories, as a "deeply divided society" and as inappropriately labelled a democracy see also Michael N. Barnett, "Thinking beyond the two-state solution," *Washington Post, Monkey Cage*, April 25, 2015, https://www.washingtonpost.com/news/monkey-cage/wp/2015/08/25/thinking-beyond-the-two-state-solution/?noredirect=on&utm_term=.ff293ce6cc2b.

13. Tanisha Fazal, "Go Your Own Way: Why Rising Separatism Might Lead to More Conflict," *Foreign Affairs* 97, no. 4 (2018): 113–23.

14. Alice M. Panepinto, "Jurisdiction as Sovereignty Over Occupied Palestine: The Case of Khan-al-Ahmar," *Social and Legal Studies* 26, no. 3 (2017): 311–32; Amir Paz-Fuchs and Yael Ronen, "Integrated or Segregated? Israeli-Palestinian Employment Relations in the Settlements," in *Normalizing Occupation*, ed. Marco Allegra, Ariel Handel, and Erez Maggor, pp. 172–92 (Bloomington: Indiana University Press, 2017).

15. Oren Barak, *State Expansion and Conflict: In and between Israel/Palestine and Lebanon* (Cambridge: Cambridge University Press, 2017).

16. Shaul Arieli, "What Israelis Aren't Being Taught in School, and Why," *Haaretz*, January 3, 2016.

17. Zvi Bar'el, "The Israeli Student's Map of Israel," *Haaretz*, June 19, 2018.

18. Smadar Perry, "Abbas rival Dahlan calls for one-state solution," Ynetnews, December 12, 2018, https://www.ynetnews.com/articles/0,7340,L -5424475,00.html.

19. Udi Dekel and Kobi Michael, eds., *Scenarios in the Israeli-Palestinian Arena*, Memorandum 186, Institute for National Security Studies (Ramat Aviv: Tel Aviv University, December 2018); Michael Milstein and Avi Issacharoff, "The Return of 'One State': How 'One State for Two Peoples' is Taking Root in the Palestinian Arena," *Strategic Assessment* 21, no. 4 (January 2019) 3–14. For the development and growing prominence of the concept of the OSR, see Meron Benvenisti, *Son of the Cypresses: Memories, Reflections, and Regrets from a Political Life* (Berkeley: University of California Press, 2007); Ben White, "The One-State Reality," The Electronic Intifada, November 13, 2007, https://electronicintifada.net/content/one-state-reality/7216; David Remnick, "The One-State Reality," *New Yorker*, November 17, 2014; Marco Allegra, "E-1, or How I Learned to Stop Worrying About the Two-State Solution," Open Democracy, August 1, 2014, https://www.opendemocracy .net/north-africa-west-asia/marco-allegra/e1-or-how-i-learned-to-stop -worrying-about-twostate-solution; Michael Schaeffer Omer-Man, "'Creeping Annexation' Is a Distraction from the One-State Reality," *+972 Magazine*, October 27, 2017, https://972mag.com/creeping-annexation-is-a-distraction -from-the-one-state-reality/130426/; Noam Sheizaf, "Two State vs. One State Debate Is a Waste of Time," +972 Magazine, September 20, 2013, https:// 972mag.com/two-state-vs-one-state-debate-is-a-waste-of-time-political -energy/79120/; Mehran Kamrava, *The Impossibility of Palestine: History, Geography, and the Road Ahead* (New Haven, CT: Yale University Press, 2016); Ian Black, *Enemies and Neighbors: Arabs and Jews in Palestine and Israel,*

1917–2017 (New York: Atlantic Monthly Press, 2017), pp. 475–80; Miko Peled, *The General's Son: Journey of an Israeli in Palestine* (Charlottesville, VA: Just World Books, 2012), pp. 215–21.

20. Ian Lustick, "The Danger of Two-State Messianism," Daily Beast, October 2, 2013, https://www.thedailybeast.com/the-danger-of-two-state-messianism.

21. Remarks made to the symposium "The Two State Solution—Is it still viable?" held at the School for Peace at What al Salam-Neve Shalom, YouTube, https://www.youtube.com/watch?v=eaSpq13k8oQ&feature=youtu.be&t=516.

22. Goel Beno, "Poll: Over Half of Israeli Jews Believe Nation-State Law Must Be Fixed," Ynetnews, February 5, 2019, https://www.ynetnews.com/articles/0,7340,L-5458296,00.html.

23. For a list of scores of such laws, see the database maintained by the Israeli legal rights organization, Adalah, https://www.adalah.org/en/law/index.

24. See "The Future Vision of the Palestinian Arabs in Israel," The National Committee for the Heads of the Arab Local Authorities in Israel," December 2006, https://www.adalah.org/uploads/oldfiles/newsletter/eng/dec06/tasawor-mostaqbali.pdf; "The Haifa Declaration," Mada al-Carmel—Arab Center for Applied Social Research, May 15, 2007, http://mada-research.org/wp-content/uploads/2007/09/watheeqat-haifa-english.pdf.

25. On the frustration of Israeli two-staters with Palestinian refusal to cooperate with two-state or coexistence-oriented projects, see Ron Punkdak, "More Relevant Than Ever: People-to-People Peacebuilding Efforts in Israel and Palestine," *Palestine-Israel Journal* 18, no. 29 (2012), http://pij.org/articles/1442. On the meaning of antinormalization, see the Palestinian Campaign for the Academic and Cultural Boycott of Israel, "What Is Normalization?," *+972 Magazine*, December 27, 2011, https://972mag.com/what-is-normalization/31368/.

26. Omar Barghouti, *BDS: The Global Struggle for Palestinian Rights* (Chicago: Haymarket Books, 2011). In December 2017 Israel's Ministry of Strategic Affairs announced a $70 million program as part of a campaign to combat BDS. Itamar Echner, "Israel vs. Boycott Movement: From Defense to Offense," *Ynet Magazine,* December 7, 2017, https://www.ynetnews.com/articles/0,7340,L-4987758,00.html. For the scale of the long-term political threat posed by BDS as seen by Israeli strategists see Amir Praeger, "Achievements According to the BDS Movement: Trends and Implications," *Strategic Assessment* 22, no. 1 (April 2019).

27. David Pollock, "Half of Jerusalem's Palestinians Would Prefer Israeli to Palestinian Citizenship," The Washington Institute, August 21, 2015,

https://www.washingtoninstitute.org/policy-analysis/view/half-of-jerusalems
-palestinians-would-prefer-israeli-to-palestinian-citizen.

28. Adam Rasgon, "Palestinian List Fails to Win Any Seats on Jerusalem City Council," *Times of Israel*, November 7, 2018. See also Amjad Iraqi, "'This Is How You Change the Status Quo': Rethinking the Palestinian Boycott of Jerusalem Elections," *+972 Magazine*, September 28, 2018, https://972mag.com/aziz-abu-sarah-mayoral-election-jerusalem-palestinian/137927/.

29. Ilan Pappé estimates that 70,000 Arabs have moved into Jewish towns and neighborhoods, commenting that small but increasing numbers of Jews appear to be moving into Arab localities (inside the Green Line). Ilan Pappé, "Indigeneity as Cultural Resistance: Notes on the Palestinian Struggle Within Twenty-First Century Israel," *South Atlantic Quarterly* 117, no. 1 (2018): 172.

30. See Dmitri Shumsky, *Beyond the Nation-State: The Zionist Political Imagination from Pinsker to Ben-Gurion* (New Haven, CT: Yale University Press, 2018), for an illuminating discussion of images of political success entertained by Zionist leaders prior to World War I.

31. "Members of Knesset: The People Want Peres," *Haaretz*, June 13, 2007.

32. "Gantz and Netanyahu Neck and Neck in Election Polls, With Clear Advantage for Right-wing Bloc," *Haaretz*, April 4, 2019. See also sources listed in Chapter 4, note 38.

33. On the fluidity of Israeli public opinion during the first eighteen years of Israel's rule of the territories, see Yadin Kaufman, "Israel's Flexible Voters," *Foreign Policy*, no. 61 (Winter 1985–1986): 109–24; Gad Barzilai and Ilan Peleg, "Israel and Future Borders: Assessment of a Dynamic Process," *Journal of Peace Research*, 31, no. 1 (1994): 59–73.

34. "Surveys: 50 Years Since the Six-Day War," Israel Democracy Institute, May 23, 2017, https://en.idi.org.il/press-releases/14606.

35. Murad A'si, *Israeli and Palestinian Public Opinion* (Washington, DC: International Center for Research and Public Policy, 1986), p. 7.

36. For details on Israeli public opinion during this period see Ian S. Lustick, *Unsettled States, Disputed Lands: Britain and Ireland, France and Algeria, Israel and the West Bank/Gaza* (Ithaca, NY: Cornell University Press, 1993), pp. 378-381 and 546-547; and Gloria Falk, "Israeli Public Opinion: Looking toward a Palestinian Solution," *Middle East Journal* 39, no. 3 (Summer 1985): 256.

37. "Israeli Public: 57% Seek Compromise with Palestinians," *Peace Now News* 12, no. 1 (December 1996), reporting a poll by the Steinmetz Center for Peace Research at Tel-Aviv University.

38. Adam Rasgon, "Poll: Under 50% of Palestinians, Israeli Jews Support Two-State Solution," *Jerusalem Post*, January 25, 2018. Polling results were the same in January 2019, with many fewer believing it was even possible.

39. Peace Index, December 2018, http://www.peaceindex.org/indexMonth Eng.aspx?num=338.

40. Jonathan Lis, "Tzipi Livni Quits Politics as Polls Show Plummeting Support," *Haaretz*, February 18, 2019, https://www.haaretz.com/israel-news /elections/tzipi-livni-to-retire-from-israeli-politics-today-associates-say-1 .6942038.

41. Dina Kraft, "Haaretz Poll: 42% of Israelis Back West Bank Annexation, Including Two-State Supporters," *Haaretz*, March 25, 2019, https://www .haaretz.com/israel-news/israeli-palestinian-conflict-solutions/.premium-42 -of-israelis-back-west-bank-annexation-including-two-state-supporters-1 .7047313.

42. "Majority Wants Israeli Law in Areas," *Jerusalem Post*, December 26, 1979.

43. Falk, "Israeli Public Opinion," p. 256; A'si, *Israeli and Palestinian Public Opinion*, p. 13.

44. Asher Arian and Raphael Ventura, "Public Opinion in Israel and the Intifada: Changes in Security Attitudes 1987–88," Jaffee Center for Strategic Studies Memorandum no. 28, August 1989.

45. Giora Goldberg, Gad Barzilai, and Efraim Inbar, "The Impact of Intercommunal Conflict: The Intifada and Israeli Public Opinion," Policy Studies 43, Leonard Davis Institute of the Hebrew University, Jerusalem, February 1991.

46. Joseph Alpher, *No End of Conflict: Rethinking Israel-Palestine* (Lanham, MD: Rowman and Littlefield, 2016), p. 134. Commenting on Israel's "notoriously flexible" polls, Alpher notes that may of these one-state advocates may also say yes to the question of whether they favor the TSS.

47. Jeremy Sharon, "Most Jewish Israelis Oppose Annexation," *Jerusalem Post*, February 8, 2017.

48. Peace index, January 2017, http://www.peaceindex.org/indexMonthEng .aspx?mark1=&mark2=&num=317.

49. Peace Index, May 2017, http://www.peaceindex.org/indexMonthEng .aspx?num=322&monthname=May.

50. Peace Index, July 2018, http://www.peaceindex.org/indexMonthEng .aspx?num=334.

51. Kraft, "Haaretz Poll," March 25, 2019.

52. Isaac Chotiner, "Michael Oren Cuts Short a Conversation About Israel," *New Yorker*, May 11, 2019, https://www.newyorker.com/news/q-and-a/michael

-oren-hangs-up-on-a-call-about-israel. See also Shlomi Eldar, "Likud's Main-streaming of West Bank Annexation," *Al-Monitor*, February 15, 2019, https://www.al-monitor.com/pulse/originals/2019/02/israel-west-bank-sovereignty-annexation-likud-elections.html.

53. Regarding Jabotinsky's originally liberal views on Arab-Jewish equality in the future state, see Mordechai Kremnitzer and Amir Fuchs, "Ze'ev Jabotinsky on Democracy, Equality, and Individual Rights," Israel Democracy Institute, 2013, pp. 1–15, https://en.idi.org.il/media/5103/jabotinsky-idi-2013.pdf. In the first version of his plan for the future of Arabs in Judea, Samaria, and Gaza, Prime Minister Menachem Begin included provisions offering them the choice of full Israeli citizenship. Seth Anziska, "Autonomy as State Prevention: The Palestinian Question After Camp David, 1979–1982," *Humanity: An International Journal of Human Rights, Humanitarianism, and Development* 8, no. 2 (Summer 2017): 290–91.

54. Translated from Hebrew by the author from a press release issued by the Office of the President. Rivlin's support of annexation with full rights to Arabs was extensively reported in the Israeli press.

55. Sam Bahour, *Asynchronous and Inseparable Struggles for Rights and a Political End-Game* (Ramallah: Palestinian Center for Policy and Survey Research, May 2016), pp. 7–10.

56. Leila Farsakh, "The One-State Solution and the Israeli-Palestinian Conflict: Palestinian Challenges and Prospects," *Middle East Journal* 65, no. 1 (Winter 2011): 62.

57. Nadim Rouhana, "Are Palestinians on the Road to Independence?," in *IEMed Mediterranean Yearbook* (2017), p. 41.

58. Diana Buttu, "I Advised the Palestinian Negotiating Team. It Was a Mistake to Negotiate at All," *Haaretz*, September 12, 2018.

59. Nadia Hijab, "Do Not Let Go of the Green Line: It Is Israel's Achilles Heel," al-Shabaka: The Palestinian Policy Network, February 15, 2017, https://al-shabaka.org/commentaries/not-let-go-green-line-israels-achilles-heel/?utm_source=Al-Shabaka+announcements&utm_campaign=9be4e56%E2%80%A6. On practical objectives worth pursuing within an overall conception of an evolving struggle, see Raef Zreik, "A One-State Solution? From a 'Struggle unto Death' to 'Master-Slave' Dialectics," in *Israel and Palestine: Alternative Perspectives on Statehood*, ed. John Ehrenberg and Yoav Peled (Lanham, MD: Rowman and Littlefield, 2016), pp. 223–42; see also contributions to *The Failure of the Two-State Solution: The Prospects of One State in the Israel-Palestine Conflict*, ed. Hani A. Faris (London: I. B. Tauris, 2013). On the appropriateness of Antonio Gramsci's concept of "war of position" for the struggles to be conducted

within the OSR, see Cherine Hussein, *The Re-Emergence of the Single State Solution in Palestine/Israel: Countering an Illusion* (New York: Routledge, 2015).

60. Dawn Teele, *Forging the Franchise: The Political Origins of the Women's Vote* (Princeton, NJ: Princeton University Press, 2018).

61. For explicit and implicit examples of this approach, see Efraim Inbar and Eitan Shamir, "'Mowing the Grass': Israel's Strategy for Protracted Intractable Conflict," *Journal of Strategic Studies* 37, no. 1 (2014): 65–90; Micah Goodman, *Catch-67* [Hebrew] (Hevel Modi'in: Kinneret, Zmora-Bitan, 2017); Noam Sheizaf, "One or Two States? The Status Quo Is Israel's Rational Choice," +972 Magazine, March 25, 2012, https://972mag.com/one-or-two-states-the-status-quo-is-israels-rational-third-choice/39169/.

62. On this general point see, Nassim Nicholas Taleb and Mark Blyth, "The Black Swan of Cairo: How Suppressing Volatility Makes the World Less Predictable and More Dangerous," *Foreign Affairs* 90, no. 3 (May–June 2011): 33-39.

63. "Humanitarian Snapshot: Casualties in the Gaza Strip; 30 March 2018–22 March 2019," United Nations Office for the Coordination of Humanitarian Affairs, Occupied Palestinian Territory, March 27, 2019, https://www.ochaopt.org/content/humanitarian-snapshot-casualties-gaza-strip-30-mar-2018-22-mar-2019.

64. For examples, see Alan Johnson, "Why the Nazi Analogy and Holocaust Inversion Are Antisemitic," *Fathom,* August 2018, http://fathomjournal.org/why-the-nazi-analogy-and-holocaust-inversion-are-antisemitic/; and Lesley Klaff, "Holocaust Inversion," *Israel Studies* 24, no. 2 (Summer 2019) 73-90.

65. "Deputy IDF Chief 's Holocaust Remembrance Day Speech Raises Ire," *Ynetnews,* May 5, 2016, https://www.ynetnews.com/articles/0,7340,L-479 9593,00.html.

66. Ibid.

67. For an early example of this effect, see Avraham Burg, *The Defeat of Hitler* [Hebrew] (Tel Aviv: Yediot Acharonot, 2007). See also Ari Shavit's interview with Burg, "Leaving the Zionist Ghetto," *Haaretz*, June 8, 2007. The prize-winning Israeli film *Waltz with Bashir* (2008) is saturated with Holocaust tropes linking Israel's behavior toward Palestinians in the 1982 Lebanon War to the savage treatment of Jews by Germans during World War II.

68. Ari Shavit, "On Gaza Beach," *New York Review of Books*, July 18, 1991.

69. For examples of the Weimar-Israel comparison, see Burg, *The Defeat of Hitler*, pp. 96–113; Uri Avnery, "Israeli Politics Bears Comparison with End of Weimar Germany and Rise of fascism," *Irish Times*, May 25, 2016, https://www.irishtimes.com/opinion/uri-avnery-israeli-politics-bears-comparison-with-end-of-weimar-germany-and-rise-of-fascism-1.2659314; Moshe Zimmermann,

"Weimar in Jerusalem: Is Israel on a Slippery Slope to Fascism?," *Tel Aviv Review* (Podcast, February 12, 2016), https://tlv1.fm/the-tel-aviv-review/2016 /02/12/weimar-in-jerusalem-is-israel-on-a-slippery-slope-to-fascism/; Mordechai Kremnitzer, "Waiving Murder Charge in Killing of Palestinian, Israel Fails to Deter Next Jewish Terrorist," *Haaretz*, January 25, 2019. For a critical response to this tendency that yet embraces the comparison, see Giulio Meotti, "The State of Tel Aviv—Israel's Weimar?," Arutz Sheva, July 8, 2012, http://www .israelnationalnews.com/Articles/Article.aspx/12023. For comparisons between the Nakba (the mass expulsion of Palestinians in 1948) and the Holocaust, see Bashir Bashir and Amos Goldberg, eds., *The Holocaust and the Nakba: Memory, National Identity and Jewish-Arab Partnership* [Hebrew] (Tel Aviv: Hakibbutz Hameuchad, 2015). On the behavior and influence of violently anti-Arab Beitar soccer fans in Jerusalem, see the film *Forever Pure* (2016), directed by Maya Zinshtein.

70. See Rashid Khalidi, *Brokers of Deceit: How the U.S. Has Undermined Peace in the Middle East* (Boston: Beacon, 2013); See also Ian S. Lustick, "New Approaches to Israel-Palestine Peace: Can Regional Powers Make a Difference?," *Middle East Policy* 24, no. 2 (Summer 2017): 9–17; Ian S. Lustick, "The Peace Process Carousel: The Israel Lobby and the Failure of American Diplomacy" (forthcoming, available at www.ParadigmLostbook.com).

71. Yanir Kozin, "Jews in the United States Say Israeli Policies Make Them Want to Vomit," *Maariv*, December 18, 2018, https://www.maariv.co.il/news /world/Article-675940. For discussion of the link between partisan polarization in the United States and prospects for a change in U.S. policy toward discrimination within the Israeli OSR, see Ben White, *Cracks in the Wall: Beyond Apartheid in Palestine/Israel* (London: Pluto, 2018).

72. Nathan Thrall, "How the Battle Over Israel and Anti-Semitism Is Fracturing American Politics," *New York Times Magazine,* March 28, 2019, https:// www.nytimes.com/2019/03/28/magazine/battle-over-bds-israel-palestinians -antisemitism.html.

73. For examples of this shift, see the extraordinarily detailed coverage given by the *New York Times* to the death of a Gaza medic at the hands of an Israeli sniper. David M. Halbfinger, "A Day, a Life: When a Medic Was Killed in Gaza, Was It an Accident?," *New York Times*, December 30, 2018. See also Michelle Alexander's Martin Luther King Day column, "Time to Break the Silence on Palestine," *New York Times*, January 19, 2019.

74. See, e.g., Yishai Fleisher, "A Settler's View of Israel's Future," *New York Times*, February 14, 2017; Carolina Landsman, "How Israeli Right-Wing Thinkers Envision the Annexation of the West Bank," *Haaretz*, August 18, 2018;

Caroline Glick, *The Israeli Solution* (New York: Crown Forum, 2014). For details on such plans by settler leaders and influential Israeli politicians such as Uri Ariel, Adi Mintz, Naftali Bennet, and others, see *Leap of Faith: Israel's National Religious and the Israeli-Palestinian Conflict*, Middle East Report No. 47 (Brussels: International Crisis Group, November 21, 2013), pp. 33–37.

75. As of this writing, Hotoveley serves as deputy foreign minister. Sophia Ron-Moriah, "Dangerous Tactics" [Hebrew], an extended interview with Tzipi Hotovely, *Nekuda*, no. 323 (July 2009): 33–35.

76. Noam Sheizaf, "Endgame," *Haaretz*, July 15, 2010, https://www.haaretz .com/1.5149140. For a Jewish law-based proposal authored by a rabbi living in the West Bank involving equal citizenship for all Jews and Arabs in an Israeli state encompassing the entire area between the sea and the river, see Rav Glickman, *Proposed Principles for a Peace Plan in the Land of Israel* [Hebrew] (Shilo: Mimeo, 2005). Readiness to accept large Palestinian populations into the state is in part the unintended consequence of years of right-wing propaganda instilling false beliefs that many fewer Palestinians live in the West Bank than is actually the case. Elhanan Miller, "Right-Wing Annexation Drive Fueled by False Demographics, Experts Say," *Times of Israel*, January 15, 2015. Fewer than 15 percent of Israeli Jews identifying as rightist have anywhere near accurate beliefs on the subject. See Peace Index, June 2016, http://www.peaceindex.org /files/Peace_Index_Data_June_2016-Eng.pdf.

77. Uri Elitzur, "To Break the Taboo" [Hebrew], *Nekuda*, no. 323 (July 2009): 37.

78. Sheizaf, "Endgame." Likud stalwarts and former ministers Benny Begin and Dan Meridor are also on record supporting equal rights for Arabs in an expanded Israel.

79. See Ian S. Lustick, "Making Sense of the Nakba: Ari Shavit, Baruch Marzel, and Zionist Claims to Territory," *Journal of Palestine Studies* 44, no. 2 (Winter 2015): 7–27.

A c k n o w l e d g m e n t s

When a project cuts deep into the life commitments and beliefs of the author, it is difficult to thank those who made the project possible. Most must be unnamed. There are simply too many, and some would not want to be thanked. Israeli Jews, American Jews, Palestinian Arabs, family members, colleagues, students, friends, activists, and argumentative interlocutors—all guided me, corrected me, and inspired me. Most importantly, none of these, including those I mention by name, can be held responsible for the argument I make in this book or for the errors it contains. I also want to honor interlocutors and readers who disagree with me but who have the courage to hear arguments and evidence that cause them discomfort. Whether you are intrigued, excited, or provoked by this book, I urge you to visit ParadigmLostbook.com for additional source material and opportunities to participate in the conversations that I hope my work will encourage.

At the University of Pennsylvania I have been privileged to benefit from the resources of the Bess W. Heyman Chair, the support of the School of Arts and Sciences, and the work of dedicated and skilled student research assistants. These included Jack Hostager, Rachel Brock, Emily True, Marissa Priceman, Dan Silverman, Clarence Moore, and Karl Sjulsen. For advice, insight, hospitality, and guidance I am particularly grateful to Chanan Cohen, Dan Miodownik, John Richardson, Ofer Zalzberg, Maya Rosenfeld, Roy Eidelson, Michael Feige, Yoav Peled, Gershon Shafir, Yoram Peri, Pnina Peri, Seth Anziska, Guy Grossman, Gabriel Sheffer, William Quandt, Amy Kaplan, Omer Bartov, Steven Rosen, Oded Haklai, Chaim Gans, Amal Jamal, Kenneth Mann, Mahdi Abdel-Hadi, David Newman, David Laitin,

Nadera Shalhoub-Kevorkian, Jackie Feldman, Roger Haydon, Yisrael Medad, Elisheva Goldberg, Yuval Orr, Taylor Valore, Nadim Rouhana, Mark Tessler, Matthew Berkman, Nathaniel Shils, Sam Fleischacker, Robert Vitalis, and Menachem Klein.

I will always be thankful for the support of the Foundation for Middle East Peace and to its visionary founder, Merle Thorpe, and especially its former president and my former colleague at the State Department, Ambassador Philip Wilcox. I am deeply indebted to Pamela Haag, whose editorial skill is matched only by the enthusiasm of her involvement in a project not her own, and to Peter Agree at the University of Pennsylvania Press, whose advice has been invaluable and whose confidence has been unwavering.

But pride of place in my heart and in the list of those to whom I am grateful is my wife, Terri, who anchors me to the worlds beyond those within which I lose myself and without whom I would truly be lost.